CONTEMPORARY ASIAN MODERNITIES

WORLDS OF EAST ASIA
WELTEN OSTASIENS
MONDES DE L'EXTRÊME-ORIENT

Band / Vol. 16

Edited by / Herausgegeben von / Edité par
ROBERT H. GASSMANN
EDUARD KLOPFENSTEIN
ANDREA RIEMENSCHNITTER
PIERRE-FRANÇOIS SOUYRI
NICOLAS ZUFFEREY

PETER LANG
Bern · Berlin · Bruxelles · Frankfurt am Main · New York · Oxford · Wien

CONTEMPORARY ASIAN MODERNITIES

Transnationality, Interculturality, and Hybridity

YIU-WAI CHU & EVA KIT-WAH MAN
(EDS)

PETER LANG
Bern · Berlin · Bruxelles · Frankfurt am Main · New York · Oxford · Wien

Bibliographic information published by Die Deutsche Nationalbibliothek
Die Deutsche Nationalbibliothek lists this publication in the Deutsche Nationalbibliografie; detailed bibliographic data is available on the Internet at ‹http://dnb.d-nb.de›.

British Library Cataloguing-in-Publication Data: A catalogue record for this book is available from The British Library, Great Britain.

Library of Congress Cataloging-in-Publication Data

Contemporary Asian modernities : transnationality, interculturality, and hybridity /
Yiu-Wai Chu & Eva Kit-Wah Man, (eds). – 1st ed.
p. cm. – (Worlds of East Asia ; Bd. 16)
ISBN 978-3-0343-0093-3 (alk. paper)
1. Globalization–Social aspects–East Asia. 2. Multiculturalism–East Asia. 3. Cyberspace–Social aspects. I. Zhu, Yaowei. II. Man, Eva Kit-Wah.
HN720.5.A8C66 2009
305.80095–dc22

2009034417

Cover illustration: © Kim Tang

ISSN 1660-9131
ISBN 978-3-0343-0093-3

Hochfeldstrasse 32, CH-3012 Bern, Switzerland
info@peterlang.com, www.peterlang.com, www.peterlang.net

Printed in Germany

Contents

Acknowledgements

We would like to thank the following units for funding and/or organizing the international symposium on "Contemporary Asian Modernities: Transnationality, Interculturality and Hybridity" held at Hong Kong Baptist University on September 9 and 10, 2006: The Arts Faculty, David C. Lam Institute for East-West Studies, Department of History, and Department of Cinema and Television of Hong Kong Baptist University. Without their financial and/or administrative supports the symposium, one of the featured events in celebration of the 50th anniversary of Hong Kong Baptist University, would not have been successful. Special thanks have to go to Kwok-bun Chan, Ricardo Mak, and Kwai-Cheung Lo for conceiving the topic of the symposium. We are honored to have the presence of Arif Dirlik, Mark Elvin and Kwok-bun Chan as the keynote speakers. Arjun Appadurai, not being able to come in person, made a virtual presentation of his keynote speech in the symposium. Last but not least, we are also grateful to the graduate students of the Humanities programme, who have contributed to the smooth operation of the symposium and editorial jobs related to this book.

Eva Man and Yiu-wai Chu

Introduction

This book is a collection of selected essays presented at the International Symposium on "Contemporary Asian Modernities: Transnationality, Interculturality and Hybridity" hosted by the Humanities Programme and co-organized by David C. Lam Institute for East-West Studies, Department of History, and Department of Cinema and Television of Hong Kong Baptist University on September 9 and 10, 2006. The essays collected here discuss the notions of "contemporary," "Asia" and "modernities" as they relate to global trend of capitalization. As "modernity" has been used to describe the cultural, economic and socio-political conditions in the Western worlds, the time in which we now live and the Asian countries where capitalization is extensively carried out are already articulating their own descriptions. Recent developments in Asia indicate some profound changes and differences that may articulate the contradictions and incoherence of modernity: the emergence of China and India, the return of traditions, religions and cultural legacies, the coexistence of different economies and social systems within one nation-state (most prominently in China), the possible appearance of a pan-Asian cultural identity as well as the American strive for maintaining hegemony in the region. Undoubtedly the idea of Asia remains problematic. While we do not intend to privilege culture for the explanations of contemporary modernity or to confirm "the clash of civilizations" as the norm of world politics, we still recognize that what provokes our concerns with the idea of "Contemporary Asian Modernities" may be a new paradigm for understanding the reconfiguration of power and ideology in today's world.

I

"Contemporary" seems to be the less controversial term in the title of this book. But if one takes a closer look, its meaning is not as clear as it seems. Besides the literal meaning of happening, existing, living, or coming into being during the same period of time, it has different meanings in different contexts. *The Encyclopedia of World History*, among others, defines the contemporary period as "1945–2000." In China, however, the contemporary period commonly refers to 1949 when Mao Zedong declared the founding of the People's Republic of China. Contemporary literature generally refers to post-1960 literary works. In Chinese literary studies, however, contemporary Chinese literature means post-1949 literary works. In the field of art, contemporary art is often interpreted as art produced at this present point, but museums of contemporary art usually define their collections as consisting of art produced since World War II. In the field of architecture, the term "contemporary architecture" suggests a theoretical position that uses architectural language not steeped in past traditions. In short, "contemporary" has slightly different meanings in different contexts. When being asked about the meaning of the term "post-contemporary," the editor of the "Post-contemporary" series published by Duke University Press made this response: "post-contemporary interpretation seeks to place the present within a historical narrative, while recognizing that the contemporary is always already disappearing. Yet the present is, so to speak, always before us."[1] The so-called "already disappearing" marks the equivocal character of the term "contemporary," which implies the present period and its diminishing at the same time. In the introduction to the founding issue of the journal *Con-temporary Monthly* published in Taiwan, the editor explains the reason to choose the term "con-temporary." As he said, "con," the opposite of "pro," might mean "against." Thus, "contemporary" also implies, in addition to the literal meaning of the term, against the

1 Cited from Scott McLemee, "Jameson and Son," *Lingua Franca* 5.5 (July/August 1995), p. 11.

present period. In this sense "contemporary" means the present and its transition at once.[2] In this volume the "contemporary" bears multiple meanings of (against) the present in the (disappearing) present period.

That the twenty-first century is *Asian* century is now a cliché. It was fashionable a couple of decades ago to celebrate the rise of Asia in the twenty-first century. While Asian politics and culture have become more and more important, it is not unproblematic to define the term "Asia." The editorial statement of the journal *Inter-Asia Cultural Studies* describes the rise of Asia in the following way:

> Since the 1980s, a pervasive rhetoric of the "rise of Asia" has come to mean more than the concentrated flow of capital into and out of the region. It has come to constitute a structure of feeling that is ubiquitous yet ambiguously felt throughout Asia. Historically, this feeling of the "rise of Asia" is complicated by the region's colonial past. While Asia's political, cultural and economic position in the global system will continue to fluctuate, there is a need to question and critique the rhetorical unities of both the "rise" and of "Asia." Wealth and resources are unevenly distributed and there is no cultural or linguistic unity in this imaginary space called Asia. On the other hand, no matter whether there are common experiences shared by sub-regional histories, there is an urgent need for forging political links across these sub-regions.[3]

The rise of Asia, in other words, has stimulated critical reflections on what "Asia" is. As Arjun Appadurai argues in his keynote speech "The Traffic of Modernity in Asia" (not included here), "Today no one can draw the map of Asia with complete confidence." Asia, according to Appadurai,

> insofar as it is a reality … is a political idea, a commercial idea, and above all a modern idea. The history of the idea of Asia as a region of identity and identification is tied up in very complicated ways with commerce, colonialism and nationalism.

Arif Dirlik also observes, "Our continued reference to Asia as an object of study, matched on the other side of the Pacific by discourses of 'Asian values,' perpetuates the assumption that there is an entity called Asia,

2 "Editor's Words" (in Chinese), *Con-temporary Monthly* 1 (May 1986), p. 4.
3 Cited from the website of *Inter-Asia Cultural Studies*, http://www.inter-asia.org/journal/; last accessed on January 16, 2008.

disguising the production of Asia spatially and temporally by these discourses."[4] "Asia" seems to have found its voice and no longer remain silent. But is "Asia" actually speaking in its own voice? If we concur that "Asianness does not have fixed contents but is articulated as critical response to the West,"[5] the indiscriminate umbrella "Asia" has a strange echo with Edward Said's "Orient." The rise of Asian studies might be interpreted as the result of the rising influence of Asia. It can also be seen as ghettoizing "Asia" as a specific area study kept away from universal topics. When Dirlik asks the question whether Asia is possible, he expresses his reservation in the following remark:

> In its class bias in privileging "cosmopolitanism" over places, a notion such as "GlobalAsia" perpetuates Orientalist ideas of Asians, whose cultural resilience supposedly overcomes all transformative cultural forces in Asia or in diaspora, to guarantee the survival of their "Asianness" (or its national subcultures) as if the latter were some genetic endowment that people carried with them in their global dispersal.[6]

In short, is there such thing as "Asia"?[7] This question has stirred up another round of debate, but this is the right place to go into details. Gayatri Chakravorty Spivak's recent *Other Asias*, among others, is an effort to challenge us to rethink if Asia should actually be plural.[8] In this volume "Asia" generally refers to Mainland China, Taiwan, Hong Kong, Singapore, India and so on. But whose Asian Century it is remains a question that must be left open here.

4 Arif Dirlik, "Asian Studies / Transdisciplinarity," http://www.asiasource.org/asip/dirlik.cfm; last accessed on January 16, 2008.
5 Toru Oga, "Rediscovering Asianness: The role of institutional discourses in APEC, 1989–1997," *International Relations of the Asia-Pacific* 4: 2 (August 2004), p. 312.
6 Dirlik, "Asian Studies / Transdisciplinarity."
7 Kwai-cheung Lo claims that "in the process of striving to represent Asia in some Asian films, there is always a signifier without a signified that carries no determine meaning, and the emptiness of its signified has been filled in by some contingent particular meaning, through the hegemonic struggle, to function as a stand-in for the meaning of Asia." Kwai-Cheung Lo, "There is no such thing as Asia: Racial particularities in the 'Asian' films of Hong Kong and Japan," *Modern Chinese Literature and Culture* 17: 1 (Spring 2005), pp. 133–58.
8 Gayatri Chakravorty Spivak, *Other Asias* (Oxford: Blackwell, 2007).

The debates centered on the notion of *modernities* have been very heated. The term itself inevitably begs the question whether it should be singular or plural. To begin with, let us start with the notion of modernity as argued in some of the essays collected in this volume. Mark Elvin examines modernity from a historian's point, noting that, "In real life, elements of modernity are intermixed with a multitude of older elements, and they produce a variety of outcomes that arise both from the collaboration and from the conflicts between them." Modernity in the singular form, in other words, silently embodies a multiplicity of references. Ricardo Mak, also a historian, uses Ma Keyao's *Shijie Wenmingshi (History of World Civilizations)* – a collection of different studies of modernization in Africa, Latin America, South Asia, Southeast Asia and the Islamic world – to present a picture "similar to what we call multiple modernities." Meanwhile, Liao Ping-hui, reminds us that countermodernity has always already been part of modernity. "In spite of Foucault's attempt to frame modernity and define it as a unique development of European societies," Liao states, "he nevertheless points out that it would be more useful to try to find out how the attitude of modernity, ever since its formation, has found itself struggling with attitudes of 'countermodernity'." It is reasonable to say that even if one agrees to a precise definition of modernity in the singular form, one has to deal with different notions of modernity. As pointed out by Chu Yiu Wai, the following questions related to modernity are worthwhile noting: "How is modernity configured – and contested – in different cultural and regional contexts? How do people in different world areas construct notions of progress vis-à-vis those of tradition or history?" These questions

> force us to confront the cultural diversity of the contemporary world while considering a larger issue: how it is that people in different world areas are coming to have more in common at the same time that they are becoming increasingly diverse, for instance, through new forms of cultural elaboration and differentiation.[9]

9 Bruce M. Knauft, "Vernacular Modernities," http://www.anthropology.emory.edu/FACULTY/ANTBK/ vernacularModernities/vernacularModernities.html (accessed May 10, 2007).

It gives the impression that when "Asian" is not as homogenous as the term implies, there should be different modernities across Asia. Critics have been arguing that it is possible to have different forms of modernities other than the capitalist one originated in the West. Andrew Feenberg's *Alternative Modernity: The Technical Turn in Philosophy and Social Theory* is an early attempt that tried to put forward the "alternative" concept by reflecting on the ideas of Jürgen Habermas, Herbert Marcuse, Jean-François Lyotard, and Kitaro Nishida to shed light on the philosophical study of technology and modernity.[10] Feenberg is still sticking to the singular form of modernity in the book while he highlights "alternative." Dilip Parameshwar Gaonkar's *Alternative Modernities* uses "alternative modernities" to "recognize the need to revise the distinction between societal modernization and cultural modernity." His edited volume tries to demonstrate, in response to Jürgen Habermas's saying that modernity is an incomplete project, that "everywhere, at every national/cultural site, modernity is not one but many; modernity is not new but old and familiar; modernity is incomplete and necessarily so."[11] In a similar vein, Liao Ping-hui's essay collected in this volume analyzes Taiwan's alternative modernity as apart from Japan's developing and China's undeveloped modernity projects. In the essay he urges us to rethink what might have inspired Chinese modernity or Asian alternative modernities, remarking that Chinese modernity projects are not only unfinished but also uneven. In sum, are there alterative modernities or simply varieties of modernity?

The concept of "multiple modernities," most cogently advanced by S.N. Eisenstadt, has added an important dimension to the debate. As Eisenstadt puts it in his edited volume *Multiple Modernities*,

> The idea of multiple modernities presumes that the best way to understand the contemporary world – indeed to explain the history of modernity – is to see it as

10 Andrew Feenberg, *Alternative Modernity: The Technical Turn in Philosophy and Social Theory* (Berkeley: University of California Press, 1995).

11 Dilip Parameshwar Gaonkar, "On alternative modernities," in his *Alternative Modernities* (Durham and London: Duke University Pres, 2001), p. 1, p. 23.

> a story of continual constitution and reconstitution of a multiplicity of cultural programs.[12]

While the book recognizes the singular origins of modernity, some contributions consider differences based on culture possible among the commonalities of modernity. Jenny Lau's edited volume *Multiple Modernities: Cinemas and Popular Media in Transcultural East Asia* endeavors to show that becoming modern happens differently in different places in Asia. In the introduction to the "Multiple Modernities Project" of the Center for Transcultural Studies, Charles Taylor and Benjamin Lee also think that it is better to speak of "multiple modernities" rather than "modernity" in the singular because "[t]he future of our world will be one in which all societies will undergo change, in institutions and outlook, and some of these changes may be parallel, but it will not converge, because new differences will emerge from the old."[13]

In Eisenstadt's view, "One of the most important implications of the term 'multiple modernities' is that modernity and Westernization are not identical."[14] Fredric Jameson would disagree by arguing that modernity and capitalism are not different. Notions about modernity, according to Jameson, must result in reliance on the capitalist status quo. "Modernity" cannot but be hopelessly tied to capitalism in Jameson's sense. And thus a singular modernity.[15] Unlike the contributors in *Multiple Modernities*, Arif Dirlik maintains that multiculturalism is itself invented by transnational corporations, and thus it "appears in this perspective as a way of managing difference within a context of commonality (without which difference would be meaningless)." As convincingly noted by Dirlik,

12 Shmuel N. Eisenstadt, "Multiple modernities," in his *Multiple Modernities* (Brunswick and London: Transaction Publishers, 2002), p. 2.

13 Charles Taylor and Benjamin Lee, "Modernity and difference," The Center for Transcultural Studies, http://www.sas.upenn.edu/transcult/promad.html; last accessed on January 16, 2008.

14 Eisenstadt, "Multiple Modernities," p. 2.

15 Fredric Jameson, *A Singular Modernity: Essay on the Ontology of the Present* (London: Verso, 2002).

> Notions of multiple or alternative modernities, in rendering into units of modernity traditions that are themselves the very products of modernity, in fact universalize the claims of modernity by appropriating them as endowments of otherwise vastly different and complex pasts.

Dirlik finds the plural form "modernities" as used in *Multiple Modernities* and *Global Modernities*[16] problematic because they tend to "sweep under the rug issues of the colonial in modernity in the name of globalization." He uses the term "Global Modernity" as a conceptual marker to distinguish the present from its Eurocentric past, while recognizing the crucial importance of that past in shaping the present. He sounds the alarm that while the seeming end of colonialism have enabled alternatives to colonialist modernity, a capitalist modernity that was deeply entangled in colonialism (to which there is now no viable alternative) has led to the universalization and deepening of colonialism. Dirlik argues in the essay collected here and elsewhere that "while Global Modernity has opened the way to conflicting claims on modernity, it has by no means abolished the inequalities of uneven development that is the legacy of colonialism to the present."[17]

In sum, whether modernity or modernities is a question this introduction cannot answer. Allen Chun asks a question about identity in his essay collected in this volume: "Yet the question is not why or if identity is *really* necessary, but rather *what is it for*? One might also add, who is it for and to what extent do alternative notions of culture provide the basis of effective counter-identities?" (original emphases). Perhaps we might rephrase the question by replacing "identity" with "modernity" to ask "who is it for and to what extent do alternative notions of culture provide the basis of effective counter-modernities." We chose to stick to the plural form to underscore the (im)possibility of Asian modernities more than the actual existence of Asian modernities. In Arjun Appadurai's words, "while Asian modernities are doubtless a pro-

16 Mike Featherstone, Scott Lash and Roland Robertson (eds) (Thousand Oaks, CA: Sage Publications, 1995).

17 See also Arif Dirlik, *Global Modernity: Modernity in an Age of Global Capitalism* (Boulder, CO: Paradigm Press, 2006).

duct of all kinds of traffic across the region, they are also shaped by the traffic jams and road blocks that define this traffic, opening up some interactions but closing others." It seems the space of flow in the global era will ensure the smooth traffic of modernity. The traffic, however, might be jammed from time to time, and our understanding of "Asia" must be influenced by the traffic conditions:

> How we reconfigure the traffic of modernity will have a great deal of consequence for how we produce our Asia in the future, and it is the Asia that we produce, not its nature, soil or cultural genius, which will in turn shape the modernities that Asia produces.

Transnationality is a good starting point to map the traffic.

II

The essays collected here are being grouped, for the sake of brevity, under three subtitles. We have no intention whatsoever to say the essays do not cut across the three fields. We first start with the highly contested concept of *transnationality* to mark the important meanings of "across," "beyond" and "through" in the age of globalization. Transnationality, literally speaking, refers to action across national borders. While "international" denotes relationship between national governments, "transnational" goes beyond national boundaries to describe relationships between individuals or other entities. The focus of much research on transnationality is in general on movements across things. The emphasis on border crossings, according to Katharyne Mitchell, "forces a reconceptualization of core beliefs in migration and geopolitical literatures ..., a rethinking of economic categories ..., [and] a rethinking in broader areas of epistemological inquiry."[18] Despite the

18 Katharyne Mitchell, "Cultural geographies of transnationality", in K. Anderson, M. Domosh, S. Pile, and N. Thrift (eds), *Handbook of Cultural Geography* (London: Sage, 2003), pp. 74–87.

effort to go beyond nation-states, "nation" is by no means dead in the seemingly borderless world. Aihwa Ong has suggested that previous studies mistakenly viewed transnationality as necessarily detrimental to the nation-state and have ignored individual agency in the large-scale flow of people, images, and cultural forces across borders.[19] National boundaries seems to have blurred in the global era, but in the new global/local paradigm, "nation," as indicated by Pheng Cheah, continued to cast a shadowy specter.[20] Trans*nation*ality rather than globality, in this sense, better reflects the shadowy specter of "nation" in the term itself.

Arif Dirlik's "Asian Modernities in the Perspective of Global Modernity" alerts that in this seemingly global era, colonialism is still very active:

> If we seem today to live in a world where colonialism has been superseded by a global modernity, in which the formerly colonized and dominated once again assert their own political and cultural claims to modernity, this global modernity is nevertheless one that has been marked indelibly by its origins in colonialism; as is quite apparent in its unevenness, as well as the uneven distributions of economic, social, political and cultural power that are the legacies to it of modern colonialism and imperialism, distinguished historically by their sources in capitalism and the nation-state.

That said, it should be clear that though transnationality implies border crossings, the movements cannot but be uneven. Arjun Appadurai's "The Traffic of Modernity in Asia" also deals with this unevenness by mapping the recent traffic conditions in Asia. Appadurai stresses that it is easy to assert that "the great cities of East Asia are hubs of an enormous amount of cultural traffic and that this traffic indeed makes Asia and its modernities real, dynamic and sustainable," but it is important for us to note the "road-blocks" as "the intensity and quality of traffic that constitutes and energizes the production of Asian modernities is

19 Aihwa Ong, *Flexible Citizenship: The Cultural Logics of Transnationality* (Durham and London: Duke University Press, 1998).

20 Pheng Cheah, *Spectral Nationality: Passages of Freedom from Kant to Postcolonial Literatures of Liberation* (New York: Columbia University Press, 2004).

in fact neither as wide nor as deep as you might think." According to Appadurai, the traffic is fast and heavy in some aspects but slow and weak in others:

> Where the traffic is fast and heavy, it is because of the force of the market of commodities and services, and capital, and its flows and of the energies of entrepreneurship. Where the traffic is weak, it is generally a matter of cultural prejudices reinforced by high-level *realpolitik*.

Asian or Chinese modernity almost always implies the traveling of modernity from the West to Asia or China. Mark Elvin's "Modernity in China in Historical Perspective" rethinks the travel of modernity to China from a historian's point of view. The essay defines "something of the paradoxical nature of the modernity that has now become a part, in varying admixtures with still enduring older cultural elements, of most of the world's societies." Liao Ping-hui's "Civility and Self-Reflexivity: Three Texts on Women and Chinese Modernity" further explores the issue of modernity in China by bringing forth bounds of race and its interrelations with nationalisms, sexualities, class distinctions, cultural identities, science and ideology. By revealing the underlying ambivalence of race and gender from the standpoint of national unity and identity, Liao tries to put us "in a better situation to investigate the complex discursive formation of Chinese modernity in light of racial and cultural antagonism, anxiety, or ambivalence."

While transnationality places the emphasis on "across," *interculturality* shifts the bone of contention to interaction as the prefix "inter" suggests. Recent cultural studies have demonstrated that culture is itself multicultural, without encounters of various groups/communities it inevitably loses its vigor. It would be helpful to distinguish between interculturality and multiculturality; interculturality can be seen as a concept fuller than multiculturality as it stresses interaction. Wolfgang Welsch's account of the concepts of interculturality and multiculturality is helpful for our issue at hand. "Compared to traditional calls for cultural homogeneity the concept [of multiculturality] is progressive," remarks Welsch, "but its all too traditional understanding of cultures threatens to engender regressive tendencies which by appealing to a particularistic cultural identity lead to ghettoization or cultural fundamentalism." Welsch also expresses his concerns with the conception of interculturality as it "drags along with it unchanged the premise of the traditional conception of culture. It still proceeds from a conception of cultures as islands or spheres." To Welsch transculturality is the most adequate concept of culture today. His judgment is based on his belief that "cultures today are in general characterized by *hybridization*" (original emphasis).[21] As we mentioned earlier when we discuss the notion of transnationality, "nation" still casts a shadowy specter in the age of globalization. And as we will demonstrate later, some critics have reservations about cultural hybridization. We thus chose to use interculturality despite its conception of cultures as islands or spheres. Interaction, as the essays collected here show, might or might not lead to hybridization.

As emphasized by Wong Man Kong, "While Hong Kong was generally taken as an ample representation of Asian modernity, its position seemed to be taken for granted without any serious academic deliberation." Hong Kong is a very good example to investigate the interaction between Chinese and world cultures. Essays in this section try to look into interculturality by using Hong Kong (and Shanghai – its counterpart in the mainland) as the focus of inquiry. Wong Man Kong's "Biculturality as Modernity: A Hypothesis about the Origins of Modern Hong Kong" underlines the significance of the notion of biculturality, showing that why and how the co-presence of two cultures became possible in the special context of Hong Kong. The making of the bicultural character of Hong Kong, in Wong's discussion of the notions of biculturality enabled by an in-depth analysis of education and medicine, can be taken as "a useful vantage point to appreciate the origin of modern Hong Kong." Allen Chun's "Hong Kong Identity after the End of History" reminds us that modernity is hopelessly intertwined with nationalism and colonialism. The history of Hong Kong, as Chun lucidly demonstrates, has "relevant and significant things to

21 For greater details refer to Wolfgang Welsch, "Transculturality – the puzzling form of cultures today," Mike Featherstone and Scott Lash (eds), *Spaces of Culture: City, Nation, World* (London: Sage 1999), pp. 194–213.

say about the nature and operation of colonial modernity." Chun uses the example of Hong Kong to show, unlike Wong's emphasis on the co-presence of two cultures, that global capitalism is "not only the abstract operation of a market society, as though a realization of utilitarian ideals, but also the end product of its own ongoing, mutating historical process." Somewhere in between the two arguments, Chu Yiu Wai's "The Donaldization of Hong Kong Society" focuses on the so-called "Donaldization" of Hong Kong society brought forth by Donald Tsang, the Chief Executive of Hong Kong SAR, using it as an example to show how Donaldization cannot but be incomplete MacDonaldization as it has been targeting upon selected modernities. In this line of thought the alternative modernities of Hong Kong, should they be possible, are limited by "its famous hot commerce and cool politics character." Chu borrows Dirlik's point to account for the Donaldization of Hong Kong society:

> If we are to speak of alternative or multiple modernities, which presently valorize the persistence of traditions and 'civilizational' legacies, we need to recognize that the very language of alternatives and multiplicity is enabled historically by the presupposition of a common modernity shaped by a globalizing capitalism.

Amy Lee's "Frozen Motion: Nostalgia and Wang Anyi's Shanghai" deal with cultural interaction by using Wang Anyi's novels as examples. Not unlike Hong Kong, Shanghai is often seen as "a paradox with its mixture of foreign and Chinese features," as proposed by Amy Lee. Wang Anyi's Shanghai have represented "the city of Shanghai in the 1930s as a cultural matrix of Chinese modernity," to borrow Leo Lees' words in his *Shanghai Modern*.[22] Amy Lee outlines the elegant and basic atmosphere, the elite and ordinary qualities of Shanghai in the essay, which can well be put alongside with Hong Kong's characteristics for a further intercultural inquiry.

Eva Man addresses the issue of interculturality under the calls of global feminism and public philosophy, and argues in her essay that

22 Leo Ou-fan Lee, *Shanghai Modern: The Flowering of a New Urban Culture in China, 1930-1945* (Cambridge: Harvard University Press, 1999).

there is the common project of a utopian form of emancipation between the two. Postmodern discourses confirm that conceptualizations of difference have constituted the relations of domination, and these are the barriers to gender equality and human liberation as a whole. If differences are originated from the construction of subjectivity and otherness, this explains why some feminist theories are read as profoundly transgressive of the binary opposition of the self to others. Thus, it is claimed that in moving to the direction of global feminisms and public philosophies, one should create (or renew) other forms of self/other relation. This essay examines these suggestions and sees into the possibility of provoking a paradigm shift, implying that the development of a sense of self is dependent on one's relations with others, and that each person's moral integrity is integrally related to the maintenance of the moral integrity of others. In addition, the notions of Global feminisms and their situations are examined, as well as the development and the current discourses of public philosophy related to the issue. The focus is on the relation of the self and others, and hence the notions of the private and the public. The traditional Confucian model of these relations is studied and compared in this essay, and it has investigated the ways the Confucian model may act as a paradigm reference to feminist thoughts, thus reflecting on an intercultural issue of contemporary Asian modernities.

The interaction of cultures seems to have provided chances for culture to hybridize. But whether it is simply mixture or really *hybridity* is not easy to tell. Hybridity, one of the most disputed terms that has dominated conceptual discussions of mixed identities in postcolonial studies, is commonly defined as "the creation of new transcultural forms within the contact zone produced by colonization."[23] Homi Bhabha, one of the most vocal theoreticians to advocate hybridity as a kind of tactic to subvert hegemonic discourse, holds that hybridity can point towards a new cosmopolitanism that can engage different possibilities

23 Bill Ashcroft, Gareth Griffiths, and Helen Tiffin, *Key Concepts in Post-Colonial Studies* (London: Routledge, 1998), p. 118.

of cultural agency.[24] The widely used discourse of hybridity constitutes a very disputed terrain of cultural theory and criticism. While Néstor García Canclini celebrates hybridity in his *Hybrid Cultures*, he still worries that hybridization might also reinforce the already existing asymmetrical relationships of domination and subordination.[25] Meanwhile, different challenges to the concept of hybridity can also be found. "The importance of hybridity is that it problematizes boundaries," but hybridity is "inauthentic" and "multiculturalism lite" according to anti-hybridity arguments.[26] Colonial modernity, in Dirlik's view, was marked by inequalities in the "hybridization" of those who inhabited the contact zones of colonial modernity. He thus criticizes hybridity as complicitous with global capitalism and affirms that Eurocentrism is the focal point around which hybridities are built. This brings us to the potential problem resulting from the uncritical celebration of hybridity.

The essays collected in this section, which examine hybridity from different angles, can further contribute different dimensions to the debate. Robbie Goh's "Cyberasian: Science, Hybridity, Modernity, and the Asian Body" uses a different example to put forward a similar argument. While "Asian modernity still carries the heavy burden of negotiating national identities," Goh uses cyborg cultures to show "another dimension of the socio-cultural, political and economic battle that Asian nations are faced with in the age of modernization" if Asian modernity is to be a hybrid in an adaptive, confident and forward-looking manner.

The "battle" continues in Lo Wai Luk's "Three Paradigms in Hong Kong Drama in the 1970s: Hybridity in Styles." Lo interprets "modern" as a reaction against the Western powers in China, and thus "modernization" was first of all a political action. But in Lo's view the battle led to a promising hybridization of cultures. Through revealing the cultural logic behind the three paradigms of Hong Kong drama in the

24 Homi Bhabha, *The Location of Culture* (New York and London: Routledge, 1994).

25 Néstor García Canclini, *Hybrid Cultures: Strategies for Entering and Leaving Modernity* (Minneapolis: University of Minneapolis Press, 1995).

26 Jan Nederveen Pieterse, "Hybridity, so what? The anti-hybridity backlash and the riddles of recognition," *Theory, Culture & Society* 18: 2–3 (2001), pp. 219–45.

1970s, Lo points out that repressed modern Chinese drama, contemporary western drama, and local creations joined together in a time when Hong Kong citizens were developing a local consciousness. In his view "[t]heir hybrid energy was so great that it changes the ecology of Hong Kong drama, and marked an important step in the non-colonization of Hong Kong culture." When compared to Lo, Matthew Chew's notion of hybridity seems less straightforward. His "Hybridization of Karaoke and Dance Clubbing Practices in Chinese Nightlife" focuses on cultural hybridity in Chinese nightlife, but he admits that "cultural hybridity in Chinese nightlife can be difficult to notice, not necessarily because they are rare, but because a large part of nightlife has been carried out in semi-underground ways." Moreover, as warned of by Chew, "even though containing a superficially postmodern mix of cultural elements, some locally created nightlife forms are so commercially driven that they barely qualify as the kind of hybridity celebrated by Bhabha or Canclini." Chew's point sums up this section by reiterating the fact that it is necessary for us to distinguish the kind of hybridity celebrated by Bhabha or Canclini – if it be possible – from a superficially postmodern cultural mixture.

This introduction has raised rather than answered questions related to the title of this volume. For this we must ask for the indulgence of the readers. We are sure the essays collected here will offer insightful inquiries into these questions. Furthermore, we would like to conclude by stating that the categorization of the essays is far from clear-cut. Some essays straddle across the sub-fields. Hopelessly intertwined with one another, these concepts made things more complicated. As reflected in our foregoing discussion of the pluriversal meanings in the title *Contemporary Asian Modernities*, we champion a problematization of the concept of modernity/modernities. If this introduction can show how the collected essays enter into the (necessarily) incomplete project of modernity, it has served its specific function.

Part 1

Transnationality

Arif Dirlik

Asian Modernities in the Perspective of Global Modernity

I will say little below on the specifics of Asian modernities, if it is indeed possible to speak of a range of modernities that may be encompassed in some space we call Asia – which is not a stage upon which modernity plays out its fate but itself a product of a modern spatialization of the world, subject in its compass to the dynamic transformations of modernity, including modernity as practices by those inhabiting the region so described. Rather, I offer a discussion of what I take to be the dynamics of modernity at the present, which I have described on a number of occasions as "global modernity," to be distinguished from an earlier period of Eurocentric modernity.[1] Global modernity as concept is intended to account for the turn modernity has taken in its globalization. It is the contradictions of this modernity, and the burden upon it of past legacies, that are my main concern in this essay. What I have to say about global modernity in the abstract will, I hope, resonate with some of the concerns that drive discussions of modernities in Asia, or Asian modernities, as the case may be.

1 Arif Dirlik, *Global Modernity: Modernity in the Age of Global Capitalism* (Boulder, CO: Paradigm Press, 2006).

Global Modernity

I understand the term global modernity in the singular, as a "singular modernity," to use Fredric Jameson's phrase, that is nevertheless productive of contradictory claims on modernity for which it has come to serve as a site of conflict.[2] My insistence on the singularity of global modernity arises out of recognition of some validity to arguments for globalization, and the global commonalities it implies. At the same time, global modernity as concept is intended to overcome a teleological (and ideological) bias embedded in the very term globalization for global commonality and homogeneity. Global modernity recognizes as equally fundamental the tendencies to fragmentation and contradiction that are also products of globalization, and of past legacies that find exaggerated expression in their projection upon a global scene. Globalization in this perspective implies not just some naive expectation of a utopian-like global village or, conversely, an undesirable global hegemony, depending on perspective, but a proliferation of boundaries globally, adding new boundaries to already existing ones even as modernity is globalized. Notions of multiple or alternative modernities, in rendering into units of modernity traditions that are themselves the very products of modernity, in fact universalize the claims of modernity by appropriating them as endowments of otherwise vastly dif-

2 I stress this point in order to distinguish the argument here from approaches to global modernity in the plural, as in the case of the essays included in the collection, Mike Featherstone, Scott Lash, and Roland Robertson (eds), *Global Modernities* (Thousand Oaks, CA: Sage Publications, 1995), or in the special issue of *Daedalus*, "Multiple modernities," edited by S.N. Eisenstadt [Vol. 129, No. 1 (Winter, 2000)]. The former volume renders "global modernities" into a stand-in for globalization. The *Daedalus* volume recognizes the singular origins of modernity, but some of the contributions nevertheless stress differences based on culture over the commonalities of modernity. These approaches are problematic, I think, precisely because of their tendency to sweep under the rug issues of the colonial in modernity in the name of globalization. For "singular modernity," see, Fredric Jameson, *A Singular Modernity: Essay on the Ontology of the Present* (London: Verso, 2002).

ferent and complex pasts.[3] These claims often are also oblivious to the historicity of the present, and assume that present differences or commonalities may be read into the future, which is quite problematic. The long historical struggle against colonialism and unequal power relations has given way over the last two decades to conflicts over modernity, informed by national or civilization-wide cultural presence in globality even as nations and civilizations are rendered more tenuous in their existence by the globalizing pressures of an expanding transnational capitalism. This is also what renders the past – colonial modernity – quite relevant to the understanding of the present, with intensifying struggles to reconfigure the relationships of power that have shaped the world as we confront it today.

The globalization of modernity needs to be comprehended not just in the trivial sense of an originary modernity reaching out and touching all, even those who are left out of its benefits, as in the ideological deployments of globalization, but more importantly as a proliferation of claims on modernity. So-called traditions no longer imply a contrast with modernity, as they did in modernization discourse. Nor are they the domain of backward-looking conservatism, except in exceptional instances – such as the Taliban, for instance. They are invoked increasingly to establish claims to alternative modernities (but only rarely, to alternatives to modernity). They point not to the past, but taking a detour through the past, to an alternative future. They have taken over from a now defunct socialism – even in formally "socialist" societies, such as the People's Republic of China, the task of speaking for those oppressed or cast aside by a capitalist modernity, and pointing to different possibilities for the future.

3 I have discussed this in a number of places for the case of China, most notably in "Confucius in the Borderlands: Global capitalism and the reinvention of confucianism," in *boundary 2*, Vol. 22: 3 (November 1995): 229–73. For an illuminating discussion of the manner in which assumptions of modernity were internalized in Indian history, see, Gyan Prakash, *Another Reason: Science and the Imagination of Modern India* (Princeton, NJ: Princeton University Press, 1999). Prakash's discussion is particularly relevant here for his deployment of "colonial modernity" in addressing this issue.

The irony is that these claims to difference in most cases presuppose a commonality where assumptions of progress and development is concerned in a fetishization of development that is, developmentalism – for which the sole model is capitalist development, with some local modifications the future of which remain highly uncertain. The contradictions they present are very real, and significant culturally and politically. Bolstered by success in development, assertions of cultural difference proliferate, breaking down the universalist presuppositions of Eurocentric models of modernity. But the cultural assumptions of claims to difference are themselves subject to disintegrative forces in their very mobilization in the cause of development, as development produces social and cultural forces, including cosmopolitan classes that are not easily containable within imagined cultural crucibles. This is what I have in mind when I refer to the universalization of the contradictions of a capitalist modernity; not just between societies but, more importantly, within them. If this indeed is the case, contemporary arguments over universalism versus particularism, homogenization versus heterogenization, and even postcolonial notions of hybridization, Third Spaces, and so on, are largely off the mark, and hinder, rather than help, analysis.[4] Firstly, because such arguments tend toward an either/or approach to these questions, avoiding the possibility – quite visible globally – that both tendencies may be at work, not in some facile process of hybridization, or the substitution of hybrid spaces for essentialized spaces of old, but in the proliferation of spaces and the contradictions they present. Secondly, the focus on Eurocentrism in such arguments, where they avoid the question of capitalism, restrict analysis to the level of abstract cultural, national, or civilizational values, ignoring the very significant transformations at work in the globalization of technological values and attendant cultural practices, that are very much bound up with the universalization of capitalism, how-

4 I have analyzed this problem at greater length, with reference to the People's Republic of China, in, Arif Dirlik, "Markets, culture, power: The making of a 'Second Cultural Revolution' in China," *Asian Studies Review* 25, No. 1 (March 2001): 1–34.

ever it may be modified otherwise to suit localized needs. The claims of Eurocentrism to universality may be dead. We may hardly say the same of the capitalist civilization which was the historical creation of Europe and North America, which now rules the world even where its origins may have been forgotten, or ignored. We need to take seriously the distinctive claims to different pasts and different futures in what someone like Guehenno perceives the "resurgence of histories" suppressed under the regime of modernity. But neither can we ignore that the cultural endowments which justify such claims have been infused thoroughly with the everyday values of production and consumption that are characteristic of capitalist society, in the invention and propagation of which Europe and North America still play key roles, even when they no longer provide directly the agents who propagate those values. The globalization of production and consumption through transnational agencies, most important among them transnational corporations still based for the most part in Euro/America, is in the process of creating a "transnational capitalist class" that shares not only similar occupations but similar education and life-styles as well.[5] One of the most important developments of recent years is the transnationalization of university education, not just with the increased attendance in first world universities of elites from the third world, but the export from the first world to the third of both models of education, and of actual university campuses.[6] The relationship is not itself new; but it is not

5 For the transnational capitalist class, see, Leslie Sklair, *The Transnational Capitalist Class* (Oxford, UK: Basil Blackwell, 2001), and, William I. Robinson, *A Theory of Global Capitalism: Production, Class, and State in a Transnational World* (Baltimore, MD: Johns Hopkins University Press, 2004).

6 This development needs much closer attention. For one illuminating discussion, see, Kris Olds, "Articulating agendas and traveling principles in the layering of new strands of academic freedom in contemporary singapore," in Barbara Czarniawska, and Guje Savon (eds),*Global Ideas: How Ideas, Objects and Practices Travel in the Global Economy* (Copenhagen: Liber and Copenhagen Business School Press, 2005). In 2003, the leadership of Beijing University (one of the premier educational institutions in the People's Republic of China) created a furor with plans to transform the university, including changing instruction to English. For a collection of the debates that ensued, see, Qian Liqun, and Gao

insignificant that what once was undertaken by missionary activity is now conducted directly by an educational apparatus (educational institutions, educational consultants, publishers), that is not only under the direct sway of corporations, but increasingly model themselves after corporate management, and play a strategic part in the technologization and marketization of education itself.[7] Multiculturalism, itself invented by transnational corporations, appears in this perspective as a way of managing difference within a context of commonality (without which difference would be meaningless).

Thirdly, therefore, debates over issues of culture are increasingly meaningless to the extent that they take as their units nations, civilizations, or so-called "cultures." The increasing visibility of a transnational capitalist class would suggest different locations for culture. This class may partake of local characteristics, but it is unified also by participation in a common organization of the political economy, a common education, and common life-styles that not only provide them with a "third space" of their own, but also distance them from their immediate environment – sometimes behind locked gates in emulation of American

Yuandong (eds), *Zhongguo daxuede wenti yu gaige* (Problems and Reform of Higher Education in China), (Tianjin: Tianjin People's Press, 2003). See also, Dai Xiaoxia, Mo Jiahao, and Xie Anbang (eds), *Gaodeng jiaoyu shichanghua* (Marketization of Higher Education), (Beijing: Beijing University Press, 2004), and, Wang Xiao, *Quanqiuhua yu Zhongguo jiaoyu* (Globalization and Chinese Education) (Chengdu: Sichuan People's Press, 2002).

7 The University of Liverpool in the UK announced at the end of October 2005 that it was establishing a campus in the PRC jointly with Xi'an Jiaotong University, that would concentrate on technological subjects. According to a report, interestingly, the campus is to be located in Suzhou Industrial Park in Eastern China, which is quite a distance not only from Liverpool, but also from Xi'an. The attraction of the location is that it is home to foreign enterprises in the PRC, including fifty-three Fortune 500 Companies. The founding of the University, in other words, is one more example of higher education as enterprise, this time as "joint enterprise," that has been the standard form of Sino-foreign business collaboration. The deal, moreover, is being backed up by Laureate Educational Limited, an on-line education transnational. See. Polly Curtis, "Liverpool to establish Chinese University," *Guardian Unlimited*, October 27, 2005.

life-styles.[8] The same may be said of other social groupings. Notions of gender are increasingly globalized, as women, depending on class, engage in similar cultural practices globally, or gather together to struggle against the ravages of globalization. Migrant tradespeople and migrant workers, at the other end of the social scale, come to partake of a common culture, as they move back and forth across boundaries of nation and continent, contributing to the appearance of globalization, but also profoundly transforming societies both of departure and origin. The point in all of this is not global homogenization or assimilation to global roles, but a question of material and cultural contexts that are at once products of these processes, and launch societies in new directions, creating new kinds of unities as well as new kinds of fractures. Any exploration of contemporary global processes needs to be attentive to this question of the "location of culture," to borrow Homi Bhabha's felicitous term (against his intentions),[9] that is no longer associated with nations or civilizations, in spite of all the apparent evidence presently of conflicts between so-called Christian, Islamic, Confucian, etc., civilizations or nations, which serve more as mobilizing ideas than as descriptions of life at the everyday level in the societies so depicted. Such conflicts need to be taken seriously, as mobilizing ideas do come into play as important historical forces, but they should not blind us to the complexities presented by simultaneous forces making for global commonality, on the one hand, and the many other dimensions of global fractures, on the other. I might add the globalization appears here as only one dimension of a historical process that has many other dimensions – an add-on to existing forces of the many dimensions of localization that has the power to reconfigure those forces, but gets reconfigured itself in the process. Such are the contradictions of global modernity.

8 For one of example of many such reports on such developments, mostly celebratory, see, "Looks like American suburbia, but it's home in India," *The Register-Guard*, Sunday, October 9, 2005, p. A19. Many a housing development in the People's Republic of China advertises itself with names derived from locations in the US, especially California.

9 Homi Bhabha, *The Location of Culture* (London: Routledge, 2004).

To summarize briefly here what I take to be the outstanding features of "Global Modernity," there are four aspects that distinguish it as a concept both from an earlier period of modernity, and globalization. Firstly, Global Modernity is in many ways the contemporary resting place of globalization. Stated differently, globalization as we have known it – driven by capitalism – is not something that is happening that has yet to fulfill its promise, or something that is about to happen. It already has happened. And the result is Global Modernity. True, "Empire" as Hardt and Negri have identified it is very much a fact of Global Modernity, with the United States as a supreme military power claiming global sovereignty for itself while on occasion denying to others even their claims to national sovereignty. But this is an Empire ridden with contradictions; which open up the spaces for alternatives to its rule. Within these spaces there are appearing challengers to Empire, legitimized not only by modern ideals of democracy, justice and popular sovereignty, but also by the revival of past legacies; which are not merely residues from the past, but represent legacies that already have been worked over by modernity; in other words, they are postmodern. The conflicts between these legacies are over alternative claims to modernity, and as they are divided by such claims, and conflicting interests, they are also grounded in a common terrain defined by a globalized capitalism.

Despite enormous differences in power, levels of material development, and incorporation within a global capitalist economy, secondly, Global Modernity is characterized by temporal contemporaneity, which distinguishes it from an earlier Eurocentric modernity. It was only about two decades ago that Johannes Fabian published his classic critique of Anthropology, *Time and the Other* (1983), where he argued that the denial of "coevalness" to the Other was fundamental to the Eurocentric teleology of modernity.[10] Already in the early 1980s, Europe's East Asian "Others" were claiming possible superiority in the development of capitalism. Modernization discourse had drawn a clear line between tradi-

10 Johannes Fabian, *Time and the Other: How Anthropology Makes Its Object* (NY: Columbia University Press, 1983).

tion and modernity, and rendered their relationship into a zero-sum relationship: the more modern, the less traditional. East Asian "tigers," so-called, already felt empowered by their success in the capitalist economy to claim that the "Confucian" tradition they drew upon was a force not of backwardness (as it had been earlier) but of success, a claim that was backed by their cheer-leaders in Europe and North America. At about the same time, the Iranian revolution of 1979 brought forth claims about the modernity of Islam. One by one, societies globally have revived or proclaimed the compatibility of their traditions (or cultural legacies) with modernity, and made it the basis for their claims to alternative modernities. The advanced-backward distinction has not disappeared from mutual perceptions between nations, "cultures" and "civilizations," but is overdetermined increasingly by differences within the same population, including the fundamental structural differentiation of those who are on the pathways of global capitalism and those who are not. Global Modernity by no means represents the "death" of the nation-state or of nationalism. On the contrary, the last few years have witnessed both a proliferation of nationalisms, and a strengthening in the power of the state vis-à-vis the population. The transformations associated with globalization have been of a different kind, in the abandonment by states of their responsibilities to large sectors of their populations, and a shift of attention from national surfaces to global nodes in the pursuit of development (not to be confused with obliviousness to national borders). I will elaborate this in the essay on Public Health in the People's Republic of China below.

The globalization of capitalism, thirdly, has reconfigured global relations. The tripartite spatialization of the world produced during the cold war years was internalized in modernization discourse. The fall of the second world of socialism, and the appearance of new centers of capital from the 1960s has ended up scrambling this neat geographical spatialization, also raising questions in the process about nations as viable units of the economy, politics or culture. What is called globalization is in reality a conglomeration of phenomena that occur at different scales, from the global to the regional to the national to the intranational and the local. This spatialization is complicated further by the persistence of earlier spatializations, such as the colonial spaces to which I have referred above, as well as spaces of indigeneity. There are presently first worlds in the third (e.g. Shanghai), and third worlds in the first (e.g. New Orleans). Global Capitalism moves along networks, with global cities at its nodes. This has also meant the shift of economic activity from surfaces to networks. I will elaborate on this shift below, in the discussion of public health under globalization. Suffice it to say here that as capital (and associated) organizations move along the networks, those who are not on the networks, or are outside of the network economy, fall through the cracks, and feel the effects of the global economy only by its inductive effects on their livelihood. The majority of the world's population is now in a process of marginalization or, as some anthropologists have put it even more strongly, "abjection-being thrown down and thrown out of the global."[11]

Fourthly, it is not entire spaces that are being left out of the global economy (which exposes eloquently the ideological basis of globalization), but also entire groups of people across national boundaries. Class structuration, in other words, has gone global with the appearance of a "transnational capitalist class," and comparable class, gender and ethnic formations at different scales. This renders misleading those arguments that continue to take nations and civilizations as their units. Such arguments ignore the transnationalization and translocalization (to be distinguished from globalization) of economic, social and cultural formations. Differences that are taken to be differences between nations and civilizations are, more often than not, also differences within the same society that are hidden from sight when the focus is on the inside/outside of national and civilizational boundaries. Classes, genders and ethnicities, as well as organizational formations of one kind or another – from NGOs to transnational corporations to professional organizations – are as much the "locations of culture" as are nations and civilizations, complicating both social formations and cultural con-

11 Jack R. Friedman, "Ambivalence, abjection, and the outside of the global: On statementality", 53 pp., p. 5, unpublished paper. I am grateful to Prof. Friedman for sharing this paper with me.

figurations. It is these complications that make it difficult to speak of imperialism, or of cultural homogenization or heterogenization. Where all this may end up is hardly predictable at this point as capital itself (not to speak of states) seems to have lost all vision of the future, beyond the manipulation of existing differences for purposes of immediate power and profit. It is for the same reason that it is meaningless to speak of "alternative modernities," as if cultural revivalisms of the present may be read teleologically into the future. It is this state of affairs, with a surplus of history but deficit of future that the concept of Global Modernity seeks to capture. It may be for the same reason that most of our contemporary vocabulary of "posts" refer primarily to the past, without the courage or the hope to name the future.

The contradictions of Global Modernity also make it difficult to speak of colonialism – not just at the present but, by implication, in the histories of which the present is a product in its own complicated and multi-directional transformations. Colonialism as concept also has lost much of its critical power with the abolition of the temporal gap between modernity and tradition, that only a generation ago justified both a progressivist and Eurocentric modernization discourse, as well as radical criticism of the colonialist impulses that informed it. This is not to suggest that those impulses have disappeared from global politics, but they appear in a far more complicated guise than they did earlier, that undercuts the ability of colonialism in an earlier sense to serve either as a historical explanation or a mobilizing political idea.

Global modernity appears at one level as the end of colonialism, a product of decolonization that has enabled the surge into modernity, as alternatives to colonialist modernity, of the formerly colonized. On the other hand, it may be viewed also as the universalization and deepening of colonialism, in the internalization into societies globally of the premises of a capitalist modernity that was deeply entangled in colonialism, to which there is now no viable alternative. This ambiguity opens up the possibility that what we are witnessing presently – from the transnationalization of capital to human motions to cultural conflict – is not so much decolonization as the reconfiguration of colonialism as capital is globalized, necessitating the incorporation in its operations of new states that are crucial to global management, and a voice for the classes of its creation who provide the personnel for that management. It is remarkable that the destructuring and deterritorialization of earlier regimes of coloniality, rather than put an end to colonialism, has intensified colonial conflicts – now rephrased as conflicts over globality, "many globalizations," in the phraseology of a recent volume.[12] Earlier colonial structurings of power, including its mappings of both the physical and the social worlds, are still visible in the palimpsest of global geopolitics. They provide both the context and the horizon of global politics even as formerly marginalized states and the subalterns of colonial capitalism enter the fray.

The End of Colonialism?

It is ironic that colonialism became difficult to speak about even as the term moved to the center of critical discourse in the early 1990s. Postcolonial criticism, responsible for bringing colonialism into the center of critical discourses, also is responsible for an inflation of the concept that has rendered it quite problematic. The concept has been rendered even more incoherent by the appropriation of paradigmatic postcolonial concepts (hybridity, borderlands, and so on) for social distinctions that have little to do with colonialism in a strict sense, such a gender, race, ethnicity, etc. The broader the concept becomes in its compass, the greater the incoherence, and the more remote its relationship to an earlier notion of the postcolonial. The incoherence also has implications for our understanding of the present. In the works of

12 *Many Globalizations: Cultural Diversity in the Contemporary World*, Peter L. Berger, and Samuel P. Huntington (eds) (Oxford and New York: Oxford University Press, 2002). The title refers to the multiplying efforts in the contemporary world to project national/civilizational values on the global scene. In other words, we are all imperialists now, though we may not be equally good at the undertaking!

theorists who are (rightly or wrongly) associated with the emergence of postcolonial criticism such as Edward Said, Stuart Hall or Gayatri Spivak, the postcolonial was of importance *because* of the relevance of colonialism to understanding the present (the "post" implying not after but more like "produced by"). This is visible even in the work of someone like Homi Bhabha, whose deconstructive efforts would contribute significantly to rendering the term meaningless. "Postcoloniality," Bhabha wrote in 1994, "is a salutary reminder of the persistent 'neo-colonial' relations within the 'new' world order and the multi-national division of labour." Nevertheless, increasingly from the 1990s, the postcolonial has dissipated into areas that had nothing to do with the colonial, and rendered into a literary reading strategy rather than a social and political concept – largely under the influence of the likes of Bhabha.[13]

The difficulties of dealing with colonialism and imperialism in the present are quite evident in the discussions provoked by the book, *Empire*, by Michael Hardt and Antonio Negri, and their argument that imperialism has now given way to an abstract Empire, without a clearly identifiable center or boundaries, where empire is as much a condition of everyday life as it is of a legal order that recognizes no outside.[14] The thesis is outrageous against the background of a United States imperialism that respects no boundaries except those of practical power, and corporate colonization of the world. And yet few have cared to reject the argument outright, as I think we are all vaguely aware that something is at work that was not there before, that this imperialism presupposes a different ordering of the world than in the days of good old-

13 For extended discussion of issues of the postcolonial, see, Arif Dirlik, *The Postcolonial Aura: Third World Criticism in the Age of Global Capitalism* (Boulder, CO: Westview Press, 1997).

14 Michael Hardt and Antonio Negri, *Empire* (Cambridge, MA: Harvard University Press, 2000). I prefer "colonial" to "imperial" in this discussion because, in my understanding, while the two terms share in common the sense of the political control of one society by another, colonial refers more directly to experiences at the everyday level, including cultural experiences, which are crucial I think to grasping the relationship between the present and the world of colonialism of which it is the product.

fashioned imperialism. Thus, two authors, insistent on the continuity of the present with the past, nevertheless feel constrained to write that:

> Using this concept, the network of institutions that define the structure of the new global economic system is viewed not in structural terms, but as intentional and contingent, subject to the control of individuals who represent and seek to advance the interests of a new international capitalist class. This class, it is argued, is formed on the basis of institutions that include a complex of some 37,000 transnational corporations (TNCs), the operating units of global capitalism, the bearers of capital and technology and the major agents of the new imperial order. These TNCs are not the only organizational bases of this order, which include the World Bank, the International Monetary fund. [...] In addition, the New World Order is made up of a host of global strategic planning and policy forums. [...] All of these institutions form an integral part of the new imperialism – the new system of global governance.[15]

The authors elide the question of why imperialism should be viewed as such in the presence of "a new international capitalist class," which creates at least some blurring of the distinction between the subjects and objects of imperialism. When imperialism arrives by invitation, is it still imperialism? On the other hand, the "new international capitalist class" is increasingly global in constitution, albeit sharing ever more visibly a common education and, therefore, a common culture. Similarly to the transnationalization of corporate capital, the transnationalization of higher educational institutions, often as "joint enterprises," is one of the foremost expressions of this common culture, and its entanglement with the culture of corporate capital, deepening the corporatization of higher education globally. If this is imperialism, it is imperialism that is to a significant degree self-inflicted![16]

15 James Petras and Henry Veltmeyer, *Globalization Unmasked: Imperialism in the 21st Century* (Halifax, NS: Fernwood Publishing/ZED Books, 2002), 12.

16 Bill Readings addressed this question in *The University in Ruins* (Cambridge, MA: Harvard University Press, 1996). The "transnationalization" of the university is visible both in the increased visibility, mostly in first world locations, of students from around the world (who can now afford education in first world institutions), as well as in the proliferation across national boundaries of the campuses of first world universities, which, if the trend continues, themselves may get to look like transnational business networks.

Contemporary ambivalence about imperialism also has implications for our understanding of past colonialism. To take one example of global significance, as recently as two decades ago, it seemed quite unproblematic to speak of imperialism in Modern Chinese history, and of the extensive educational activities conducted by foreigners – most importantly missionaries – as one of the most important media in the production and consolidation of Euro/American cultural hegemony. Education in the hands of missionaries seemed designed to complete the job begun by gunboats. For nationalists in China as elsewhere, with their ideological investment in state-directed education as the most effective instrument of creating a homogeneous culture and loyal citizens, foreign involvement in education meant ideological subjugation and, consequently, compromise of national sovereignty.

It is remarkable how problematic this view of education as a tool of imperialism has become over the last decade. It is not that nationalist objections to foreign-sponsored education have disappeared, or that historians are no longer concerned with issues thrown up by the confrontation between nationalism and imperialism (or colonialism). "Decolonizing the mind" still appears as an urgent task to conservative as well as radical postcolonial intellectuals obsessed with unfinished national projects, and conservatives globally (including the US) contemplate with anxiety if not outright hostility any effort to introduce greater social and ethnic complexity to the writing of national histories, which they feel might weaken the nation ideologically. In the People's Republic of China itself, patriotic education is very much the order of the day, and the postsocialist regime finds in the reaffirmation of civilizational values a source of legitimation as a substitute for the waning faith in socialism.

There has been a proliferation in recent years of doubts concerning the historical status of both imperialism and nationalism. What is most important in recent transformations, I would like to suggest here, is the challenge presented by the progressive blurring of the distinction between the inside and the outside that has been crucial over the last century to the sustenance of the seemingly unbridgeable opposition between the national and the colonial (or imperialist). The blurring of this distinction is not just ideological, but social in a very significant sense. Structural transformations in global relationships have endowed with a new significance social groups that are the products of two centuries of global interactions between colonizers and colonized, who long were objects of suspicion in nationalist ideology but find themselves valorized in new ways as they increasingly occupy a strategic position in the global economy. It is not very surprising that the education that produced these groups is also subject to re-evaluation accordingly. As an intense desire for incorporation in global capitalism replaces in Communist Party policy the radical anti-imperialism of Maoist revolutionary socialism, it is not very surprising that we should be witnessing in the People's Republic of China a similar reevaluation of modern Chinese history, and of the role in it of imperialism, and its cultural legacies, including education.

In a provocative study of cultural imperialism published in the early 1990s, John Tomlinson argued the entanglement of cultural imperialism in issues of modernity, and urged that in the assigning of "blame" for the ills of domination, a distinction be made between "the critical discourse of modernity and the other discourses of cultural imperialism." He wrote:

> In the latter, some clear, *present*, agent of domination was identified: the mass media, America, multinational capitalists. There was the idea that this agent was responsible – that criticism meant laying the blame at its door. But here we have to think of a *situation* being to blame and this is less satisfying to the critical spirit. Thinking in terms of modernity seems to mean thinking in a rather different critical mode from that employed in the discourse of cultural imperialism. It seems to mean, for example, accepting that our cultural discontents have complex multiple determinations that have arisen over time and thus that no *present* agent is responsible in any full sense.[17]

Tomlinson's substitution of modernity (a "situation") for cultural imperialism (an "agency") was informed by a further distinction he made in the unfolding of modernity through a period of imperialism to a

17 John Tomlinson, *Cultural Imperialism* (Baltimore, MD: Johns Hopkins University Press, 1991), 168–69.

present condition of globalization, beginning roughly in the 1970s. "Globalisation may be distinguished from imperialism," he wrote,

> in that it is a far less coherent or culturally directed process. [...] the idea of imperialism contains, at least, the notion of a purposeful project: the *intended* spread of a social system from one centre of power across the globe. The idea of 'globalisation' suggests interconnection and interdependency of all global areas which happens in a far less purposeful way.[18]

I would like to bracket here for the moment the possibility that Tomlinson's questioning of "cultural imperialism" at the moment of the fall of socialisms and the global victory of capitalism is only one more example of an enthusiasm over a non-imperial globality that was characteristic of the 1990s, that since then has been rendered largely irrelevant by an intensified United States imperialism that may well be unprecedented in its urge to "spread [...] a social system from one centre of power across the world." The idea of an empire without center or boundary and, therefore, agency, would be argued even more forcefully by the end of the decade by Antonio Negri and Michael Hardt. These questionings of "imperialism" have been accompanied, most importantly in postcolonial criticism, by questions concerning the relationship between nationalism and colonialism that further have called into question the utility of the concepts of colonialism and imperialism in understanding not only the present, but the past as well. In some contemporary works, the colonial and imperial pasts appear merely as stages of an inexorable globalization that has presently replaced an earlier modernization discourse as a paradigm for understanding the development of the modern world – of which Tomlinson's own work provides one example.[19]

It is possible also to reverse the relationship here, as I will suggest below: that rather than the history of colonialism disappearing into a

18 Ibid., 175.

19 See, for example, the essays collected in A.G. Hopkins (ed.), *Globalization in World History* (London: Random House, 2002). The volume offers a new periodization of world history in terms of four periods of archaic, proto-, modern and postcolonial globalization.

new teleology of globalization, globalization itself may be understood as the fulfillment of a modernity of which colonialism and imperialism have been constituent moments: colonial modernity. Contrary to Tomlinson, moreover, modernity is no more "just" a situation than the capitalism which dynamizes it, which has its own agencies. Colonialism has been a preeminent agency in the globalization of modernity. If we seem today to live in a world where colonialism has been superseded by a global modernity, in which the formerly colonized and dominated once again assert their own political and cultural claims to modernity, this global modernity is nevertheless one that has been marked indelibly by its origins in colonialism; as is quite apparent in its unevenness, as well as the uneven distributions of economic, social, political and cultural power that are the legacies to it of modern colonialism and imperialism, distinguished historically by their sources in capitalism and the nation-state.

The Colonial Modern in the Making of Global Modernity

Whatever name we may employ to describe the present, it is hard to overcome a sense of modernity gone wrong; which inevitably makes one wonder if it was wrong all along! While this sense may be stronger in some locations than in others, it is there regardless of where we may look. There are no longer havens from modernity, backward or progressive. This is the condition of global modernity. It is the product of the globalization of colonial modernity.

The idea of colonial modernity has appeared with some regularity over the last few years, largely as a consequence of postcolonial criticism. It appears in these writings as a concept intended to overcome the binarism of the modern and the colonial, one centered in Euro/America and looking-forward, the other covering much of the third world – the term that came to denote colonial and semi-colonial regions after World War II – and identified with backwardness. Colonial modernity affirms the contemporaneity and the complicity of the modern and the colonial, rendering the terms into two inextricable constituents of a relationship.[20] The colonized, rather than being left out of history by virtue of being colonized, as was conceived both in colonial and postcolonial nationalist historiography, now acquire a history as agents in a colonial modernity which they helped fashion with their participation in its workings.[21]

20 Tani Barlow, "Introduction," in T. Barlow (ed.), *Formations of Colonial Modernity in East Asia* (Durham, NC: Duke University Press, 2000), 1–20.

21 "Colonial modernity," at least in some usages, is endowed with normalcy as any other kind of modernity. Thus, the editors of a recent volume on Korean modernity write that, "'True modernity' here would mean that an independent and discrete Korean modernity was interrupted by the imposition of Japanese colonial rule. Yet this precolonial modernity is also described using a Western-centered conception of the key elements of modernity. It is thus impossible to separate different models of modernity in such a manner," *Colonial Modernity in Korea*, Gi-wook Shin, and Michael Robinson (eds) (Cambridge, MA: Harvard University Press, 1999), 382, n.18. Shin and Robinson stress the unequal power relations that shaped this colonial modernity, including the unevenness that resulted from it (p. 11). Their work nevertheless has been received with some resentment in Korea for erasing or downplaying colonialism (I owe this to a personal communication from Prof. Paik Nak-chung). In some discussions of modernity under the aegis of colonialism, the word colonial itself does not even appear with any prominence. See, for example, Leo Ou-fan Lee, *Shanghai Modern: The Flowering of a New Urban Culture in China, 1930–1945* (Cambridge, MA: Harvard University Press, 1999), that deliberately privileges the colonial modern as *the* modern. For an elaborate affirmation of the modernity of colonial modernity against its nationalist and Marxist critics who stress its deficiencies (its "lacks"), see, Dipesh Chakrabarty, "Subaltern histories and post-enlightenment rationalism," *Habitations of Modernity: Essays in the Wake of Subaltern Studies* (Chicago: University of Chicago Press, 2002), 20–37. With his own commitment to the postcolonial, Chakrabarty is vague on the coloniality of the modern at the present. The deployment of "colonial modernity" that comes closest to my argument here is in Andrew F. Jones, *Yellow Music: Media Culture and Colonial Modernity in the Chinese Jazz Age* (Durham, NC: Duke University Press, 2001). Jones underlines the transformative power of the colonial, its foundations in political economy, and its persistence even in its radical or right-wing appropriations for nationalist purposes. He is vague, however, on its long-term applications, partly because his study stops in 1937, and partly because of a tendency to merge the colonial into the transnational.

This perspective is neither wrong nor unreasonable. But it is as partial as the earlier view it has replaced, that valorized not the hybrid products of colonialism, which it did recognize, but the revolutionary subject, equally a product of the colonial encounter, who rejected the possibility of an accommodation with colonialism, and sought through the anti-colonial struggle to overcome bourgeois modernity in general in search of an alternative – not to modernity as such but to bourgeois modernity. The alternative modernities which now assert themselves against Euro /American paradigms of modernity are products of the interaction between particular colonialisms and precolonial native legacies, fashioned into localized modernities by the subjects of colonial modernity. These are now also the subjects of global modernity, asserting themselves on a global scene in the ideological spaces seemingly evacuated by a "provincialized" Euro /America, in tenuous negotiation over the future of modernity that frequently degenerates into the reassertion of colonial practices.

Colonial modernity in much of this contemporary postcolonial writing is intended, on the one hand, to reaffirm the modernness of the colonized, and, on the other hand, to undermine Eurocentric claims to a modernity that can be conceived apart from colonialism. Without questioning either the historical or the political validity of this impulse, I would like to suggest nevertheless that the urge to rescue the colonized for history also calls for some caution against tendencies to a reductionist equation of the modern and the colonial which, though inextricably related, nevertheless are not reducible to one another; to the dispersal of modernity into an endless number of modernities which, accompanied by a rejection of totalities, deprives modernity even of synecdochal unity, depriving it of all meaning; downplaying structural inequalities that globally shaped colonial modernity; and, dissolving dialectical interplays between the actors of colonial modernity into diffuse borderlands hybridities that dispense with the necessity of accounting for power relations that shape the borderlands, and their social, political and cultural products.

I would like to suggest that rather than collapse the two terms, it may be more productive both intellectually and politically to identify the colonial in the modern, and the modern in the colonial; which may enable both an avoidance of the teleology of modernization, and the somewhat naive urge in third worldist anti-colonialism to overcome the modern. At a time when reactionary fundamentalism is on the surge globally, some caution is necessary politically in casting the modern into the prison-house of the colonial. On the other hand, an unqualified identification of the colonial as modern – except in the very specific historical sense of locating it in terms of relationships – obscures conflicts over modernity among the colonials themselves, but may also end up depriving criticism of its ability to deal with reactionary elements in formerly colonial societies, as all are now qualified as modern out of historical location, as if modern itself could have no substantial content aside from such relationships.

Colonial modernity is best viewed as a structural relationship, made dynamic by a capitalism emanating from Euro/America, that is a product of the dialectics between the structuring forces of capitalism that have been global in scope and reach (not universal or homogeneous for being global), and the many local forces transformed by these forces but also transforming them into many local guises, which then could act back upon Euro/American societies with transformative effects of their own. The term "colonial modern," in its original deployment in earlier, colonial, times, was infused with a sense of power relations that might be useful to recall presently. Robert Rydell writes of what he describes as "the 'coloniale moderne' sensibility" in early twentieth century universal expositions that:

> Rooted in the exotic fascination with the "Other" cultivated at European fairs before the Great War, coloniale moderne – a conjuncture of modernistic architectural styles and representations of imperial policies that stressed the benefits of colonialism to colonizer and colonized alike – developed from the desire by European imperial authorities to decant the old wine of imperialism into new bottles bearing the modernistic designs of the interwar years. More specifically, the coloniale moderne practice – *habitus* may be a better expression – crystallized around efforts by governments to make the modernistic dream worlds of mass consumption on view at fairs unthinkable apart from the maintenance and extension of empire.[22]

22 Robert Rydell, *World of Fairs: The Century-of-Progress Exhibitions* (Chicago: The University of Chicago Press, 1993), p. 62. The participants in the production of

Colonial modernity, in other words, was marked not only by inequalities in power structurally, but also inequalities in the "hybridization" of those who inhabited the contact zones of colonial modernity. The term "colonial modernity" was deployed in specifically colonial situations, but it may be productive in hindsight to view it as a defining characteristic of modernity in general; even where colonialism, technically speaking, did not exist – as in China or Turkey, for example. Some of these societies had colonial ambitions of their own, but efforts to find some kind of equivalence between these world empire colonialisms and the colonialism of capitalist or socialist modernity of the kind associated with actually existing socialisms, with the nation-state at its center, are not very convincing.[23] These were the societies that, following formal decolonization, would be renamed the third world. Now the third world itself has lost much of its meaning, but the global inequalities that informed the deployment of the term are still very much with us, even if new mappings have been superimposed upon earlier delineations of the nations and regions encompassed by the term.

Aside from the hegemonic relationships produced by Euro/American power, it seems to me that the most important instrument of colonialism in the modern age was the nation-state which, as I have argued above, itself was a colonizing force as an agent of modernization. The colonialism of the nation-state is even more starkly evident in third world situations, where the nation-state has claimed for itself a civilizing mission in bringing modernity to the population it claims as its own. Whether we view the nation in class, gender and ethnic, or urban-rural and regional terms, nation-building, representing the demands of those who view themselves to be the most modernized elements in society, has served as the most thorough-going instrument of the colonization of the world in the name of modernity, that is both extensive

---

various forms of art identifiable as "colonial modern" included the indigenous people, colonials of European origin, and Europeans influenced by the exoticism of the colonies.

23 For one such effort, see, Laura Hostetler, *Qing Colonial Enterprise: Ethnography and Cartography in Early Modern China* (Chicago: University of Chicago Press, 2001).

and intensive: the colonization of physical space as well as the spaces of everyday life and the interior spaces of individuals.

On the other hand, it is also important to note that colonialism also shaped modernity in its original homelands by practises that were evolved in the process of the colonial invasion and transformation of the world. Gauri Viswanathan has shown the impact on literary education in England, including the teaching of English, of methods developed with great success teaching colonial subjects in India.[24] Susan Thorne has brought out the importance in the cultural formation of nineteenth-century England of missionary attitudes and practices that had evolved in the colonies.[25] French colonial officials, bringing to the colonies the most modern methods of governance, believed "that the arts of government [...] deployed in the colonies were also applicable in France."[26] We are already well aware from scholarship on the third world, of which Edward Said's *Orientalism* and *Cultural Imperialism* are seminal examples, of the ways in which conquest of the world has shaped modern Euro/American learning and its organization – which, for all practical purposes, *is* modern learning, and the ways in which this learning has appropriated for itself the learning of the world, discarding ways of knowing that do not fit in with its imperial claims to truth. Most fundamentally, capitalism itself may be incomprehensible without reference to colonialism. The history of capitalism is in many ways coeval with the history of colonialism which, as Fernand Braudel has argued, included the colonization of Europe itself by a world economy expanding from the Mediterranean in all directions of the globe.

24 Gauri Viswanathan, *Masks of Conquest: Literary Study and British Rule in India* (New York: Columbia University Press, 1989).

25 Susan Thorne, *Congregational Missions and the Making of an Imperial Culture in Nineteenth Century England* (Stanford: Stanford University Press, 1999). See also, Catherine Hall, *Civilising Subjects: Metropole and Colony in the English Imagination, 1830–1867* (Chicago: The University of Chicago Press, 2002).

26 Paul Rabinow, *French Modern: Norms and Forms of the Social Environment* (Cambridge, MA: MIT Press, 1989), 281.

We may have come full circle at the present, when it is possible to speak of the structures and the de-structurations-cultural as well as material – generated by the colonial past in their deterritorialization from the nation-state; where motions of capital, commodities, peoples and cultures have in turn put into motion national or civilizational claims on modernity, giving global modernity its fluid appearance. Colonial modernity is still visible not only in the unevenness of modernity as it appears in static mappings of the world, but also in the persistence of colonial spaces and the power relations that direct global flows. Capital and production are in the process of being exported to the third world, completing the task of economic colonization, now in the name of development and globalization. There is an apparent redistribution of wealth among the laboring populations even as it is concentrated simultaneously in the hands of a global elite cutting across national, regional or other boundaries of first, second and third worlds. The jobs of blue and white collar workers are exported from the first to the third world, even as former colonials travel home to mother in the colonial spaces that refuse to vanish with talk about globalization. If globalization so-called does not look like the colonialism of old, it is because the unevenness and inequality created by colonialisms globally is deterritorialized from the nation, and wealth and power are concentrated in the hands of a global elite. One conservative commentator (Paul Craig Roberts) predicts that the United States will become a third-world country in twenty years! Some parts already have. We may recall in this regard that the contempt for the colonials of nineteenth century colonialists was also extended to the oppressed and marginalized at home, including the working populations and women. On the other hand, we need to note also that the state in countries such as India and the People's Republic of China is by now complicit in the colonial activities of capital, which provides it not only with new opportunities for development but also with a means to carry through its own colonial projects internally and externally.

The legacy of colonialism is also evident in conflicts over cultural and political identity. Despite a commonplace tendency these days to invoke varieties of traditions in claims to separate identities, these traditions now appear in forms that have been reworked (if not created) by colonialism. The difference now is not between the colonized and the colonizer, but differences among those who have been shaped by the colonial past in different ways, and now mobilize against one another identities that are equally – not identically – products of colonialism, but still subject to the inequalities of cultural power that are the legacies of the past. What I have in mind here is cogently expressed in a study by Ulf Hedetoft of the cultures produced by British colonialism not just among the colonials but in Britain as well, which now are visible in conflicting claims to British citizenship.

> It is not only in the identity, and identity-crisis, of the modern English character that the colonial past makes its presence felt, however. At the other end of the spectrum, the different forms of British colonialism produced a variety of colonial subjects and identities whose self-image and conceptions of the world were fully as much the product of the confrontation with the British as the latter's feelings of superior character were the result of the clash with and suppression of colonial "barbarians"; interestingly, however – and embarrassingly for the British, these colonial products were not *all* simply left to cope with their own problems in their "third world" countries following decolonisation, but some of them reversed the colonial migratory movement and, as a result of the *form* decolonisation assumed (British attempts to cling to the spoils of Empire through the Commonwealth), re-appeared on the British scene as immigrants, would-be settlers and British nationals.[27]

It makes some sense, in addressing the relationship between capitalism, colonialism, the nation-state, and cultural modernity, among other

27 Ulf Hedetoft, *British Imperialism and Modern Identity* (Aalborg, DK: Institut for Uddannelse og Socialisering, AUC, 1985), 2. Colonialism transformed both the colonizer and the colonized, Hedetoft shows, but did so in unequal ways that now persist in English attitudes toward immigrants – the formerly colonized coming home to mother, in other words. See also the essays collected in, Alec G. Hargreaves, and Mark McKinney (eds), *Post-Colonial Cultures in France* (London: Routledge, 1997), especially the editors' introduction, pp. 3–25. These essays deal both with the colonial transformation of French and Maghrebi cultures, and the persistence of colonial difference and inequality past decolonization, and the relocation of Maghrebis in France; attesting to the persistence of colonial modernity in the very context that invented the term and the idea.

things, to keep them separate analytically while recognizing their entanglement in the processes that we have come to encapsulate under the term modernity. It is possible to suggest that colonialism in a trivial sense is as old as the history of humankind. What distinguishes modern colonialism from earlier colonialisms is its relationship to capitalism and nationalism; which also guarantee its persistence even after colonialism as a formal system of international relations has come to an end – with the important exception of indigenous peoples around the world who serve as a constant reminder of the persistence of colonialism. The culture of modernity, too, may be incomprehensible without reference to colonialism, both in its formation, and in its diffusion over the world, which were part and parcel of the same process.

The totality created by these relations needs to be kept in mind in any serious critique of colonialism. Modernity as I understand it, is the name we have given to the historically changing totality that is the product of these relationships. An analytical separation of the various moments that have gone into its making is crucial, nevertheless, to grasping these relationships as contradictions – relationships of unity as well as opposition. If colonialism has undermined the best ideals of an Enlightenment utopianism – including the ideal of cosmopolitan co-existence – by mobilizing them in the service of world conquest, the same ideals have inspired struggles against colonialism at home and abroad, not to speak of the critical perspectives we bring to the appreciation of modernity. Those struggles, too, are by now part of an unfolding modernity.

There is a great deal to be said for recognizing colonial history as history, rather than as history gone underground (as in nationalist historiography), which indeed may be crucial to understanding colonialism not simply as a structural concomitant of capitalism or nationalism, but as a condition of everyday life. It is also necessary to recognize the ways in which the colonial encounters with native societies have produced not only alternative modernities, but alternative modernities that have produced their own colonialisms if only in the form of nation-states. The "janus-face" of the nation-state may be most clearly visible in colonial states where the nation is indispensable to warding off one kind of colonialism while it seeks to make possible its resistance by a colonial appropriation of local differences.[28]

The nation-state, in other words, did not put an end to colonial history, but inaugurated a new phase within it, playing a crucial role in its globalization – by which I mean, as I noted above, the proliferation of those participating in colonial activity who, if they do not form a transnational class, nevertheless share a certain outlook on the world in common, as may be perceived in the rapid global spread in the use of "terror" to curtail democracy and social justice.[29]

Asian Modernities

The perspective afforded by colonial modernity suggests that while Global Modernity has opened the way to conflicting claims on modernity, it has by no means abolished the inequalities of uneven development that is the legacy of colonialism to the present. Three points are particularly worthy of note by way of conclusion.

First, the proliferation of claims on modernity by no means suggests that all these claims receive equal hearing globally. It is possible to suggest, in fact, that many of these claims remain as local claims, appropriate to the particular locality (however defined), while the modernity represented by Euro/America remains as the only one with

28 We owe the term, "janus-faced," to Tom Nairn, *The Break-up of Britain: Crisis and Neo-Nationalism* (London: Verso, 1981).

29 The British sociologist Leslie Sklair has been the foremost advocate and analyst of the idea of a "transnational capitalist class" for over a decade, most recently in *The Transnational Capitalist Class*, op. cit. His contributions in this regard would be greatly enriched if he were to attend more closely to the increased (and increasingly important) participation in this class of personnel-including intellectual and cultural personnel – from outside of Euro/America, and outside of corporate structures alone. Such participation also points to the contradictions within this class, and the way culture has become a medium for their articulation.

universal claims as part of all modernities globally. Eurocentrism may have been no less ethnocentric than any other ethnocentrism, but it is the one ethnocentrism that has been global in scope and effect. This legacy of colonial modernity by no means has been relegated to the past.

Secondly, while the claims to alternative modernities are voiced more often than not from different national locations, and in the name of nations and civilizations, the difficulties of identifying national and civilizational boundaries presently should warn us against the easy identification of alternatives in modernity with particular nations and civilizations. The spatial locations of alternative modernities, such as they are, are overdetermined structurally by constituents ranging from the place-based through the national, the regional and the global.

Finally, it follows from the above two points that while it is possible presently to speak of localized modernities that are products of particular historical structurings, these differences are mediated by the legacies of a modernity that found its fullest expression in Euro/American modernity, which still accounts for the commonalities that in the midst of proliferating differences call for a recognition nevertheless of globality as a condition of the present. This legacy is not just a legacy of the past, but a dynamic moment of modernity at the present. Crucial to it is the globalization of capital, and the social and cultural practices it calls forth, which provide the reference from which both commonality nor difference derive their meaning and dynamism.

MARK ELVIN

Modernity in China in Historical Perspective

I would like to share with you my basic vision of the difficult and tangled topic of modernity as it relates to China's history from about 1600 to the present day. You may not find that you can agree with me, but I hope that at least it stimulates some interesting discussion.

My observations will cover four main topics. These are, firstly, the problem of the lack of, by a narrow margin, the creation of a home-grown modern science in late-imperial China; secondly, the difference between late-imperial and modern economic growth in China; thirdly, the impact of late-imperial and modern economic growth in China on the natural environment; and, fourthly, the Chinese form of the social and psychological consequences of modernity worldwide, which I call "the crisis of absurdity," and the efforts made to remedy it. The first example of this last development in the West, let us note, was the French Revolution, which did away with the discredited monarchy and tried to do away with the Church, and then struggled only half successfully to find something to put in their place – leaving French society torn in two. There is not the time to treat even one of these topics properly. I will simply offer you some opinions. Their main job is to flag an agenda of questions that I think could usefully be discussed in more depth, not to pretend to provide substantial answers.

Definitions

First, though, a word about the concept of "modernity." I have found that if one is to talk coherently about this topic one must consider it as, almost always, only *one* ingredient among the many that determine people's actions or thoughts. There is no general condition of humanity that can usefully be described overall simply as "modern." In real life, elements of modernity are intermixed with a multitude of older elements, and they produce a variety of outcomes that arise both from the collaboration and from the conflicts between them. Some of these older elements come from millions of years ago. As De Waal has shown, human person-to-person politics are not very different in their essentials from those found among chimpanzees.[1] Others come from more than a thousand, or even thousands, of years ago, notably the roots of our main religious traditions; and these differ from culture to culture. Modernity confronting Confucianism as developed by Neo-Confucianism has led to different mixtures from those that arose when it confronted a traditional form of Christianity, or Islam.

If we want a definition of "modern" that is *analytically stable* we also need to put the calendar aside. There is no point in using a term that can change its content year by year. What we need is a criterion that remains usable, in principle, indefinitely.

We also need to avoid using a criteria phenomena that occurred quite widely in what we would generally agree are "premodern" times. For example, if we focus on skeptical rationality, together with a view of the world mainly based on empirical evidence, and a belief that humanity since its primitive beginnings has mainly risen through hard-won technical progress, we can find all of these already to a rather surprising degree in the scientific epic by the Roman poet Lucretius, *De rerum natura*, "On the nature of things." It is a tightly argued exposi-

1 Most recently in F. de Waal, *Our Inner Ape* (New York, NY: Riverhead Books, 2005).

tion, over 7,000 lines in length, written more than 2,000 years ago.[2] Characteristics used for identification thus need to be sharply defined.

From a historian's point there is a simple criterion of "modern," though using it with sufficient subtlety when analyzing specific cases is anything but simple. It runs as follows: the application of the term "modern" is justified *only if* it describes any component of a pattern of intellectual, economic, political, or social activity that demonstrably derives directly, or indirectly, primarily from *modern science*.[3] This might seem to be circular because of the use of the adjective "modern," but it does not have to be, as I will show in a moment.

In most aspects of life, the elements that are *indirectly derived* are probably in the majority, especially those shaping ways of thought, and ways of perceiving and valuing. This is probably why the usefulness of the criterion I have just given is not always immediately obvious. One usually has to look some way beneath the surface, and back to some depth in time.

The most important indirect pathways run through the increasing role played by science in making possible the technology underpinning modern economic growth,[4] and its proliferation of effects of this growth on our environments, our jobs, what we buy and consume, and how we travel and communicate, hence also how we interact with each other. Without a continuous input of new or improved technology deriving, ultimately, from modern science, the growth of economic productivity at the leading edge could not be long sustained. This has been overwhelmingly true since the early part of the nineteenth cen-

2 Titus Lucretius Caro, *De rerum natura*, with an English translation by W. Rouse, revised by M. Ferguson (Cambridge, MA: Loeb Classical Library, Harvard University Press, 1975).

3 The core of this conception goes back to Simon Kuznets. See, for example, his Nobel Prize Lecture in 1971, printed in A. Lindbeck (ed.), *Nobel Lectures in Economics 1969–1980* (Singapore: World Scientific Publishing Co., 1992), and also accessible on the web at www.geocities.com/econ_555jim/kuznets-lecture.html.

4 For various definitions of "modern economic growth" see Simon Kuznets, *Modern Economic Growth: Rate, Structure and Spread* (New Haven and London: Yale University Press, 1966).

tury, though its partial relevance goes back somewhat further, at least to the creation of workable steam-engines (and the understanding of partial vacuums).

The possibility of *borrowing* and adapting existing technology has also been such an important part of much economic growth in most parts of the world that, again, the justification for asserting the strategic primacy of the underlying science is not always evident at first glance. I would however maintain that, in the last analysis, it is virtually always there.

Provided, then, that we define "modern science" independently, a workable definition of the "modern" in modern economic growth can be acceptable even if apparently circular: it is growth in which an important part is played by a continuous use of improving inputs of technology derived from modern science.

To backtrack for just a moment, the economic historian Simon Kuznets long ago provided a set of the symptoms of *economic* modernity that are still useful today. One of the most basic of these markers for the appearance of MEG (his well-known acronym for "modern economic growth") is the shifting of a large proportion of the labor force from the primary sector, mainly farming, to the secondary sector, which is essentially manufacturing, and also to the tertiary, which are services. He suggested that a shift of at least thirty to forty-nine percent of the primary workforce out of the primary sector is an appropriate minimum benchmark, though he also considered some other factors.[5] On this broadly Kuznetsian basis, the degree of the "modernity" of the present-day Chinese economy *as a whole* is still slightly questionable, notwithstanding the remarkable achievements of China's economically advanced sector. It is, however, obviously approaching this point, and the more developed regions in China have clearly been well past it for some time.

Bearing these points in mind, let us now go back to framing our definition. There is a short way, and also a longer way, of formulating a

5 Such as per capita rate of growth in production, the rate of the introduction of innovations, and so on.

workable definition of "modern science" that distinguishes it from the sciences of the Mediterranean classical age, of imperial China in various periods from the Han through the Song to the late Ming, of mediaeval Islam, and of the Western European high Middle Ages, its immediate predecessor:

> We will begin with the short one: this is that distinctively "modern" science requires the formulation of laws of nature in *quantified form*, ideally as functional relations or equations, in continual interaction with testing through precise measurements derived from *experiments* whose results are made routinely publicly available, and so subject to *criticism, refinement, and recasting*. In summary: numbers from experiments condensed into testable formulae, accessible to a reasonably wide public, and continuously being improved upon. This is a demanding list, yet sixteenth-century China in one or two instances just crossed the line as specified by this short definition. The key exhibit in proving this is the work on acoustics of the Ming prince, Zhu Zaiyu, toward the end of the sixteenth century. His experimentally validated and printed results on the mathematical basis of equal-temperament tuning still stand unshaken today in every properly tuned piano in the world.[6]

Incidentally, at this level, that of correct results, and at this level only, there are no cultural differences between China and Europe, or any other culture. Here you must forget postmodernism and the hocus-pocus that is sometimes talked about there being multiple *valid* sciences. To make the point by a somewhat dramatic but illuminating example, you could risk losing a lot of money by ignoring crucial shared cross-cultural realities. People gambled by tossing six-sided dice and also two-sided coins both in premodern Europe and premodern China. In both cultures winning or losing in such activities was determined by just one, identical, underlying pattern of probabilities, as it is today. There was significantly different success, however, in finding the intellectual paths that have to be taken if one is to discover and understand

6 The factual foundations underlying my evaluation of premodern Chinese science are presented in my "Some reflections on the use of 'styles of scientific thinking' to disaggregate and sharpen comparisons between China and Europe from Sòng to Mid-Qing times (660–1850 CE)," in *History of Technology* 25 (2004), 53–103.

these patterns, and their uniquely correct results, at least at an elementary level.[7] In late-imperial China, understanding went a long way toward achieving this understanding, but still insufficiently to formulate an integrated theory of basic probabilities, whereas Europe with Cardano, Pascal, Fermat and their successors eventually did manage to do this. Culture of course comes back in again at this point, often with a vengeance. To switch back for a moment to our example of musical tuning, where China was for a brief time ahead, Zhu Zaiyu thought that correct tuning would ensure not just musical harmony but also social and even cosmic harmony. His advocacy of equal-temperament tuning thus had more than a trace of subversion and political heresy. It implied that the ruling Ming imperial house, of which he was a minor member, had not solved the problem correctly, so causing social and cosmic discord. Social and cosmic disharmony had serious philosophical links in Confucian thinking. The emotional driving force behind Zhu's work was in good measure a desire to put the situation right. Perhaps ironically, though, it was only in the middle of the Qing dynasty that his ideas were openly described as politically and ideologically dangerous, and he was posthumously attacked by the authorities. If we consider another celebrated scientist, this time from Europe, who was also seen as, at least approximately speaking, dangerously heterodox, namely Galileo, the latter's interests and motives, and the dangers to the Christian faith attributed to aspects of his thinking by the religious authorities, were obviously of an almost completely different – culturally different – nature from those of his great Chinese near-contemporary.

Modern science in China during the late Ming and early-to-mid-Qing nonetheless proved to be a largely unsustainable endeavor, apart from some work in the reconstruction historical pronunciation that

7 In introducing this qualification, I am thinking of such problems as the differences arising from the contrast between the Bayesian and non-Bayesian approaches. See Deborah Mayo, *Error and the Growth of Experimental Knowledge* (Chicago and London: University of Chicago Press, 1996) for interesting comments on this issue.

has also stood the test of time, though less perfectly. All the same, Zhu Zaiyu's breakthrough shows that the question is a very subtle one. Its failure, the absence of a breakthrough of such a type as to lead to continuing progress, relates to aspects like those I have called the inadequate "density of interest"[8] in the science in late-imperial China. Why were there not enough intercommunicating scholars in China who found such matters sufficiently interesting to keep the development of the field alive? That the intellectual capacity needed – the potential for modern science – was present has just been proven. And there was at least some interest: the tough-minded Jiang Yong defended Zhu Zaiyu's results, more than a century after the prince's death, against the hostile views of the by no means untalented musical bureaucrats employed by the Qianlong emperor.

In sum, using the simple list of criteria, imperial China by 1600 was close to having the minimal intellectual foundations needed for a science-based modernity. But it didn't break through. It is broadly the same, but with some interesting added qualifications, when we turn to a more complex and adequate definition of "modern science."

The late Alistair Crombie saw modernity in science emerging in Western Europe with the accelerated improvement of five, originally largely separate, older styles of scientific thinking, plus the invention of a new one, and, crucially, the ever-increasing *fusion* of these styles of thinking into what was eventually an intellectual armory unprecedented in human history.[9] His *disaggregation of the question* of scientific thinking into separate styles of thought sharpens analysis, as it gives us a precisely formulated checklist against which we can test China's historical record more accurately than we can have if we use only a general formulation. In the case of China, the results show different levels of achievement for the different styles.

From the Crombian point of view, a "style of thinking" is a way of arguing that is designed to carry culturally accepted conviction on the

8 In two lectures at the Collège de France in October 2005.

9 A. C. Crombie, *Styles of Scientific Thinking in the European Tradition*, 3 vols (London: Duckworth, 1994).

basis of certain particular criteria. For non-scientific thinking, these could include accepted or imposed or revealed authority. For a scientific style of thinking – no.

The six styles of scientific thinking that he identified as having been historically critical for modern science were as follows:

1. The first was what he calls "postulational" thinking. This means argument based on the definitions of terms and axioms, using deductive procedures, and systematically structured. The Western archetype is Euclid's geometry. China could not match this in rigor, but was honorably represented by works such the commentaries by Liu Hui on the *Jiuzhang suanshu* [Nine Chapters on the Mathematical Art]. This bulky work could do some tricks in late antiquity that were not yet fully mastered in the west at that time, notably the rapid manipulation of most sorts of fractions. Karine Chemla has also recently argued that it has a more systematic structure than appears at first sight.[10] There is an interesting question here as to the degree that formal deductive proof actually matters from the historian's point of view: could it not be argued that the reliability of procedures is what mattered most? A great amount of modern Western mathematics (such as the differential/integral calculus) was used to great effect a long time before its validity was fully rigorously proven.

2. The second style was that of experiment. China did not have an impressive record here if we take the strict definition that requires holding all the factors in a small-scale physical situation constant except for one, and repeatedly measuring the results of changing this one. But the idea was clearly understood, and at least a few, like Zhu Zaiyu, practiced it. Needham, unfortunately, in his great *Science and Civilisation in China*,

10 See K. Chemla and Guo Shuchun (eds), *Les Neufs Chapitres. Le classique mathématique de la Chinese anciennne et ses commentaires* (Paris: Dunod, 2004), and K. Chemla, "Mathematics, nature and cosmological inquiry in traditional China," in G. Dux and H.U. Vogel (eds), *The Understanding of Nature in China and Europe from the 6th Century BCE to the 17th Century CE* (Brill: forthcoming 2008/09).

constantly confuses the notion of experiment with that of a single observation requiring intervention, like the celebrated late-Ming medical naturalist Li Shizhen looking – once – at the contents of a dead animal's stomach by cutting it open.[11]

My favorite example of a thought-experiment is the proposal by Xie Zhaozhe, who compiled a famous miscellany early in the seventeenth century, of a way to disprove a popular folk-belief. This belief was the idea that all the hares in the world were female, and that only the hare in the moon was male, which meant – course – that people thought that female hares had to be exposed to moonlight if they were to become pregnant. To disprove this, he suggested keeping a number of hares for a year in a room darkened to block out the moon's light, and seeing if any young hares were born or not.[12] To us, the details are whimsical, but the grasp of procedural principle is sound.

3. The third style was building "hypothetical" models in the mind, to represent theories and to study them, but Crombie's examples (like Archytas's famous model bird) show that he tacitly included physical models as well. Simple models were common in Chinese astronomy, such as imitation celestial spheres covered with the constellations and rotated by water-powered clockwork to match the turning of the night skies. Less well-known was the attempt, by Zhu Zhongyou in the fourteenth century, to make a physical model of the tidal bore in Hangzhou Bay to test his theory of how this shock-wave was caused. He got it wrong, probably producing what is called hydraulic jump instead, but to have done it right at his epoch would have required considerable sophistication, especially as regards questions of scaling. The behavior of aggregates of substances can change significantly with scale. Thus the working model of Hangzhou Bay that exists today at Hangzhou

11 It was a pangolin. See J. Needham and Lu Guizhen, *Science and Civilisation in China*, Vol. 6, section 38, "Botany," 318. See the discussion in Elvin, "Some reflections on the use of 'styles of scientific thinking'," 62.

12 M. Elvin, "The man who saw dragons: Science and styles of thinking in Xie Zhaozhe's *Fivefold Miscellany*," *Journal of the Oriental Society of Australia* 25–26 (1993–1994), 1–41.

uses a special type of sawdust to imitate the movements of sediments – that is, mud – which is, at first sight, surprising. But the imitation mud is more accurate, at a reduced scale in the model, than the real thing. It is mental models, though, that are in many ways at the heart of modern science.

4. The fourth style was systematic taxonomy. In taxonomy, coherent subsections of the world of experience – for example, flowering plants – are categorized hierarchically with, ideally, only one criterion distinguishing each branch in the structure from the others at the same level. You will find a multilevel illustration of this for the "hundred diseases" *(bâi bìng)* in Li Shizhen's late-sixteenth-century herbal, the *Bencao gangmu*. It begins with general symptoms and works down to more specific ones, and then to particular types of patient such as children, and it does this so carefully that one feels one could put it into a computer model. Many of the medicinal categories are not those of modern medicine, but this has little bearing on the principle: Li Shizhen knew as clearly as anyone in the world in his time what a taxonomic structure ought to be. Outside the categorization of diseases, he did not, however, find a way to create them, except in little subsets that were not ruled by consistent principles. His taxonomy for plants and animals is in fragments, and was behind comparable efforts in the west even when it appeared late in the sixteenth century. It was still farther behind 150 years later, especially following the work of Linnaeus.

5. The fifth style was new: thinking in terms of probabilities. This is a way of characterizing predictable patterns of events that only emerge when large numbers of events that are individually unpredictable are repeated over and over again. It flickered in and out of existence in Europe during the sixteenth century, but took root in the middle of the seventeenth. In China, all of the mathematical components for this sort of thinking – notably permutations and combinations, Pascal's triangle, and skill with manipulating fractions – had long been known. It was fitting them together into the analysis of the probabilities of possible pathways through the labyrinths of chance that was never achieved. Or,

more accurately, it appears never to have been recorded as having been done. There were empirical results applicable to gambling by the end of the Qing (for example in *fantan*) that suggest that more was known than was put into the public domain. Trade secrets, perhaps.

6. The sixth style was an explanation in terms of sequential historical stages. The paradigm case in Europe was the analysis of the long-term changes in the structures and semantics of the Indo-European languages. It was here that European thinkers first used the idea of "descent with modification" that ended by being one of Darwin's inspirations. It was found that when words changed over time this was in accordance with patterns that had some consistency within each language descended from an original one, but differing as between these different groups of descendants. Only in this last general domain was China still up to world levels as of 1700, and possibly even later still. This was notably so for the reconstruction of the pronunciations of ancient Chinese pioneered by Chen Di and Gu Yanwu. The history of this last style, analysis via the sequence of historical stages, shows that when *the social density of interest* was great enough, late-imperial China could create good *networks* of scholarly communication, an essential requirement for modern science. And, equally important, it could pursue a *program* of research shared among a number of scholars down through a number of generations.

Interestingly it is in the early-nineteenth-century novel the *Jinghua yuan*, *The Destinies of the Flowers in the Mirror*, by the phonologist and historian of pronunciation, Li Ruzhen, that you will find the first Chinese estimation of the distance of a peal of thunder based on using a clock to measure the time it took to travel from one spot to another after the lightning-flash, using a fairly good estimate of the speed of sound.[13]

In spite of such flickers of interest, when we look back at Crombie's checklist of the components whose accelerating advance and synergistic combination made the new European science distinctively "modern," what is striking is that, the sixth style, that of historical analysis, ex-

13 Li Ruzhen, *Jinghua yuan* (Hong Kong: Zhonghua shuju, 1958), 589–90.

cepted, China in 1700 or even 1800 was not at a much higher level than she had been in 1600, provided we except some items assimilated from the Jesuits. Something quite subtle was holding China back. What was missing, I would suggest, was a dynamic of self-sustaining improvement outside certain philological and historical domains (where it did indeed exist). Science is not just abstract styles of thinking. It is a complex socio-intellectual process.

China in Late-Imperial and Early Modern Times

The foregoing may seem a little remote from practical life. It is when we turn to the economy that the point about science being in a strategic sense at the heart of modernity hits home. Full of good things though Pomeranz's book, *The Great Divergence*, is on the comparison between China and Europe in the eighteenth and nineteenth centuries, modern science is the elephant in the drawing-room that he failed to notice.[14]

Otherwise, the economy of late-imperial China would seem to have had almost every feature that economic modernity would have required.[15] These included:

1. The quest for the rational mastery of nature. The huge hydraulic undertakings of the Ming in the sixteenth century, and those of the middle part of the Qing, are evidence enough of this.[16]

14 K. Pomeranz, *The Great Divergence. China, Europe, and the Making of the Modern World Economy* (Princeton: Princeton University Press, 2000). See my review in *The China Quarterly* 167 (September, 2001).

15 For the general picture, see the second and third parts of M. Elvin, *The Pattern of the Chinese Past* (Stanford: Stanford University Press, 1973).

16 For example, M. Elvin and N. Su, "Action at a distance: The influence of the Yellow River on Hangzhou Bay since A.D. 1000," in M. Elvin and Liu Cuirong (eds), *Sediments of Time. Environment and Society in Chinese History* (New York: Cambridge University Press, 1998), 344–407.

2. An economy that was extensively, almost universally, commercialized and monetized, much of it since Song times, and with a significant range of mechanisms for providing credit.
3. A scale of at least some of the trading operations that was huge. One can find a merchant in Suzhou, for example, who sold a million bolts of cotton cloth a year. Imports of raw cotton into the province of Guangdong alone around 1800 were about the same as the total raw cotton imports into Great Britain at the same time. If there was an obvious weakness from the point of view of technical development it was the preference of businessmen for using subcontracting rather than unified management. But in terms of short-term economics, it usually made sense to do so. Artisans could be set to compete against each other, and investment costs for productive facilities largely shifted to them, except where major technical sophistication was required, as with some silk-weaving.
4. The bimetallic monetary system, based on silver and copper, might have been made more efficient, and caused less frictional loss in assaying and conversion and transport costs, but on the positive side, it was a barrier against the state-driven inflation that would almost inevitably have happened if the government had imposed a national fiduciary currency.
5. The labor-force on the whole worked hard, skillfully, and in a disciplined fashion.
6. The legal security of property ownership was probably not as solid as in parts of Western Europe, but usually just producing three years'-worth of receipts for tax-payment was accepted as proof of legitimate possession of land. I think its fragility has been somewhat exaggerated.
7. The honesty of commercial transactions across long distances and extended periods of time is an issue that has not been as thoroughly explored as it has for early modern Europe, but I do not have the impression it created major problems. Brokers and interprovincial and trade guilds probably served as effective guarantors.
8. Internal disorders did sometimes cause difficulties. The slow spread of firearms through the civilian population after the middle of the

> eighteenth century – an often overlooked fact that was first documented by the Japanese scholar Suzuki Chûsei [Nakamasa] – was a symptom of this; but it would be hard to argue for a major negative impact on the economy in general, at least until the middle of the nineteenth century.

But there was no takeoff into an early stage of modern economic growth, either in terms of the criterion of at least some modern scientific input, or in terms of Kuznets's tests of symptoms, such as a significant shift in the labor-force out of the primary sector. One can find some fascinating examples in mid-Qing times of large-scale organizations in private industry, with a division of labor among specialists, and some innovative artisan-level technology, but in terms of the framework of ideas suggested here they do not qualify as "sprouts" of modern economic growth.

It should be remembered that one can have quite a significant level of capitalism without necessarily having MEG. The concepts are not synonyms.

Why, then, this absence of home-grown MEG in late-imperial China?

More than thirty years ago Radha Sinha and I suggested that late-imperial Chinese farming was caught in what we called a high-level equilibrium trap.[17] The yields per unit of area in lowland fields were enormous by European standards. In seed-to-yield ratios, rice in the prefecture of Jiaxing in mid-Qing reached around seven times the ratio for wheat in England in the eighteenth century.[18] Of course this particular comparison uses different crops and different climates and different soils, but even so the gap is substantial. But – and here is the

17 M. Elvin, "The high-level equilibrium trap: The causes of the decline of invention in the traditional Chinese textile industries," in W. Willmott (ed.), *Economic Organization in Chinese Society* (Stanford: Stanford University Press, 1972), 137–82. Reprinted in M. Elvin, *Another History. Essays on China from a European Perspective* (Sydney: Wild Peony, 1996).

18 M. Elvin, *The Retreat of the Elephants. An Environmental History of China* (Yale: London, 2004), 208–9.

point – it seems that pre-scientific Chinese technology in farming, and perhaps some other sectors like inland water-transport, had come close to a ceiling, a high ceiling, but a ceiling. It lavished labor-time, and organic and other natural fertilizers, on the land, using a level of skill in cultivation so sophisticated that it was often compared to gardening rather than farming. It had only a few competitors in the world in yields per unit area on lowland fields, perhaps in some parts of Japan and India at most. It poured labor-time and other resources, including valuable organizational and political skills, into creating and maintaining an immense variety of irrigation and drainage systems against the inevitable annual undermining inflicted by natural hydrological forces. But – without new inputs, like the chemical fertilizers invented by von Liebig in Prussia in the middle of the nineteenth century, yields per unit area, or in terms of the ratios between the seeds put in and the grains harvested, could barely go any higher. That was one reason why it we called it a "trap."[19]

Worse, the population had grown to a size where the unceasing continuation of these high yields was in general essential to sustain the population at a bearable level of nutrition. I say "in general" because the upland fields, a proportion of which were in shifting cultivation, require a separate analysis. The main consequence of this trap is obvious: strategic economic flexibility was lost, and paradoxically, in an economy with great tactical flexibility. Thus:

1. It was all but impossible under such circumstances to have any widespread surge in consumer demand to underpin new initiatives.
2. Workers could not be permanently shifted out of farming because of the intensity of labor needed in the peak seasons.

19 But not necessarily in every sector. See M. Elvin, "Skills and resources in late traditional China," in D. Perkins (ed.), *China's Modern Economy in Historical Perspective* (Stanford: Stanford University Press, 1975), 85–113. Reprinted in Elvin, *Another History*. There is an environmental analysis of the trap in Elvin, "Economic pressures on the environment in China during the 19th century seen from a contemporary European perspective: the Jesuit Mémoires," in the *80-year History of the Toyo Bunko*, Vol. 2 (Tokyo: The Toyo Bunko, 2007).

3. There was a high cost to using any potential farm land to produce crops other than cereals, unless these could be grown within the year-round cycle with food crops. Late-imperial Chinese farmers were on the whole brilliant at doing this, but they thus used up most of the potential of multi-cropping, which had surged in the later Ming, by around the middle of the Qing.

Inputs from modern science would have broken late-imperial China's high-level equilibrium trap, and in recent times they have done just this. But the science, or the technology based on it, had first to be imported from outside.

The capacity of the late-imperial Chinese handicraft sector to handle modern technology, once models were available, was remarkable. This is illustrated by the non-stop growth of the Chinese machine-building industry in Shanghai after the late 1860s. I did a special study of this sector, a summary of which was published in 1993,[20] and came to the conclusion that, by the start of the Pacific War early in 1937, at least one Chinese firm in this city could build virtually any given piece of machinery needed in a modern civilian economy apart from airplanes and some armaments, and that it could design the majority of them as well.

The basic explanation of how the Chinese engineers acquired this capacity is straightforward, but interesting. Shanghai had a solid late-traditional handicraft base. Then, during the disorders of the middle of the nineteenth century, the city acquired an influx of skilled manual workers from the regions around, artisans seeking safety and work. Three fine new engineering schools in the area also were in effect: the government's Jiangnan arsenal, with many foreign experts, and the two British shipyards, later merged, of Farnhams and Boyds. The city also enjoyed what was in effect a non-stop international exhibition of machines from all over the advanced world that were in use in foreign firms and often on sale as well.

20 M. Elvin, "Le transfert des technologies," *Nouveaux Mondes* 2 (1993), 73–85. The full version was accepted for publication in a collective volume about ten years ago but this book has never appeared.

Skilled Chinese engineers typically began their careers as independent businessmen by repairing foreign machinery, or by making parts under contract. They then moved on to buying it, or using a mix of both strategies, and rapidly progressed to making copies, which were usually much cheaper. Before too long they were often designing their own versions. By 1936, the Dalong works, the leading Chinese-owned and Chinese-run manufacturer of textile machinery, was negotiating overseas export orders – a development stopped by the war. Parts that were difficult to make could usually be imported from overseas. There was a supply of skilled workers, and also of short-term finance, some of which came in via Chinese banks linked with foreign banks.[21]

Very little was missing from what was needed for a purely technological modernity even a century ago; and modern Shanghai's growth in recent decades rests on foundations that are actually at least 150 years old, even if the city was mauled in the War. What was missing before the arrival of the West was modern science and its derivatives, and not much else. But, ultimately, strategically, these were all-important.

Modernity and the Natural Environment

The most important change made possible by the modern elements in society has been modern economic growth. And this brings us face-to-face with the question of what MEG has been doing to the environment. Swiftly growing China is becoming one of the most important contributors to this environmental impact, and no discussion of modernity in China can sensibly push it to one side.

By the end of the imperial period, China's premodern economic growth had left her in what was in many ways a uniquely difficult situation for such a large country as regards the natural environment.

21 Elvin, "Le transfert des technologies."

She had a population, around 430 million at the midpoint of the nineteenth century, that pressed quite hard on almost all the land-area that was potentially easily adaptable for farming. Manchuria, now but not then the Dongbêi sanshêng, was the only major exception, as the Manchus did their best until after 1859 to keep Han Chinese from settling in most of it. In China Proper the previous century and a half had seen a great influx of migrants into the upland areas, where stable continuous farming was difficult, and also into parts of the non-Han southwest. Some of the southwestern shift was backed by military force, and formed part of what I have described as a form of Chinese "colonialism." The early twentieth century, especially the 1920s, saw a demographic flood into Manchuria, mostly carried by the railroads and steamships, an eloquent testimony to the pressures of land shortage.

Also, in the rice-growing regions more than two-thirds of the cropping area depended on irrigation from a supply of water that had been pushed, given only premodern technology, close to the limits of what made technical and economic sense. The maintenance of the water-control systems required, in many areas, a significant input of energy, cash, resources, and, for larger schemes, managerial skill just to keep going at the same level. It is also my impression that by the mid-Qing very few suitable locations for developing profitable new water-control systems remained available within the limits of the old technology. In other words, there was little spare water and little spare land by the final years of the period of premodern economic growth.

To make matters more difficult, the Qing period saw the intensification of the age-old long-term trend towards the deforestation of China. Wood had become in very short supply in many areas, both for use in the construction of houses and boats, and for fuel. There is extensive qualitative evidence of the lack of both wood and water from this time, albeit with important local variations.[22]

So the environmental situation in China was difficult from the start of modern times, and not just the result of later MEG.

22 See chapters 3 and 4 of *The Retreat of the Elephants*.

It was, however, only in the later twentieth century that it became unambiguously evident, in the world as a whole as in China, that the capacity of natural ecosystems to absorb the ever-increasing contamination caused by modern economic growth, to supply the ever-increasing demand for raw materials required by modern economic growth, and to continue to provide valuable natural services, of which the pollination of crops by insects may be taken as a representative example, was likely to be limited.[23]

It is evident that there are question-marks over the longer-term viability of the enterprise of MEG, at least in its current form. In China and in the developed parts of the world alike there is, to speak in general terms, an ongoing conflict between the vigorously pursued particular short-term interests of certain companies and the ruling groups of certain states on the one hand, and the much more poorly supported longer-term collective interests of the human population as a whole on the other.

Seen from the historian's point of view, one could describe what has been happening to the environment as the paradigmatic case of the difficulties of combining the modern and premodern elements in human society. We have some amazingly powerful environment-changing tools furnished courtesy of modern science, and also, if we are interested enough to pay attention, an impressive knowledge of the dangers that we are getting ourselves into, also courtesy of modern science. But our political and social systems, of virtually all kinds, seem incapable of doing what would appear to be eminently sensible: namely, pursuing modern economic growth at a slower and more prudent rate.

Why is prudence important? Firstly, many environmental processes are, or probably are, non-linear. That is to say, at some point a steady

23 Books that are relevant here include V. Smil, *The Bad Earth: Environmental Degradation in China* (Armonk, NY: Sharpe, 1984) and his *China's Environmental Crisis: An Enquiry into the Limits of National Development* (Armonk, NY: Sharpe, 1993). For a factual summary, see Liu Jianguo and J. Diamond, "China's environment in a globalizing world," *Nature* 435 (June 30, 2005), 1179–86. For the politics of the first quarter-century of the PRC, see J. Shapiro, *Mao's War Against Nature* (Cambridge; Cambridge University Press, 2001).

and predictable process changes its rate of change dramatically. A well-known example is the acidification of water. There is a lake in the northern United States, Great Elk Lake, that for about forty years absorbed acid effluents from industry without the water quality changing very much. In the next few years, it flipped, and became as acidic as to be poisonous.[24] Currently the world's oceans are becoming more and more acidic. Some of China's offshore waters, like Bohai, are already reported to be deadly to much present-day marine life. I leave you to imagine the problem of answering the obvious question that follows.

Secondly, the speed with which environmental pressures are likely to intensify is unclear, but this speed is probably critical for the ability of humankind to cope, or fail to cope, with the accumulation of problems. Scientific and technological innovation are powerful tools, and can deal with a lot, but they need time and money, and the training of people if they are to be created, paid for, and put into effect. If problems accumulate at too high a speed, even those that are in theory soluble become insoluble in practice, because of insufficient time, an insufficient quantity of trained people, and insufficient cash. China is probably moving faster at the moment than any other major economy, even if the real growth rate for the country as a whole is probably overstated for a variety of reasons, including the need to deduct a percentage point or two each year to allow for environmental damage, as Vaclav Smil has argued.[25] So speed is a critical consideration.

Thirdly, a great deal depends on political intelligence, and the political capacity to identify the necessary measures and actually make them work. Neither of these requirements should be taken for granted. Let me give you an example from the Three Gorges Dam on the Yangzi. The researches of Lin Chengkun, at the University of Nanjing, made it clear some time before work started that there was a risk of huge mid-gorge landslides once the unstable porous rock – crumbly shales,

24 F. Schmidt-Bleek, *Wieviel Umwelt braucht der Mensch?* [How much of the environment does mankind need?] (Berlin: Birkhäuser, 1993), 44.

25 V. Smil, *Environmental Problems in China: Estimates of Economic Costs* (Honolulu: East-West Center, 1996).

sandstones, limestones, coal and so on – had become impregnated with water following the planned mid-gorge rise of the water level by about ninety meters.[26]

The main danger spot is at Xintan, twenty-seven kilometers upstream of the dam. In 1985 a landslide here released over seventeen million tons of rock, and put more than 1.5 million tons of it in the river. There are also large quantities of debris left by previous events of this sort, and these could be reactivated by a heightened water level. The worst known catastrophe in the historical record occurred in the year 317 AD, when a rockslide here caused the river to rise on the order of thirty meters and flow backwards for over fifty kilometers. Much worse damage could occur under the new conditions. Nonetheless it is obvious that it would have taken quite extraordinary political courage and political self-confidence for the PRC leaders to stop the dam once started, or to drastically reduce its height on the basis of such information – assuming, as now increasingly seems to be the case, that the balance of probabilities supports Lin's evaluation. So now we are waiting for a disaster almost certainly to happen – some time or another.

Most students of contemporary China have some idea about such current problems as the strategic water-shortage in north China, which is ever more dependent on mining the diminishing reserves of underground water, and the worsening pollution of most water supplies. The Huai River, by the way, though sometimes held up as an awful example, is by no means the worst. The Hai-Luan river system contains over 100,000 parts per million of industrial liquid waste, and 25,000 parts per million of domestic sewage, much worse than the Huai. In other words it has ceased to be a river and become a sewer.[27]

26 Lin Chengkun, *Changjiang sanxia yu Gezhouba-de nisha ji huanjing* [Sediment and the environment in the Three Gorges and at Gezhou barrage on the Yangzi River] (Nanjing: Nanjing daxue chubanshe, 1989), with long English abstract. Note how long it has taken for any serious attention to be paid to Lin's well-documented warnings.

27 See the official data summarized in M. Elvin, "Water in China past and present: competition and cooperation," in *Nouveaux Mondes* 12 (2003), 103–28.

One further figure about water may be worth bearing in mind. Using Chinese official statistics it appears that, in approximate terms, the total amount of all the run-off of water plus the amount mined from subsurface sources each year, comes to a bit over 2,000 cubic meters per person per year. This is about the same as the quantity currently directly economically *used* per person in the United States. China's actual direct economic use per person was probably somewhat under 500 cubic meters around 1990; I don't have more recent figures to hand at the moment, though there almost certainly will be some somewhere. About four-fifths of China's water is used for farming, and the only modernized countries that have a use as low per person are the few like Britain that can mostly rely on natural rainfall for agriculture. Can China, or at least North China, ever realistically hope, in the foreseeable future, to catch up in this respect? Water is needed for making almost everything.

The Crisis of Absurdity

We come now to our last theme, which is the most difficult: the crisis of absurdity. Encountering a partially modernized world is a serious shock, both for a non-modernized society as a whole and for the individuals in it. Even for a civilization as sophisticated as late-imperial China this was the case.[28]

The rich late-imperial Chinese world of human experience – perceptions, emotions, symbols and representations, and institutions – was strategically subverted in the minds of the leaders of the thinking classes during the fifty years between the end of the 1840s and the end of the 1890s. The story is well-known, but the onset of the process is puzzling. China was humiliated, both militarily and diplomatically, but she was not occupied, let alone ruled, by a foreign power – except

28 M. Elvin, "How did the cracks open? The origins of the subversion of China's late-traditional culture by the West," *Thesis Eleven* 57 (May, 1999), 1–16.

for a few tiny patches of land like the one where we are meeting today. In comparison with the greater part of the non-Western world, areas such as India and Africa, let alone Australia or the Americas, China retained a large measure of control over her own destiny. How did *cultural* autonomy slip from her grasp?

The most striking feature of this period was the death of what may be called "scriptural Confucianism." By this I mean a system of beliefs, and modes of conduct, based primarily on the conviction that the Confucian classics, or scriptures, were a uniquely privileged repository of truths about human life in its cosmic setting as they related to Heaven, and the values by which this life should be lived.[29]

Of course what we tend, rather too loosely, to call "Confucian" values did not disappear from daily life, at least in diluted fashion; but the framework of justification largely vanished. The ending, in 1905, of the old-style government examinations for degrees that entitled a successful candidate to be considered for a post in the bureaucracy is perhaps the best-known symbol of the acknowledgement that the Chinese world had changed.

If you want an image to remember, consider that in 1821 the imperial authorities condemned a military graduate to be put to death by being flayed alive in public, that is, having his skin cut off, for the crime of physically beating his wife's mother. (1) His wife was branded on the forehead as an accomplice; (2) Their house was then destroyed and the site dug up to a depth of three feet, and banned in perpetuity as a place where anyone could live – so ineradicable was the moral contamination of unfilial behavior felt to be; (3) The neighbors and relatives who had failed to report the unfilial behavior were flogged with varying numbers of lashes with the bamboo; (4) The county magistrate and education officials who had failed to spread filial virtue in their jurisdiction were banished. That was late-imperial Confucianism in action, still convinced of its moral and scriptural rectitude. You will find the documentation in the mid-nineteenth-century collection made

29 See Elvin, "The Collapse of Scriptural Confucianism," chapter 11 in *Another History*.

by Yu Zhi called the *Deyi lu* (roughly translatable as "Records on attaining perfection").[30]

China being a huge and complicated country, and change always being patchy, I would hesitate to say that nothing of this sort would have been possible a hundred years later, but it is hard to imagine the central government or most of the various authorities who held sway locally at this later time acting in this way.

The severity and suddenness of the collapse of scriptural Confucianism was in contrast with what happened to other major systems of belief when they met modernity. Christianity and Judaism had their problems with it, and still do in some respects – the new Pope, Benedict XVI, has been reported recently in the press as feeling uncomfortable with the idea of evolution – but they have adapted and adjusted in one way or another, and are very much still around. So are Islam, Hinduism, and of course Buddhism, which is probably the religion least challenged by the ideas of modern science. So, among the major players, Confucianism was something of an exception – a point recognized long ago by Liang Qichao.

A summary answer to the question of why this collapse was relatively extreme and sudden would probably begin by looking at four points, but they are only a beginning:

1. The first is the unusually important role played in the late-imperial Chinese polity, as compared to most others, by *prestige structures*. A prestige structure depends on the creation and maintenance of an image that not only inspires admiration and fear among actual and potential participants in it, but also successfully presents itself as the repository of a future that is destined to arrive, and with whom a group or an individual must be associated if they are to enjoy good fortune.

One traditional concept that evokes the importance of prestige is the familiar *tian ming* "the Mandate of Heaven." It could be seen in modern times as also having applied to systems of beliefs, values, and

30 There were a number of editions printed in various places. The earliest seems to have been in 1864. I have used the 1869 edition from Shanghai (no publisher listed).

systems governments as a whole, not just dynasties. China's world-historical cultural success story prior to the nineteenth century, and its diminished success thereafter, strongly suggested the loss of the mandate once held. In the twentieth century, the Chinese Communist Party in effect substituted a "Mandate of History," though this term does not seem to exist in Chinese.

Prestige structures are relatively rigid. More than a modicum of perceived overt change implies past error, and this damages the image. Behind the scenes they can be relatively flexible. However, once the image begins to suffer damage, little happens at first but then a process of positive feedback develops that eventually leads to a sudden collapse. Once people think that change is inevitable, there is a bandwagon effect, and they shift allegiances fast.

Formal institutional democracy is not an intrinsic part of "modernity" as I have defined it. It also existed in some places both in antiquity, notably ancient Greece, and in the middle ages: the Icelandic Althing, the world's most ancient parliament still in existence, was founded in 930, just before the Northern Song dynasty began. But it seems that some measure of democratic spirit at least is in most cases important for the safety of those who introduce new ideas, which include those of modern science, and for the operation of the networks of critical discussion required to prevent conceptual ossification. Hence it enters the debate in terms of a probable prerequisite for the home-grown creation of new elements of modernity.

For politicians who are operating a prestige system, maintaining a facade is the key to success and survival. They grasp at every small symbolic increment, and resist even the smallest decrement, since there is no knowing when positive feedback may trigger catastrophe. Hence, too, the concern with control over the population's mental attitudes and information. There are thus attractions in cultural isolation, state control of communications, and a more-than-usually strong tendency to make public statements that express what *should* be so rather than what *is*. This is complemented, but not counterbalanced, by cynicism among the intelligent, who grasp the logic underlying the prestige system, about what is really going on behind the scenes.

Even limited British and French military success in the middle and later nineteenth century, and later the gradual exposure of more and more Chinese to aspects of economic and technical modernity as a result, undermined the old Chinese prestige-structure facade behind what was, for about two generations, its still largely resolute front. This evaporation of belief can be seen from the trends in the writings of Chinese scholars between the so-called "foreign affairs movement" *yangwu yundong* just after mid-century to those of the 1898 reform movement, the *wuxu bianfa*.

2. The second point to look at is the presence of powerful but usually latent iconoclastic and social-revolutionary tendencies *already* at work in late-imperial society. They are not, by and large, a part of our story of modernity, but certain more rational theological tendencies, notably in the writings of Hong Ren'gan, the cousin of the leader of the Taiping insurrectionary régime, and his remarkable modernization program of 1859, however dictatorial and intolerant it was in some of its aspects, deserve to be mentioned.

3. The third point is complementary to the first. This was the psychological reorientation, in one way or another, of the majority of the younger leading Chinese scholars who wrote on current affairs. They agreed that something was, indeed, seriously wrong with their country. They disagreed over what it was, and what should be done about it.

More specifically – they asked themselves if this national sickness was due to a weakening of familiar Chinese virtues, still intrinsically valid, and only needing to be strengthened by neo-Confucian moral rearmament. If so, were Western weapons only paper tigers, and morals and morale the only factors that mattered? Or, on the other hand, did rifles, warships, telegraphs and railroads and the like, have a necessary if supplementary part to play in safeguarding the country? Or were novelties like these a menace that would subvert the literary-agrarian social and economic order inherited from the past?

If the answer to the first question was, on the contrary, "no," then what was needed? No writer holding to this second viewpoint would have questioned that it was desirable to revitalize older Chinese values.

But he would have demanded more. He would have expressed dissatisfaction with the Chinese character, and, for example, its tendency to gloss over unpleasant realities. He would have seen Western forms of social and political behavior as having an effectiveness that old China could not match.

Some argued that Western states maintained close ties with business interests, and democratic institutions that let them draw on the ideas, enthusiasms, and purses of their peoples. Those who took this line wanted greater technical expertise, and a reawakening of Chinese creativity, and thought modern machinery would make life better, as against their opponents who thought it brought unemployment and other problems.

Was China superior to the West, either in past glory, or future destiny, or intrinsic moral quality? Or was she inferior? Was the correct strategy simple rejection, or was it a combination of adaptation and assimilation? Should China isolate herself again? Or should she intensify her contacts with the West. Or even engage in copycat imperialism?

Was development a good thing; or was it a violation either of nature or of Chinese culture? Was the appropriate sort of economic theory one that stressed the limits on natural resources, and treated transactions as zero-sum games? Or was what was required a Promethean vision of increasing benefits for all? Was the right goal stability regained, or was it ceaseless innovation?

Going further still, had the very nature of history altered? Was the present crisis just another conflict between China and the "barbarians"? Or was it qualitatively new? If it was genuinely new, could China remain essentially "China" by making concessions to foreign style only where operationally useful? Or was a radical reorientation needed? Were the foreigners themselves merely profiteers, or were they deadly enemies? Could they be both struggled against and made use of? Should they be treated with sincerity, or with deception, or with some blend of both?

These widely varying ideas can be found in the works of scholars like Liu Xihong, Xue Fucheng, Fang Junyi, Wang Bingxie, Guo Songdao, and Wang Tao, to name just a few; they are a mixture of penetrating insights and of prejudices and misunderstandings. But the foundations of the feeling of a crisis of absurdity were being laid.

By the middle 1890s the opinion among the educated was beginning to crystallize that something basic had to change. One of the earliest forceful statements of this point of view was Zheng Guanying's well-known *Words of Warning to a Prosperous Age* of 1894. He recast the older Chinese conception of history, which had indeed contained the idea of development, in terms of interstate commercial and technological rivalry, and of Social-Darwinian competition. He argued for the need to set people's minds free so that they could master experimental science, so as to be able to struggle and survive. Experimental science, he thought, "exhausts the hidden springs of the changes of Heaven and earth" and so allows human beings to "supplement the workings of Heaven with human actions, and to put the workings of Heaven into the service of human affairs."

Seventeen years later, in 1911, the old political system was wreckage, even as the modernizing parts of the economic system, limited but growing fast, were doing well. This, though, is a story to be told another time. Why do I speak of a looming "crisis of absurdity?"

The encounter with a crisis of absurdity is the least well understood aspect of the genesis of modern China. To grasp it intuitively one has to read fiction-writers and satirists, of whom the most eloquent – for me – is the largely forgotten best-selling author of Shanghai in the middle-1930s: Ping Jinya, or, to give him his pen-name, Master Spider-in-the-web: Wangzhu sheng. His masterpiece is the five volumes of *Tides in the Human Sea*. It is the equivalent for China of the scathing mockery of Viennese society before and after World War I by the Austrian satirist Karl Kraus.[31]

This comparison brings us to a crucial point. The crisis of absurdity is typically a product of the rapid onset of limited but disruptive modernization. It has arisen in Western societies just as much as it did in Chinese society. In its inner nature it thus has little if anything to do

31 On whom see E. Timms, Karl Kraus, A*pocalyptic Satirist. Culture and Catastrophe in Habsburg Vienna* (New Haven, CN: Yale University Press, 1986).

with imperialism. It is intensified by the demoralization caused by defeat in war, as in imperial Germany and Austria-Hungary, or Tsarist Russia, or a more diffuse sense of defeat generally, as in China. But its root cause lies in the psychological dislocation caused by the intrusion of elements of modernity into a still little-changed social system. In the words of Edward Timms, the biographer of Kraus, what is critical is "a contradiction between the given social structure and the forms of consciousness in which it [is] apprehended."

In societies that have been seriously dislocated, especially by external and/or civil war, and where the mechanisms of social and political control have become impaired, the anguish brought on by a crisis of absurdity leads to a massive effort to remove it. Typically this takes the form of a struggle to exorcize the perceived pollution or moral evil that is believed to have caused the problem. Examples of such scapegoats are capitalists and kulaks (the Soviet term for rich peasants), or Jews in Austria and Germany, or landlords and other "reactionary" or exploiting elements in China. The reaction against perceived absurdity seems always to be associated with a period of mass killing. This is commonly accompanied by the imposition of a system of social, political, and ideological discipline and indoctrination justified by the presentation of a vision of a shining, prosperous, heroic, and above all meaningful, future. The details vary from culture to culture, but the hidden cause is close to identical. In most societies, with more durable mechanism of control, the crisis is contained, though not dissolved.

If we look at *Tides in the Human Sea* we find a Shanghai where both traditional values and the Chinese heritage are mocked, and at the same time Western cultural values also laughed at as pretentious nonsense, though Ping Jinya is happy enough with modern technology like telephones and motorcars. Almost everything in the city is deceit, the "selling of appearances" *(mai xiang)*, from beggary to high politics. At a deeper level an insistent theme is the complete absence of traditional karmic justice: the evil more often than not flourish, while the good and honest suffer. Any notion of later retribution or recompense during life or after it is dismissed as illusion. Ping excels at conjuring up subplots that seem absurd but are chains of events each of which is perfectly possible. This includes making fun of the traditional kinship system and its values, contriving, for example, that a person ends up in two contradictory kinship roles. The world he depicts, ruled by money, sex, and violence, is real enough, observed with his lawyer's clinical eye, and in a way entertaining and instructive, but senseless. At the deepest level of all is a dismayed humanism, which is why the book is not, in fact, as trivially horrible and as horribly trivial as it can at moments seem.

There is time to give only a brief flavor of the panorama of absurdity that his pages summon into existence. In his portrayal of the society of beggars, who are shown as mirroring the structure and values of "respectable" society, even to the extent of "reforming" the techniques of begging, there is a character, a degree-holder from the former Qing dynasty called Doctor Duplex. On one occasion Duplex declares:

> My only hatred is against my parents. Why did they have to make me study since my earliest youth? Why did they have to teach me to recognize written characters? Why did they want me to take the examinations and advance in my studies, so inflicting on me this sort of misery?
> If, instead, from my earliest days, they had sent me to a house of pleasure to learn how to boil water, or to a rickshaw company to learn how to pull a rickshaw, I would have been content from then till now, and in no way obliged to suffer for these many years.[32]

Ping Jinya is as brutal with reform rhetoric and Western philosophy and science as he is with the old examinations. A young man who has obtained a degree in modern psychology in France is effortlessly fooled by a group of worldly-wise Shanghai prostitutes. A debauchee who frequents such ladies is described as practising the philosophy of "utilitarianism" *(shili zhuyi)*. And so on, and so on.

The key point is that *Tides* was, in its day, a best-seller, and in this respect it was more representative of how people thought at that time than, say, the works of Lu Xun. One book can only be an illustration,

32 "Wangzhu sheng" [Ping Jinya], *Renhai chao* [Tides in the human sea] (Shanghai: Zhongyang shudian, 1935), II, 118.

not in any sense a proof. But if you want to see what is on my mind when I talk of a "crisis of absurdity" in China on the eve of the Communist era, have a look at it. In present-day times, different though they are from the mid-1930s, *Xiongdi* [Brother] by Yu Hua may perhaps be seen as perhaps another evocation, in a Chinese setting, of the inherent absurdity of much of life created by diverse influences derived from modernity, directly or indirectly.[33]

Summary

If we put together all the perspectives discussed in this brief talk, it is possible to define something of the paradoxical nature of the "modernity" that has now become a part, in varying admixtures with still enduring older cultural elements, of most of the world's societies. Its historical roots lie in the unique phenomenon of modern science, originally western European, then gradually increasingly ecumenical, which is in many ways the most penetrating and subtle, and powerful, of all the ways of thinking of which humanity has been capable. The infiltration of its ways of thinking and creating into technologies, and hence economies, has been a key element (necessary, though not in itself sufficient) for converting social structures, and the environment that is our home, in ways that have been both admirable and disastrous. Its impact on philosophies and religions have undermined or transformed older values and understandings of life and the universe in ways both painfully disruptive and exhilaratingly liberating, sometimes deepening insight and at other times tearing away the various fabrics of meanings, both insightful and spurious, by which peoples have in the past made existence at least bearable, at times inspiring. It survives in its present political forms mostly by brainwashing, overt and covert, but also opens

33 Yu Hua, *Xiongdi*, 2 vols (Taipei: Maitian chuban, 2005). I am most grateful to Professor Eva Man for the gift of this book.

access to a wealth of information and understandings unimaginable in former times. And, ultimately, it has often provoked both idealistic but also dogmatic and unrealistic, and, more often than not, crude, dictatorial, and mass-murderous reactions in societies too weakened and humiliated by events to find the psychological resources adequately to resist the onslaught of perceived absurdity.

It is at the heart of a web of transformations for which historical sociology has yet to find an adequate conceptual framework.

RICARDO K.S. MAK

The Idea of Modernity in World History Studies in Contemporary China

Introduction

The concept of modernity, though widely used, means different things to different people. Basically, it can be conceptualized as a process of societal and cultural differentiation and pluralization propelled by the complex interplay of a series of developmental dynamics including industrialization, urbanization, democratization, the general capitalization of social life, the rise of individualism and the growth of civil society since about the fifteenth century. At the same time, it can also be seen as the social conditions created by free market activities, modern political practices, new class and gender structures, intensive international competitions and rational and pragmatic cultures, which modern men need to live with.[1] Furthermore, modernity refers to the experience of modern men. As Berman writes:

> modernity is a mode of vital experience – experience of space and time, of the self and others, of life's possibility and perils – that is shared by men and women all over the world today. Modern environments and experiences cut across all boundaries of geography and ethnicity, of class and of nationality, of religion and ideology: in this sense, modernity can be said to unite all mankind. But it is a paradoxical unity, a unity of disunity that pours us all into a maelstrom of perpetual disintegration and renewal, of struggle and contradiction, of ambiguity and anguish.[2]

1 These features are discussed in detail in Stuart Hall and Bram Gieben (eds), *Formations of Modernity* (London: Polity, 1992).

2 Marshall Berman, *All that is Solid Melts into Air: The Experience of Modernity* (London: Verso, 1983), 15.

The formation of modernity has been the major theme of numerous economic, historical and sociological researches, but the experience of modern men seems to attract attention across different academic disciplines. Since the eighteenth century, Western thinkers look at modernization, which has dramatically transformed traditional lives founded upon religions, collectivism, premodern customs, agricultural economy, etc., in joy and fear, and in hope and anxiety. Connolly summaries their mixed feelings as follows:

> Even if modernity is not unique (it is too early to tell), it is at least distinctive. In its optimistic moments it defines itself by contrast to earlier periods which are darker, more superstitious, less free, less rational, less productive, less civilized, less comfortable, less democratic, less tolerant, less respectful of the individual, less scientific and less developed technically than it is at its best. Its opponents often endorsed these differentiations while grading them differently. Modernity has lost a world of rich tradition, a secure place in the order of being, a well-grounded morality, a spiritual sensibility, an appreciation of hierarchy, an attunement to nature; and these vested places have been filled by bureaucracy, nationalism, rampant subjectivism, an-all consuming state, a consumer culture, a commercialized world or, perhaps, a disciplinary world.[3]

Alberto Martinelli, tracing the origin of the concept of modernity, highlights Western thinkers' changing attitude toward cultural and social changes since the Middle Ages. At the height of Christendom, "sharp distinction between the sacred time and profane time and the City of God and City of Man encourages devaluations of the new as an expression of superficiality and vanity."[4] However, social, economic and intellectual movements since the twelfth century redirected men's interest in secular life and awakened them to their ability to decide their own future. In the eighteenth century, driven by a growing penchant for empiricism, science and rational reasoning, by a new faith in universalism, progress, individualism and uniformity of human nature, and by a strong

3 William E. Connolly, *Political Theory and Modernity* (Oxford: Basil Blackwell, 1988), 1.

4 Alberto Martinelli, *Global Modernization. Rethinking the Project of Modernity* (London: Sage, 2005), 5.

desire for toleration, freedom and secularism, etc.,[5] Europeans celebrated the "depreciation of the old and traditional" in modern society. Modernization, the development toward modernity, seemed to promise them "permanent innovation" and "continual creation of the new."[6]

Cultural elite of the nineteenth century, however, were sad to see that the withering away of moral absolute, stable social structure and consistent human relations in a mobile, commercialized and surveillance society was a price for modernization. The rather gloomy face of modern society and the fate of men in it became core issues of classical social theories. While August Comte and Herbert Spencer insisted optimistically on the continual progress of mankind as a whole, Karl Marx, Emile Durkheim and Max Weber joint force to expose the inhumane face of modernity.[7] Karl Marx's critique of fetishism and the commodification of men in capitalist society, Emile Durkheim's investigation into anomie in individuals in urban society and Max Weber's prophesy of the birth of an "iron-cage" life administered by bureaucracy vividly showed the unintended consequences of modernization. In the next decades Western thinkers such as Freud and Foucault, echoing with Nietzsche, were at pain to point out the limitations of rationalism. Since the 1990s, Anthony Giddens has kept on talking about the risk and insecurity that men encounter in modern society.[8]

All these have not entirely destroyed the optimism of the modernists. Jürgen Habermas, for instance, though admitting that the actual administration of modern society has created terroristic features such as bureaucratic instrumentalism and excessive state violence, rejoices

5 Peter Hamiliton, "The Enlightenment and the birth of social science," in Stuart Hall and Bram Gieben (eds), *Formations of Modernity* (London: Polity, 1992), 21–22.

6 Martinelli, *Global Modernization. Rethinking the Project of Modernity*, 5, 7.

7 Anthony Gidden's *Capitalism and Modern Social Theory: An Analysis of the Writings of Marx, Durkheim and Max Weber* (Cambridge: Cambridge University Press, 1971), though a book published three decades ago, remains a comprehensive work that bring together the three thinkers' critique of modern society.

8 See, for instance, his *The Consequences of Modernity* (Cambridge: Polity Press in association with Basil Blackwell Oxford, 1990).

the emancipation of individuals in modern society. For him, "instead of giving up modernity and its project as a lost cause, we should learn from the mistakes of those extravagant programs which have tried to negate modernity."[9] Shmuel Eisenstadt, who was once a representative among modernization theorists, has recently turned to develop his theory of "multiple modernities," which explains how the forces of modernization emerging from the West synergize with local values, behaviors and institutions within different cultural frameworks to produce different types of modern societies.[10] Having reevaluated the role of traditions in modernization, he says, "modernity does not dissolve traditions, but rather they serve as resources for modernity's perpetual constitution and reconstitutions."[11] Nevertheless, he assumes that different paths lead eventually to the destination modernity.

Obviously Western thinkers' reflections on modernity and modernization have provided important ingredients for contemporary social sciences and cultural studies. It is, however, important to know if thinkers in the non-Western nations, which are assumed to be modernized through contacts with Western nations in the last centuries, share similar intellectual concerns. In fact, the impacts of modernization has become no less controversial an issue in the non-Western world. In the 1960s modernization theorists were once so optimistic as to believe that development models built upon historical experience of Western industrial nations could help modernize non-Western societies. However, underdevelopment and dependency theorists such as Paul Baran, Paul Sweezy, Andre Gunder Frank, Celso Furtado, and Theotonio Dos Santos have concluded from the less than impressive result of modernization experiments in many Third-world countries that such attempts, instead of generally improving the social and economic conditions in Latin America, Asia and Africa, retarded development in these areas, forcing the people there to face problems that

9 Jürgen Habermas, "Modernity – an incomplete project," in Hal Foster (ed.), *Postmodern Culture* (London: Pluto, 1985), 15.

10 See for instance, Shmuel Eisenstadt's *Multiple Modernities* (New Brunswick, NJ: Transaction Publishers, 2002).

11 Ibid., 10.

Western nations had never met, including debt, hyperinflation, pollution, economic stagnation, etc.[12]

China, which has begun to extensively absorb foreign investment less than three decades ago, possesses now one of the most active capitalist markets on earth. Skyscrapers in Shanghai towering over China's fast-growing economy gradually erase traces of socialism, while vital urban life in Guangzhou reaches a point of bewilderment. The Chinese people's reactions to and reflections of their new life experience have become subjects of investigation among Chinese cultural theorists.[13] At the same time world historians in China have made great effort to explain how modern life emerged in the West and then became a global phenomenon. Their arguments, which this essay strives to analyze, in many ways reveal their understanding of modernity and their perception of China's past, present and future.

Chinese Historians and the Modern World

The formation of the modern world was never central to traditional Chinese historiography and systematic study of world history began rather late in China. Although Chinese scholar-officials' exploration of the wider world in the mid-nineteenth century according to the prin-

12 For critical analyses of the underdevelopment theory, see John G. Taylor, *From Modernization to Mode of Production* (London: Macmillan, 1979); Anthony Brewer, *Marxist Theories of Imperialism: A Critical Survey* (London: Routledge, 1990); Mitchell A. Seligson and John T. Passé (eds), *Development and Underdevelopment: The Political Economy of Inequality* (Boulder: Lynne Rienner Publisher, 1993); and Sing C. Chew and Robert A. Denemark (eds), *The Underdevelopment of Development* (Thousand Oaks, Cal.: Sage, 1996).

13 See for instance, Shen Xiangping, *Quanqiuhua yu Xiandaixing* (Globalizaition and Modernity) (Changsha: Hunan People's Publishing Co., 2003) and Xie Lizhong and Yuen Sun Pong (eds), *Xiandaixing, Houxiandaixing yu Shehuililun: Quanshi yu Pinglun* (Modernity, Postmodernity and Social Theories: Interpretation and Analysis) (Beijing: Beijing University Press, 2004).

ciple of "learning from the barbarians in order to control the barbarians" produced rather scanty descriptions of non-Chinese nations, they, having briefly encountered Western nations, came gradually to realize that a new type of society characterized by technological advancement, political liberalization, administrative efficiency, etc. had come to shape in the Western world.[14]

Chinese intellectuals in Republican China, progressive as well as conservative, displayed growing interest in the recent developments of leading Western nations. For the young Turks who were busy drafting their reform blueprints for the new born republic, the industrialized Western nations served as ready national models and the secret of their success became a core subject of their investigations.[15] The "traditionalists," who endeavored to reinvent China's tradition, found the study of world history equally useful, because it was through a comparison with Western civilizations that the values and the uniqueness of Chinese civilization could best be reassured.[16] The study of world history in this period, however, was limited to the teaching of a number of general Western history courses in major universities and the introduction of methods and achievements of Western historiography. Even the early Chinese Marxists, who had acquired a basic understanding of the materialist conception of history, were interested in reinterpreting the history of Chinese society rather than formulating a new perspective of the world. Non-Chinese histories were thus mentioned in their works unsystematically.[17]

14 For a discussion of these Chinese thinkers' impacts on the study of world history in Modern China, see Ricardo K.S. Mak, "The middle kingdom struggles to survive: The Chinese worldview in the nineteenth century," in Benedikt Stuchtey and Eckhardt Fuchs (eds), *Writing World History 1800–2000* (London: Oxford University Press, 2003), 291–308.

15 For a detailed study of modern Chinese scholars' search for a national model, see Danny S.L. Paau, *Wenming de Chongjing* (The Vision of Civilizations) (Hong Kong: The Chinese University Press, 1999).

16 Q. Edward Wang, *Inventing China through History: The May Fourth Approach to Historiography* (Albany: State University of New York Press, 2001), esp. chapter 5.

17 Arif Dirlik, *Revolution and History: The Origins of Marxist Historiography in China 1919–1937* (Berkeley: University of California Press, 1978).

The study of world history after the founding of the People's Republic of China in 1949, unfortunately, was on the one hand confined by an ideological straitjacket, and on the other hand plagued by the shortage of experts and education and research resources.[18] Before 1978 the teaching and research of world history sought solely to reconfirm the Soviet Union's official worldview founded upon orthodox historical materialism. The scope of world history was so broad that it practically pieced together historical accounts of all non-Chinese peoples. Analyzing the history curriculum in Chinese schools, Edward Q. Wang points out that:

> History teaching in schools, for example, was carved into two blocks in curriculum: Chinese history and world history, which, by and large, remain the same today. The former was taught and researched according to the Marxist theory, with the aim of developing a new interpretation of China's past. The latter was introduced initially for the purpose of carrying out the Communist mission of the "world revolution," which has by now become irrelevant.[19]

World history written by Chinese historians appeared to be a mosaic of different non-Chinese histories, with Western history as the core, repackaged in Marxist language. In addressing a number of historical questions, they needed to, nevertheless, deal with the emergence and the characteristics of the modern world directly or indirectly. These include (1) How far had Chinese society, compared with other societies, developed in Marx's scheme of history? (2) Was there a stage of capitalism in China? If yes, when had it begun? If no, why did it not occur? (3) What were the impacts of imperialism on China?

The intellectual climate for the study of world history has changed tremendously in the last decades. The introduction of the "four modernizations" under the leadership of Deng Xiaoping and China's

18 Chen Qinan (ed.), Introduction to *Jianguo Yilai de Shijie Shi Yanjiu* (World History Studies since the Founding of the People's Republic of China) (Beijing: Archives of Social Sciences, 1991), 5.

19 Q. Edward Wang, "Encountering the world: China and its other(s) in historical narratives, 1949–89," *Journal of World History* 14, No. 3 (September, 2003): 331.

growing contact with foreign nations gave birth to a new group of world historians who took a less dogmatic approach to world history. The fact that 30% to 40% of the teaching staff at departments of history in various universities was specialized in world history showed that this unexplored area now attracted a greater public interest.[20] By 1989 no less than sixteen national associations were active in the research of world history. The Peking University, Nankai University, Nanjing University and the Institute of World History of the Chinese Academy of Social Sciences (founded in 1984),[21] etc. became centers of world history studies in China. Major journals about world history such as *Shijie Lishi* (World History), *Shijie Lishi Yanjiu Dongtai* (Trends in the Study of World History), *Waiguoshi Zhishi* (Knowledge of Foreign Nations' History) and *Shijie Lishi Pingcong* (Critical Studies in World History), most of whom were founded in the 1980s, facilitated exchange between world historians in China.

According to *Zhongguo Lishixue Nianjian* (Annals of Historiography in China) which began since 1982 to provide bibliographical information about world history in China, the number of world history books published has increased from 43 in 1982 to 171 in 1997, while articles on world history increased from 351 in 1982 to 1,280 in 1992. A glance at the titles of articles published in *Shijie Lishi* in the 1990s is enough to show that Chinese historians were interested in a much wider range of topics, including the ancient Greek democracy, medieval economic transformation, the influence of the Reformation, history of individual European nations, the rise of the USA, etc. Some of them ventured to examine how different histories developed into a coherent whole in the modern era.[22]

The Marxist worldview lost gradually its appeal for the Chinese intellectuals in the reform era. Before the 1990s, the three-volume

20 *Zhongguo Lishixue Nianjian* (1990), 18.
21 *Zhongguo Lishixue Nianjian* (1994), 664.
22 *Zhongguo Lishixue Nianjian* (1994), 17 and Liu Jiahe, "Bijiao Shi he Shijie Shi" (Comparative History and World History), in *Zhongguo Lishixue Ninjian* (1996), 21 and Wu and Qi, *Shijie Shi*, 424–7.

Jianming Shijie Shi (A Brief History of the World) jointly edited by prominent Chinese historians including Ma Keyao, Zhu Longhua and Zhang Zhilian appeared to be a paradigm of world history writings, whose structure, organization and explanations were adapted by numerous monographs as well as textbooks.[23] Completed in 1972, revised in 1974 and eventually published in 1978 by the Beijing Renmin (People's) Publishing Co, this book continued to use concepts such as labor, class struggle, dialectical materialism and the antagonism of productivity and production relations to explain the beginning of early human communities, the rise and fall of slavery in Egypt, Mesopotamia, South Asia and the Greece, the history of feudalism in Korea, Japan, India, the Middle East, Western Europe, South of Sahara and even the United States, the development of capitalism and its transmission to the non-Western world through imperial expansions, and so on. In this narrative structure, the conditions of modern men and social problems within industrial societies that contemporary Western thinkers have long been striving to explain and the new generation of Chinese intellectuals have begun to encounter, were either overlooked or seen as inevitable results of economic exploitation in the stage of capitalism. It has proved especially incapable of explaining the function and operation of the modern international system, and global developments in the post-Cold War era such as the transformation of the Communist Bloc, the growth of regional co-operations, the rise of American hegemony after the Gulf War, China's great reform and its integration into the world economy, and the growing importance of Southeast Asia.

23 Great world history projects such as *Jianmin Shijie Tongshi* compiled by twenty historians under the leadership of Li Chunwu and Shou Jiyu (Beijing: Beijing Renmin Publishing Co., 1981) and *Shijie Shi*, a joint venture undertaken by twelve universities including Liaoning University, Huadong Normal University and Nanjing University (Beijing Renmin Publishing Co., 1983) are modeled on *Jianmin Shijie Shi*. Even works published in the 1990s, such as Wu Yujin and Qi Shirong's *Shijie Shi* (World History) and Cui Lianzhong's six-volume *Shijie Tongshi* (A General World History) do not go far beyond this framework.

As the capitalist mode of production has in effect penetrated various realms of Chinese society, the questions of how capitalism emerged in the West, how elements of modern life originated in the West were transmitted to China and what particular experience the Chinese people in the process of modernization have had begin to preoccupy world historians in China, whose findings reflect their new perspective of the world as well as the political reality in China.

The Political and Ideological Bases of World History Studies in Contemporary China

Guided by leading reformer Deng Xiaoping's pragmatism, China put aside the "politics takes command" strategy and concentrated on modernizing its agriculture, industry, technology and national defense since the late 1970s. Since the lack of capital and technology have long been a stumbling-block to China's reforms in the last centuries, the reformers in the post-Mao era boldly reconnected China with the Western world, in the hope that through importing foreign capital, manpower and technology, China could in the short run significantly increase its productivity and in the long run build up a solid industrial base that enabled China to stand on its own feet. To attract foreign investment and to increase Chinese people's incentive to improve their own situation, the reform tolerated to a certain extent private property and free economic activities. In terms of economic growth, "socialism with Chinese characteristics" has worked surprisingly well, transforming China into the "workshop of the world" as well as one of the biggest markets for consumer, industrial and financial products.

The growing quest for political liberalization and the threat of foreign intervention left two major challenges that the reformers needed to contain. Internally, the Chinese government since the Deng era responded to public political demand by emphasizing collective rule, regularizing procedures and reforming political institutions.[24] Externally, China defended its sovereignty by taking a tough stand against any unfriendly foreign activities within its territory, while refraining from interfering into other countries' domestic affairs. Diplomatic measures derived from this strategy drew China in a number of cases into conflicts with the USA, particularly over Taiwan and Tibet.[25] To encounter the USA's growing influence in various areas, China not only attempted to stabilize its relations with Asian countries, but also to intensify its cooperation with European countries such as France and Germany.[26]

Social problems resulting from the economic reform also took the Chinese government to task. In fact, the policy of "letting a small group of people get rich first," which aimed originally at creating room for private economic initiatives, resulted in the boom of private enterprises, massive urbanization, the rise of living standard in seaports and commercial cities and the birth of new cultural and economic elite. But at the same time, it widened the urban-rural gap, fragmented the society and created social and economic inequalities. In order to prevent massive disorders, the government has not only launched a series of "education" and iron-hand policies, but also played down since the 1990s the role of class struggle in China's development. This explains why

24 Merle Goldman and Roderick Macfarquhar, "Dynamic economy, declining party-state," in Merle Goldman and Roderick Macfarquhar (eds), *The Pardox of China's Post-Mao Reforms* (Cambridge, MA: Harvard University Press, 1999), 11.

25 See for instance Wang Lixiong, "The Tibetan question: Nation and religion," *Exploring Nationalisms of China: Themes and Conflicts* (Westport, Connecticut: Greenwood Press, 2002), 151–72; C.L. Chiou, "Taiwan's evolving nationalism: Ideology for independence," in *Nationalism, Democracy and National Integration in China* (London: Routledge 2004), 93–119 and Joseph Cheng and Kinglun Ngok, "Chinese nationalism and Sino-US relations: The NATO bombing of the Chinese Embassy in Belgrade," in *Nationalism, Democracy and National Integration in China*, 88–92.

26 See for instance Christoph Nebhöver, *Die Chinapolitik Deutschlands und Frankreich zwischen Aubenwirtschaftsföderung und Menschensrechtsorienterung (1898–1997): auf den Suche nach Balance* (Hamburg: Institut für Asienkunde, 1999).

capitalists are now welcomed by the Chinese Communist party and why Premier Wen Jiabao kept emphasizing in early 2007 that a "harmonious society" is what China now very much needs.[27]

Taken together, China strives to create a haven in which it can gradually build up its economic and technological strengths with the help of peaceful cross-cultural interactions and co-operations. Such an attitude underlies in many ways the discussion of the modern world among Chinese world historians.

The Birth of Modern Industrial Civilization

It has long been a tradition that speculative philosophers of history such as Friedrich Hegel, Arnold Toynbee and Oswald Spengler used cultures and civilization instead of nations as units of analysis in their schemes of history. In the 1960s, the Western world historians who found the vast study area that covered human past and present and nations inhabiting the five continents too huge for them to handle, saw cultural interaction as a possible theme around which a system of world history could develop. William McNeil's *The Rise of the West* published in 1963, though criticized for being Eurocentric, represented one of the earliest successful attempts. From a leftist perspective, Immanuel Wallerstein perceived modern world history as a process in which the industrial West, which continued to absorb economic and social resources from all parts of the world, condemning the impoverished non-Western people to an inferior position, from which very few of them were able to escape. Chinese historians, though not going so far as to replace nation-states with cultures or civilizations as subject matters, pay growing attention to forces of civilizations that gradually blur political boundaries. History of civilization *(wenmingshi)* has be-

27 *Singtao Daily*, March 16, 2007.

come popular in China and works on it have recently increased tremendously in number.[28]

Generally speaking, many of the Chinese world historians agree that civilization is made up of ideas, institutions and material inventions. Through confronting and transforming the state of nature, humans create civilizations and raise themselves from barbarism. Chen Qinzhuang, Zhan Tianxiang, and Ji Xiangxiang, drawing on Fernand Braudel's view, go further to emphasize that a mature civilization is able to create its sphere of influence, to borrow from and to resist foreign civilizations.[29] In the premodern times, since contacts between civilizations were obstructed by geographical barriers, even the most advanced civilizations were able to extend their influence only to people living around them. Each civilization, together with its sphere of influence, existed and developed quite independently from the others. However, it seems a consensus among Chinese world historians that Western industrial civilization characterized by industrialism, rationalization, urbanization, social differentiation, consumerism, technologization of life, etc. has continued to expand from the West to every part of the world since the sixteenth century.

In contrast to orthodox Marxist historians who hold capital as the leitmotif of modern historical development, world historians in China refocus their attention on the role of technology in the making of industrial civilization. For many of them, capital, though the most important factor of production, becomes a real power after it is converted into technology. Assessing the importance of this paradigm-shift, Crozier says "the emphasis on science and technology, in Marxist terms 'the force of production,' opens the way for a modification of historical

28 These include Ma Kayao, *Shijie Wenmingshi* (Beijing: Beijing University Press, 2004); Li Shian and Meng Guanglin, *Shijie Wenmingshi* (History of World Civilizations) (Beijing: Renmin University Press, 2002); Chen Qinzhuang, Zhan Tianxiang and Ji Xiangxiang, *Shijie Wenmingshi Jianbian* (Hangzhou: Zhejiang University Press, 2000), etc. Wang Side's *Shijie Tongshi* (Shanghai: Huadong Normal University, 2001) is consisted of three volumes with subtitles pre-industrial and regional civilizations, the rise of industrial civilization and the directions of modern civilizations respectively.

29 Chen, Zhan and Ji, *Shijie Wenmingshi Jianbian*, 3.

theory that is applicable to more than just twentieth century history."[30] In many of their accounts, technology is the prime mover of global changes since the third industrial revolution, intensifying international division of labor, giving rise to multinational enterprises and widening the gap between the "have" and "have not" nations.[31]

The fact that industrial and technological advancements are seen as indicators of national strengths further testifies Chinese world historians' belief in the omnipotent power of technology.[32] For them, it is to the first industrial revolution that Britain's leading position up to the last quarter of the nineteenth century was due. The second industrial revolution in the late nineteenth century marked the beginning of German industrial and military supremacy, and the third industrial revolution has prepared for the American hegemony in the twenty-first century.[33]

Surprisingly their explanation of the rise of modern science and technology also breaks with the orthodox base/superstructure model, which perceives intellectual developments as "superstructure" produced by social and economic conditions. Turning this model upside down, quite a number of Chinese world historians attribute the rise of modern industrial civilization to intellectual movements in early modern Europe, including the Renaissance, the Reformation, the Scientific Revolution, and the subsequent commercial revolution,[34] all of which culminated in the industrial revolution in the eighteenth century. Taken together Chinese world historians' emphasis on technology and intellectual development is in line with the China's reform program which gives increasing weight to these factors.

30 Ralph Croizier, "World history in the People's Republic of China," *Journal of World History* 1, No. 2 (Fall, 1990): 166–67.

31 Wang Jinxin and Zhou Gonggu, *Shijie Shigang*, 2 vols (Shanghai: People's Publishing Co., 1999), 2: 777–82.

32 Ibid., 2: 787–4.

33 Li Zhitan, *Ershi Shiji Shijie Shi* (Twentieth Century World History) 2 vols (Wuhan: Hubei Jiaoyu Publishing Co., 1997), 2: 138–45; Cui Lianzhong (ed.), *Shijie Tongshi* 6 vols (Beijing: Renmin Publishing Co., 2000), 6: 209–11; Wang and Zhou, *Shijie Shigang*, 2: 777–86.

34 Li and Meng, *Shijie Wenmingshi*, chapter 7.

Shijie Tongshi[35] (General World History) highlights the narrative structure of contemporary world history writings in China. Consisting of three parts: premodern civilizations and regional history (history before 1500), the rise of industrial civilization (world history between the sixteenth and the nineteenth centuries) and modern civilizations: developments and choices (twentieth century world history), this work puts old and new elements together in the same pot. For instance, like most world history writings in the 1990s, it sees the fifteenth century as a turning point of world history, because different civilizations began to grow into one coherent whole in this century. At the same time, in addition to abandoning most Marxist concepts and terminologies, it shifts its attention to the continuous development of a multi-polar world in the late twentieth century. More importantly, it sees science and technology as a force of modern transformation. In individual nations, science and technology increase the productivity and transform the mode of production, speed up social differentiation and eventually create modern governments. On the international level, the technological revolution in the post-World War II era further redistributes knowledge, wealth and power among nations, consolidating the multipolar world.

For world historians in China, the domination of industrial civilization seems to be irreversible. However, the consequences it has produced, such as social inequality, excessive individualism, environmental problems, vulgarization of cultural taste, etc., are not yet their major concerns. The Chinese government's quest for a "harmonious society" is reflected by the fact that class struggle and working class movements, two core concepts of Marxist interpretation of history, are sidelined in contemporary world history writings in China. In Li Shian and Meng Guanglin's *Shijie Wenmingshi* (History of World Civilizations), for instance, not even one single chapter is given to socialism or working class movement. In Wang Side's three-volume *Shijie Tongshi* only the chapter "Critique of industrial civilization" covers the rise of socialism and working class movement.

35 Wang, *Shijie Tongshi*.

Cultural and Political Rivalries in a Multi-Polar World

Western leftist sociologists, as mentioned above, are convinced that the transmission of Western industrial civilization through imperial expansion to non-Western societies has created a world system dominated by the West. The Chinese world historians, however, are more optimistic. For them, local cultures in the non-Western world, instead of being homogenized by Western industrial civilization, hybridize with it to create new social conditions that Western peoples have never experienced. Nation states in the non-Western world, whose role in the global era is more important than ever, will join force to form different regional powers that counter-balance the USA, which has become the only superpower. A "multi-polar world" is on the rise.

Ma Keyao's *Shijie Wenmingshi* (History of World Civilizations), which is a collection of different studies of modernization in Africa, Latin America, South Asia, Southeast Asia, and the Islamic world, presents a picture similar to what we call multiple modernities. Essays in this edited volume tell a story about modern technology and management style, rationalism and parliamentary system originated from the West meeting "bureaucratic authoritarianism" in South America, the legacy of colonialism and multi-racial problems in South Asia, Confucianism in East Asia, Islamism in the Arabian world and traditional cultures in Africa. The "third road" in India, which has combined a mixed economy and a democratic political system, and the revival of religious fundamentalism in some Muslim countries are products of these encounters. The so called "East Asian Model," in which Western free trade and industrialism coexist with parental governments and traditional values, further generates a great variety of societies with different structure and configuration, some of them more resistant to Western culture, some of them better integrated into the capitalist world system.[36]

The modern world is for the Chinese world historians by no means free of conflicts. Since the 1990s the term *duoji shijie* (multi-polar world)

36 Ma, *Shijie Wenmingshi*, 288–9.

has become widely used by them to depict the international setting after the dissolution of the *liangji shijie* (bi-polar world) dominated by the USA-USSR rivalry.[37] A series of political and economic changes in the last phase of the Cold War, including the formation of the European Union, whose members such as Germany and France have long been trying to overcome the American influence; the establishment of economic communities in various regions; the enviable growth of South East Asia; the rise of China; and the growing military strength of India have witnessed the flow of wealth and power from the East and West blocs to other regions. Europe, China, America, and South Asia, though not equal in strength, now appear to be the four most powerful regions in the world, each of which develops under the leadership of one or a few core nation states. Conflicts and co-operations among these regions are thus unavoidable.[38]

The nature of the "multi-polar" world is clearly conceptualized in Zhu Ning's *Bianluan zhong de Wenming* (Civilizations in Disorder).[39] This book suggests that in the course of history, powerful nation states, which have the potential to extend their influence beyond their geographical boundaries, tend to absorb neighbors into their orbits of development. This process of absorption and incorporation has become ruthless than ever since the late nineteenth century, reaching a new peak in the post-Cold War era and resulting in several "pan-"areas: pan-North American, pan-Western European, pan-continental European and pan-East Asian areas, etc.[40] A "pan-"area remains stable as

37 See also Zhang Hongyi and Rui Xin, *Ouzhou Youshi, Meisu Duizhi, duoji Shijie* (The European Superiority, the USA-USSR Confrontation and the Multi-polar World) (Beijing: Zhongguo Qingnian Publishing Co., 1999) and Li Zhitan, *Hongguan Shijie Shi* (World History) (Wuchang: Wuhan University Press, 1999).

38 Jin Zhongyuan, *Ershi Shiji de Shijie. Bainian Lishi de Huisu* (The World in the Twentieth Century. A Retrospection), 2 vols (Shanghai: Fudan University Press, 2000), Vol. 1, part 4.

39 Zhu Ning et al., *Bianluan zhong de wenming* (Beijing: Renmin University Press, 2000).

40 Ibid., 63–4.

long as nation states within this area are able to achieve a balance of power, and as long as its "core nations" are able to guarantee other members the minimum justice and security.[41] Although the USA is now the only superpower, it is compelled in many areas to co-operate with other "pan" areas in an age of globalization.

Liu Jinghua, a historian of the Wuhan University uses the term *yichao duoqiang* (one superpower and several powers) to describe relations among these regions.[42] For him, the USA is inarguably the only economic and military superpower today, but it needs to work with other powers such as Western Europe, which is undergoing a modest revival, China, which is growing in importance, the former USSR, and the new rising industrial countries in Asia, if peace and sustainable growth are to be achieved.[43] Multi-lateralism, instead of unilateralism, should be the answer to growing international conflicts over distribution of resources, crashes of religions and civilizations, political and economic inequalities, etc.[44]

Obviously many of these works use milder terms such as *chongtu* (conflicts) and *maodun* (contradictions), instead of *douzheng* (struggle) to depict differences and disagreements among nations in the post-Cold War era.[45] Despite continuous conflicts among nations, a global war is for them unlikely, because no nation has the reasons and abilities to wage one that will result in a nuclear holocaust.[46] At the same time, believing that international organizations such as WTO and IMF have created platforms for international dialogues and co-operations,[47] they optimistically predict that problems threatening the existence of mankind such as pollution, poverty and population growth, and even drugs,

41 Ibid., 64.

42 Liu Jinghua, *Renlei Liuqian Nian* (Six Thousand Years of Human History), 2 vols (Guangzhou: Huacheng Publishing Co., 2000), 2: 715.

44 Ibid., 2: 723.

44 Ibid., 2: 724–5.

45 Liu, *Renlei Liuqian Nian*, 724–5; Li and Meng, *Shijie Wenmingshi*, 237–40; Zhu Ning et al., *Bianluan zhong de wenming*, 311.

46 Wang and Zhou, *Shijie Shigang*, 2: 813–14.

47 Cui, *Shijie Tongshi*, 6:584; Wang and Zhou, *Shijie Shigang*, 2: 805–8.

AIDS and terrorism can be solved by peaceful means.[48] To create a better understanding between nations, the existing North-South dialogue and South-South cooperation, as Li Zhitan, a young Chinese world historian, maintains in his *Ershi Shiji Shijie Shi* (World History of the Twentieth Century), should be supplemented by more intensive cross-cultural dialogues in an age of growing international connections and competitions.[49]

Interestingly China's foreign policy seems to set the tone of discussion over China's position in the contemporary world, a subject that has long been neglected. Participants in this discussion share the opinion that China, in order to achieve peaceful coexistence with other nations, should develop a multi-directional foreign policy that helps maintain friendships with all major powers on earth.[50] Since national independence is the wish of all nations, China has no reason to interfere into their domestic affairs.[51]

Concluding Remark

In many world history writings in contemporary China modernity, which means wealth and power, seems to be a national goal for the Chinese people to attain rather than something to be worried about. How modernity emerged in the West and was transmitted to different parts of the world, and what the Chinese people can learn from the historical experience of other modern people, so as to create modernity in a Chinese context are the central questions to be addressed. In contrast, the task of investigating the conditions and sufferings of modern

48 Jin, *Ershi Shiji de Shijie. Bainian Lishi di Huisu*, Vol. 2, part 2.

49 Li, *Ershi Shiji Shijie Shi* (Twentieth Century World History) 2 vols, 1: 12.

50 Jin, *Erhxi Shiji de Shijie. Bainian Lishi de Huisu*, Vol. 2, 444–6; Cui, *Shijie Tongshi*, 6: 602–8.

51 Li, *Ershi Shiji Shijie Shi*, 663–6.

men, into which Western thinkers in the last two centuries have thrown themselves in great zeal, have attracted the attentions of few Chinese world historians.

An essay written by the historian Anran and collected in Ma Keyao's *Shijie Wenmingshi*, which is one of the very few historical researches that touches upon the human conditions in modernity, reflects the new generation of Chinese historians' hope for the continuous development of modernity. Attributing Western thinkers' pessimism to their static and one-sided understanding of modernity, which is still in the making, Anran criticizing them for mixing up the nature, the limitations and the excesses of technology and instrumental rationality, for underrating modernity's ability to reform itself, for overlooking institutions and cultures that twist the development of modernity, for romanticizing traditional cultures and societies and for playing down deliberately the progress produced by technology. Speaking in the tone of Habermas, he maintains that a better developed modernity offers solutions to the problems of contemporary modernity.[52]

In light of this optimism, the dark side of modernity, if it ever exists, is a condition that modern men need to temporarily live with. Chinese people, most of whom are still standing on the threshold of modernity, should face up to modernity courageously.

52 Anran, "Keji Jinbu yu Chixu de Gongye Geming (Technological Advancements and the Continuous Industrial Revolution)" in Ma Keyao, *Shijie Wenmingshi*, 39.

PING-HUI LIAO

Civility and Self-Reflexivity: Three Texts on Women and Chinese Modernity

Accounts of Asian modernities have been informed by a sense of lack and inadequacy (Chakraparty), malcontent and misfit (Haroontunian), or entanglement and improvization (Mbembe). It is often against Western models that Asian modern experiences are judged. A recent example is the poll conducted by Canadian Reader's Digest which placed New York, Zurich, and Toronto as the top three cities in the global courtesy ratings, with Taipei, Singapore, Seoul among the rudest and least tolerant, slightly better off than Mumbai which finished last (no. 36). While the result is revealing albeit unsurprising, this is hardly anything new if we take into consideration the long tradition of Chinese cultural criticism from within that raises question of civility and self-reflexivity, as seen in the works of Li Juchen (1763–1830), Wu Cho-liu (1900–1975), and Dung Kai-cheung (1967–). These writers have notably suggested alternative ways to re-define Chinese civility and modernity from the perspective of comparative cosmopolitanisms.[1]

1 There are at least one hundred women literati in Li Juchen's *Romance of the Mirrored Flowers*, but I want only to single out a black lady to make the point on cultural critique from the edge. As for Wu's *Nanking Journals*, it does touch upon a young girl on the train who leaves shoe marks on her seat and thereby reveals to the dismay of Wu an untidy image of Chinese in the public spaces. I have discussed this telling episode elsewhere (in Rojas and Wang, 289–92), but here my concentration is on general comparative accounts.

Figures and Discourses of Incorporation and Distancing in *Ching-hua yuan*

In the middle Ch'ing novel *Ching-hua yuan* (or The Romance of the Mirrored Flowers, 1828) by Li Juchen, problems of China confronting the West are displaced and then recast as a narrative about a group of new women – one hundred in total – attempting to revive the T'ang dynasty.[2] Among the distinguished woman scholars, local and foreign, two black woman scholars stand out as problematic "neither-nor" figures that register the difficulty for China to come to terms with its Others: they are from the Kingdom of Black Teeth and have not only black skin but red eyebrows and black teeth. And it is in Li Hung-wei, the black woman scholar who often dresses in red, that Li Juchen's anxiety concerning China's modernity is revealed in terms of the sexual, racial, and cultural politics of incorporation and distancing. For Li Juchen, the black figure in red – most often called Hung-hung (or Red-red) – represents an ambivalent element on the "interior frontier" which calls into question the very criteria by which Chinese traditionalism can be identified, membership in a imagined community may be accorded and nationality assigned.[3] Not quite Chinese and yet in many

2 Li Juchen, *Hui-t'u ching-hua yuan* (Peking: Chungkuo, 1985).

3 As Fichte defined it, an "interior frontier" entails two dilemmas: that the "purity" of the community is prone to penetration on its interior and exterior borders, and that the essence of the community is an intangible "moral attitude," "a multiplicity of invisible ties." Etienne Balibar recently elaborated the concept in "Fichte et la Frontiere Interieure: A propos des Discours a la nation allemande," *Les Cahiers de Fontenay* 58/59 (June, 1990). He suggests that a frontier locate both a site of enclosure and contact, of surveilled passage and exchange. Coupled with the world "interior" it carries the sense of internal distinctions within a territory (or empire); at the level of the individual, it marks the moral predicates by which a subject retains her/his national identity despite location outside the national frontier and despite heterogeneity within the nation-state. Ann Stoler draws on Balibar to discuss sexual affronts and racial frontiers in relation to European identities and the cultural politics of exclusion in colonial southeast Asia, see her *Carnal Knowledge and Imperial Power* (Berkeley: University of California Press,

ways more conversant with Chinese Classics than many scholars, Hung-hung is a figure neither to be incorporated easily nor to be rejected as totally foreign. She is such a problematic "in-between" figure that registers the difficulty for China to come to terms with its Others in the early nineteenth century.

Completed a hundred years after the severance of all diplomatic ties with European nations and only two decades before the disastrous Opium War, the novel consists of a series of international trade adventures and of events about forming an intellectual community of women poets to restore the glory of the T'ang dynasty. Produced in a period of deceptive stability that witnessed the resurgence of Chinese exegetic science but also the degeneration of the Ch'ing empire in its futile struggles against foreign intervention and influence, the novel deploys a series of adventures to debunk the metropolitan myth of China as the "middle kingdom," "center of the world." In inventing the Other to be looked upon as a site for self-reflection, the author urges his readers to revitalize traditional virtues and learning, so as to rescue China from global commercialism and colonialism of the time. However, in displacing and redescribing the nationalist issues as an event involving dangerous sexuality displayed by Empress Wu Tse-t'ien, the novelist actually elaborates on the complex relationship between nationality and sexuality, between modernity and identity. On the one hand, Empress Wu is set up as a victim, an allegorical name for a specific historical failure in response to a coherent sense of modernization. On the other hand, women scholars, who are said to be the very incarnations of one hundred Flower goddesses, are means to straighten out that historical rupture. In between the extreme positions, Hung-hung stands as an ambivalent figure to be incorporated and excluded simultaneously.

2002). I am indebted to her work for the racial politics of incorporation and distancing, though we are dealing with different problems. Balibar and Immanuel Wallerstein's recent book, *Race, Nation, Class* (London: Verso, 1990) is also very helpful.

In his succinct criticism of Partha Chatterjee's reading of the nationalist paradigm, R. Radhakhishnan writes:

> It is important to notice how nationalist ideology deploys the inner/outer split to achieve a false and repressive resolution of its identity. Forced by colonialism to negotiate with Western blueprints of reason, progress and enlightenment, the nationalist subject straddles two regions or spaces, internalizing Western epistemological modes at the outer or the merely pragmatic level, and at the inner level maintaining a traditional identity that will not be influenced by the merely pragmatic nature of the outward changes. In other words, the place where the true nationalist subject really is and the place from which it produces historical-materialist knowledge about itself are mutually heterogeneous. The locus of the true self, the inner/traditional/spiritual sense of place, is exiled from processes of history while the locus of historical knowledge fails to speak for the true identity of the nationalist subject. The result is a fundamental rupture, a form of dissidence, a radical collapse of representation. Unable to produce its own history in response to its inner sense of identity, nationalist ideology sets up Woman as victim and goddess simultaneously.[4]

Now, in Empress Wu and T'ang Kui-ch'en, the heroine of the novel and incarnation of Goddess of a Hundred Flowers, we see the point about setting up Woman as victim and goddess, as Radhakrishnan suggests. But, in inventing the quarrel in Heaven – between Moon Goddess and Flower Goddess – and the disruption of the T'ang in the hand of a woman, both of which have to be resolved by women from different geographic spaces, Li Juchen is not simply elaborating the sexual politics here. He in fact projects historical contradictions and difficulties on to non-synchronic spaces, asking geography to provide answers to history and social reality. As a consequence, the first part of the novel – up to chapter 40 – is devoted to the heroine's father T'ang Ao and his adventures in other countries. These countries are fictional constructs drawn from traditional travel narratives – *Shan-hai ching* (The Classic of Mountains and Seas), for example – or contemporary accounts of voyages and explorations. The introduction of these exotic

4 R. Radjakrishnan, "Nationalism, gender, and the narrative of identity" in Andres Parker et al. (eds), *Nationalisms and Sexualties* (New York: Routeldge, 1992), 85.

subjects, with their marvelously variegated races, colors, customs, languages, writings, rituals, etc., is to the end of self-criticism through an invented gaze or, to quote Stephen Greenblatt, of experiencing cultural "resonances" in the form of "wonders," of recognizing the self in the presence of the supposedly radical difference.[5] Here, the key word "mirror" in the title of the novel indicates the psychosocial effects of the self-image reflected by and through the Other, even though mirror also has Taoist-Buddhist connotations about ephemeral nature of things.

Li Juchen deliberately uses the invented gaze strategy to urge his readers to reform, and one of the most obvious examples is the episode of two black women scholars in the Kingdom of Black Teeth. It is interesting that throughout the novel the two black women scholars are referred to as Hung-hung (red-red) and T'ing-t'ing (pretty) by their nicknames, whereas other women scholars maintain their proper names. Names and the power of naming are in some subtle ways related to hierarchy formation in the novel. T'ang Hsiao-shan (small hill; screen), for instance, changes her name into Kui-ch'en – meaning "loyal subject." It is as if by gaining a more dignified and therefore appropriate name, the heroine is finally able to carry out what she is predestined to do and to form an intellectual community based on sisterhood. As T'ang Hsiao-shan changes her name and her role after a divine revelation, the name change indicates self-knowledge, a new direction, and social bond. With it a new identity is created to make clear a new enunciative positionality. However, the two black women scholars are designated according to their favorite colors of dresses, not in terms of their personality or any other essential features. The intimate but somehow superficial system of naming them actually goes hand in hand with the racial politics of incorporation and distancing. The color of their skin and their dresses remains a major indicator of their racial and cultural difference even though they may be incorporated into the

5 Stephen Greenblatt, "Resonance and Wonder," in Peter Hollier and Helga Geyer-Ryan (eds), *Literary Theory Today* (Ithaca: Cornell University Press, 1990), 74–90; *Marvelous Possessions: The Wonder of the New World* (Chicago: University of Chicago Press, 1991), 1–25.

imagined community. It is such a politics of incorporation and distancing that enables the Other to be uncannily apart and yet compellingly near.

Together with T'ing-t'ing, Hung-hung stands out as learned and admirable. Both black women scholars understand Chinese Classics much better than T'ang Ao and his friends. Though no longer a professional scholar, T'ang Ao has spent some thirty years reading Chinese Classics. He may have well passed the Civil Exam if not intervened by a political scandal. But, to his astonishment, the two black women scholars not only offer new interpretations of texts he has never heard of before but master Chinese calligraphy beautifully. Compared with other episodes, the encounter with the black women scholars is given more detailed description, and the event takes up almost four chapters (15–19). The reader certainly detects the implied presence of the author in these two women scholars when the debate is on Chinese phonetics and exegesis of the Book of Change. For Li Juchen himself is a phonetician by profession. As a matter of fact, in the second part of the novel, in which T'ang Kui-ch'en meets with the other ninety-nine women scholars, the author simply indulges himself in discussing phonetic issues. But curiously enough, it is via the black women scholars that Li Juchen suddenly reveals his lifetime interest and for the first time in the novel touches upon Chinese phonetics and Classical learning.

In the Kingdom of Gentlemen episode, which features in chapter 11, the implied cultural criticism concerning the rise of despicable commercialism in China has forcefully been made. China has been famous for its civility, but now it seems the virtue belongs to residents of the Kingdom of Gentlemen alone. Greed and selfishness are common vices among people who used to regulate themselves in light of Confucian ethics. In the encounter with the black women scholars, the message hits even harder. For the black are more cultivated and learned in Chinese philosophy and literature. The citizens of the Kingdom of Black Teeth, of which Hung-hung is but a representative, are said to be so devoted to reading and book-keeping that they have to books in their cellars to avoid any unwanted circulation. The object of ridicule here is the book collecting and publishing industry for which Ch'ing government is famous. For two hundred years or so, Ch'ing government's policy is to enslave the colonized – especially the Chinese intellectuals – by keeping them busy in editing and collecting books, instead of creating the social imaginary or subversive counter-discourse. Book collecting is hence related to containment and manipulation, a strategy of literacy and control. As more books are collected, less authentic knowledge of Chinese tradition is generated, to the extent that the true learning simply disappears from the home land.

It is interesting that two black women scholars should be portrayed in more than favorable terms, whereas a white male scholar from the Kingdom of the White is later on ridiculed for failing to get punctuations right in spite of his awfully impressive systematic ways of going about Chinese studies. The white Sinologist, or, in Edward W. Said's terminology, "Orientalist," develops his pseudoscience of Chinese texts simply by displacing, ignoring, and even making superfluous what is "really" in the texts. The contrast between the textual practice of the black women scholars and that of the white is vivid because of the black-white stereotype, a peculiar form of racism or, in Kwame Anthony Appiah's word, "racialism" that starts to take root in Chinese popular culture as foreign trade has by then become more frequent in southern China. Traditionally, the black are slaves from the Middle East, and the contrast between black and white is simply to distinguish beautiful, valuable objects from those terribly unappealing and thereby establish the order of things. But, with the European white and the African black population in view, a peculiar form of racism has by mid-Ch'ing been constituted to criticize the patronizing behavior, condescending attitude, and in particular colonial practices of the white – the "foreign demons." The fear of the foreign forces and the Other's power is further complicated by cultural, political, and military encounters between China and the West. In overgeneralization, the white become objects of aggressivity, envy, abomination, abjection and disgust, etc. In the form of cultural racism, the perceived threat of the racial Other to undermine order is, as David Theo Goldberg suggests, "displaced and countered by appealing to an absolute, reassuring, mystic law incorporated in the body, family, nation, race, and tradition."[6] Thus, in the novel, the white male scholar becomes an object of ridicule, an Other to be rejected in the racialized construction of cultural identity and in terms of the politics of nationalism. However, in depicting the white scholar as a Sinologist, the author also expresses the desire to incorporate the Other in spite of his desire to negate or at least slight the Other. It is at the ambivalent intersection of the politics of nationalism an the poetics of narcissism – of seeing the self in the Other both incorporated and distanced at the same time – that the black and white scholars are deployed in the novel to suggest terms by virtue of which Chinese intellectuals may perceive modernity and recognize identity.[7]

The racialism or cultural racism issue in the novel has often been bypassed or occasionally discussed in terms of allegory and satire.[8] But, as the bounds of race and its interrelations with nationalisms, sexualities, class distinctions, cultural identities, science and ideology, etc. become important topics in contemporary cultural studies,[9] we are in a better situation to investigate the complex discursive formation of Chinese modernity in light of racial and cultural antagonism, anxiety, or ambivalence. My point here is not to resort to race as a universal category, but simply to reveal the underlying ambivalence of race and gender from the standpoint of national unity and identity. After all, what the one hundred women scholars set out to do is to help reunite the T'ang dynasty and to fashion women scholars' poetic identities.

6 David Theo Goldberg, *Anatomy of Racism* (Minneapolis: University of Minnesota Press, 1990), p. xix.

7 *Modernity and Identity*, cf. Scott Lash and Jonathan Fridman (eds) (Oxford: Blackwell, 1992) for their mostly Eurocentric views on the subjects.

8 Hsin-sheng C. Kao, *Li Juchen* (Boston: Twayne, 1981); Angela Wang, "Ching-hua yuan and Gulliver's Travels." (Ph. D. dissertation, National Taiwan University, 1991).

9 Louis Gates, *"Race," Writing and Difference* (Chicago: University of Chicago Press, 1986); David Theo Goldberg, *Anatomy of Racism* (Minneapolis: University of Minnesota Press, 1990); Dominick LaCapra, *The Bounds of Race* (Ithaca: Cornell University Press, 1991); Etienne Balibar and Immanuel Wallerstein, *Race, Nation, Class* (London: Verso, 1990).

From the perspective of race and gender, then, we may be able to see how the black women scholars operate in the text. For in the black women scholars, especially in Hung-hung, we witness the strange mechanism of exclusion and inclusion in the very construction of Self and the difference of Otherness. They are said to be radical but conservative, similar to Chinese women and yet very different, more advanced but in some way less civilized. In the episode of fan in acquisition, for example, both are said to have inscribed two pieces of literature on the fan to advocate traditional feminine virtues. However, in a later episode, Hung-hung is described as totally different species that is not capable of arousing man's interests in her and is hence to be alienated or at least dealt with independently.[10]

Onto Hung-hung and T'ing-t'ing hence are inscribed two texts, one remonstrating transgressive behaviors in women, whereas the other expressing an abandoned woman's desire to remain chaste and to long for her husband's return in a combination of anagrams and acrostics. We gather from their psychic identification with the traditional woman that the two black women scholars are by no means feminists, being complicit with the dominant gender technology or engendering discursive system that through the process and product of representation and self-representation subjugates women.[11] The novel has been hailed by many critics, most notably Hu Shih, as a masterpiece about women's liberation. On the surface, it appears to celebrate the creativity of new women. Yet, deep down, it abides by patriarchal rules, as manifested by the introductory remarks in chapter 1 on what constitutes femininity. On the one hand, Empress Wu sets up the Civil Exam for women scholars and endows them opportunities to make a difference. But, on the other, the Empress is revealed, if not reviled, to be a disrupter who not only usurps the throne but causes the one hundred floral goddesses to be expelled from Heaven. The novel is about the rise and fall of the matron and "intimate enemy," the enabler and disabler;

10 Li, *Ching-hua yuan*, chapters 49–50.

11 Teresa de Lauretis, *Technologies of Gender* (Bloomington: Indiana University Press, 1987), 10–26.

about the ambivalent movement on the part of these new women to disempower their empowerment, to restore the, ironically, masculine tradition – the Symbolic order.

The ambivalent movement operates in the logic of double-bind, i.e., of enabling and disabling at the same time. And the movement is further perpetuated by the sexual, racial, and cultural politics of incorporation and distancing. For it is the curious mirroring of the Self in the Other that constitutes the function of cultural criticism in an invented gaze. And Hung-hung is but a case of such mirroring, a figure in the "mirror phase," an imaginary projection and self-construction (or, in Greenblatt's words "self-fashioning"): it is as if Hung-hung were one among us but at a closer scrutiny she is the Other that urges the Self to construct the "real me." Such is her role in being a student of Chinese literature and at the same time sexually repulsive or at least undesirable foreign body, i.e., in being a surplus and a minus simultaneously. In the latter instance, Hung-hung is depicted as a sex object unappealing to the head of robbers and his wife. She is regarded by both parties as an "unworthy catch," not even qualified to be a maid or a concubine. Because of her black skin, Hung-hung is looked upon as an undesirable Other, despite her good looks. Being black, she serves as a point of contrast against which T'ang Kui-ch'en and other Chinese women stand as "normal" and attractive objects of desire. As a contrasting presence, Hung-hung in fact causes the fight between the wife and her husband. As a result, the head of robbers is severely punished by his wife, who is portrayed as "extraordinary" and "remarkable."[12] (This episode has frequently been used to make a protofeminist out of Li Juchen. However, the rhetoric the wife deploys is that of a weaker vessel: she would rather die if her man finds another woman worthier. When her husband is touched by her pretended suicidal performance, she utilizes the opportunity to beat him up on the ground that he wants to start another affair. Cunning and manipulative, but by no means "radical," she relies on her feminine charm and tactics to manage the man and thereby set other women free.)

12 Li, *Ching-hua yuan*, chapter 1.

There is an ambivalent psychic structure of identification and distinction working simultaneously that attempts to cut the other women apart but always already finds her within. As a matter of fact, it is within a similar but larger ambivalent and hybrid structure of feelings that modern Chinese intellectuals reacted and continue to react to what Andre Malraux calls "the temptation of the West." In a case like Chang Ping-lin, an important scholar at the turn of the century who is in many ways like Li Juchen, we sense the difficulty to separate Westernism from nativism (or traditionalism). To him, the slogan of the time, "Chinese learning forms the main body, while strategically purring Western science and technology to use," actually comes down to mean a modification of Chinese tradition, if and only if that tradition is still available. The modified version is then one that is underwritten neither by the Western subject of Enlightenment nor by a simple reactionary or essentialist nativism. It is more an invented rediscovery of Westernism within Chinese tradition than an innocent assimilation of European science and technology into Chinese learning. The foreign bodies of leaning do not dissolve altogether but they are drawn into the renegotiated space and zone of intersection in which all culturally determinate significations are put into question by the hybrid figure that disseminates in the endless process of incorporation and distancing. In other words, instead of redefining the Self in the hypostatized structure of gaze, Chang Ping-lin and many others find themselves caught in a dynamic doubling – rather than dialectical or oppositional – movement toward modernity in which the Chinese subjectivity motions and shifts in between denial and identification. Now, the "neither-nor" or "in-between" structure of feelings can be detected in the figure of Hung-hung, the black woman scholar who is one of the members of the one hundred but at times still regarded as an outsider, an alien element that helps fashion the "true" self. There are times when the one hundred floral goddesses form their highly integrated sisterhood; however, race, ethnicity, class issues still emerge to make distinctions inevitable. An example of this is the episode of Yin Johua being recalled to the Kingdom of the Amazons by her mother. The dying mother's request is further enforced by Empress Wu's decree to urge

Johua to return to her motherland. Seeing her return inevitable, Johua agrees to it on the condition that Hung-hung and T'ing-t'ing accompany her. As a result, four women from other lands – the fourth being Chih Lan-yin from the Kingdom of Split Tongue – have to leave China. Empress Wu's demand on the four women scholars' departure infuriates most members of the community. Together, they condemn the Empress for being unfair to the foreigners and for causing political upheavals in the nation. After a short period of gathering together and reciting poems, a scene much grander in scale than that in a much later *Dream of the Red Chamber*, the one hundred women decide to battle against Empress Wu and her brothers to restore T'ang.

Yet in condemning Empress Wu, these women scholars also disempower their power giver. It is the Empress who makes possible the women scholars to stand out and gain important positions. But, it is the Empress who had earlier caused the downfall of these women in their pre-existence as floral deities, who despite their will to do otherwise submit to the Empress's decree and bloom in winter to the dismay of the King of Heaven. In fact, what Empress Wu does in dethroning her husband and raising women's social position or at least level of literacy is nothing dissimilar to what the wife of the head of robbers does to her husband. Whereas one is blamed and eventually defeated, the other is upheld as a heroic case. A major difference lies in the distinct impacts of their actions on the public (or national) and private (or domestic) spheres. Empress Wu is seen as a threat to the order of things both for her disruption of T'ang rule and for her whim to demand all flowers to come into full blossom in the midst of winter. Mysteriously related to Moon Goddess Ch'ang-e, she represents the demonic aspects of Woman: irrationality, arbitrariness, sensuality, wickedness, uncontrollability, and in particular dangerous, if not threatening, sexuality. Of course, Li Juchen didn't live to see the rule of another Empress – Tz'u-hsi – and the decline of the Ch'ing dynasty. But, in the novel, there are places where Empress Wu or a woman deity (such as Moon Goddess) is said to be responsible for the moral degeneration and social disintegration. Evidently, woman becomes the allegorical name for a specific historical failure here, as Radhakrishnan indicates.

The specific historical failure in question happens to be that of Chinese modernity, and that in the figure of women who symbolize crisis and the possibility of cultural recreation, women who operate from the very start in the logic of enabling-disabling or of doubling such as Flower Goddess in T'ang Kui-ch'en, the Self in the other, the disempowering in the empowering, interior-exterior hybridity, and so on.

What I want to suggest is that the problem of Chinese modernity, posited in *Ching-hua yuan* as feminized bodies of knowledge and power that are helplessly caught in the unresolvable doubling and hybridity, may actually allow us to explore other forms of cultural affiliation – those that come to use through a subtle political rearticulation of private values and public virtues, for instance – instead of those fixed or hypostatized structure of traditionalism vs. Westernism polarity.[13] Modernity is often characterized in terms of consciousness of the discontinuity of time: a break with tradition, a feeling of novelty, of vertigo in the face of the passing moment. At least this is what modernity means to Michel Foucault. However, in spite of Foucault's attempt to frame modernity and define it as a unique development of European societies, he nevertheless points out that "it would be more useful to try to find out how the attitude of modernity, ever since its formation, has found itself struggling with attitudes of 'countermodernity'."[14] In other words, attitude of countermodernity has always already been part of modernity. And Foucault himself also suggests that modernity is "an attitude" of history and that "Enlightenment must be considered both as a process in which men participate collectively and as an act of courage to be accomplished personally."[15] As a political problem, not simply an epistemological one, Enlightenment affects all humanity. Of course, as many critics indicate, Foucault fails to probe further the historical ironies, disjunctive temporalities, and much-vaulted crisis of

13 I draw on Homi Bhabha's essay in Goldberg and also his contribution to *Critical Fictions: The Politics of Imaginative Writing*, Philemena Mariani (ed.) (Seattle: Bay, 1991), 64–5.

14 Michel Foucault, "What is Enlightenment?" in Paul Rabinow (ed.), trans. Catherine Porter, *The Foucault Reader* (New York: Pantheon, 1984), 39.

15 Foucault, "What is Enlightenment?" 35.

representation of Western modernity.[16] Homi Bhabha writes, for example, "the Eurocentricity of Foucault's theory of cultural difference is revealed in his insistent spatialising of the time of modernity." The point is to remind us neither to reduce the colonies and the Third World to some homogeneous other of the West, nor to vacuously celebrate the notorious multiculturalism.

Completed in 1820 and published eight years later, *Ching-hua yuan* has been looked upon as a feminist text, an encyclopedic novel in Chinese literati tradition, a political satire and allegory,[17] a somewhat "antiquarian" mode of romance produced in the age of unbelief to make fun of social reality,[18] an utopian projection outside of one nation's borders, of the cultural practices it deems exotic but at the same time instructive,[19] and so on. Hsin-sheng Kao commented in 1981 that Li Juchen "has enjoyed little popularity or discussion in the light of modern theories of criticism."[20] The situation has changed a great deal since then, though the majority of scholarships still consist of efforts to identify and relocate the geographical sites or historical events the novel refers to. A more recent trend is to pair the novel with its Western counterparts – *Utopia* or *Gulliver's Travels*, for instance – and reflect on cultural differences.[21] However, as a literary text that rejects coherence or unity, the novel in fact urges us to relate it to the difficult cultural situation of modern China, and instead of following "the teleological thread that makes progress possible," to isolate episodes and small nar-

16 See Edward W. Said, "Foucault and the imagination of power" in *Reflection on Exile* (Cambridge: Harvard University Press, 2002); Gayatri C. Spivak, *The Postcolonial Critic* (New York: Routledge, 1991), 201, 209–10.

17 Kao, *Li Juchen*.

18 Yen Chuan-ying, "Ishikawa on taiwan feng-ch'ing yu shui-ts'ai hua," (Ishikawa on Taiwan Landscapes and Watercolors), paper delivered at Asian Art in the 1930s Workshop, Institute of History and Philology, Academia Sinica, Taipei, May 14, 1999.

19 Wang, "Ching-hua yuan and Gulliver's Travels."

20 Kao, *Li Juchen*, p. iv.

21 Chiang T'ai-fen, "Ching-hua yuan and Utopia." (Ph.D. dissertation, National Taiwan University, Taipei, 1990); Wang, "Ching-hua yuan and Gulliver's Travels."

ratives (of those uneasy incorporation and distancing) that rupture historical continuity, as Foucault suggests.[22] It is illuminating that the novelist celebrates the birth of new women and yet puts before them a rather gloomy future: discrimination, segregation, and tragic death. Since Li Juchen never lives to complete the novel, we cannot but remain in doubt about the fate of these women and Chinese modernity. To seek answers or at least clues, we will have to turn elsewhere to stories of the other two women from different societies, as ancient singers of vernacular tales would say, "while the flower bursts into just one blossom, the narrative now heads toward an opposite direction."

Travel and Translation in Early Twentieth Century Asia[23]

While the novel *Asia's Orphan* (Ya-hsi-ya-te-ku-erh, 1945) by Wu Cho-liu is often hailed as a masterpiece about Taiwan's difficult transition from its colonial period to postcoloniality, his travelogue "Nanking Journals" (Nanking tsa-kan or literally, Mixed Feelings toward Nanking, 1942–1943) has gained relatively little attention.[24] Brief and sketchy as it is, "Nanking Journals" in fact prefigures the plot and theme

22 Michel Foucault, *Politics, Philosophy, and Culture* (New York: Routledge, 1988), 90.

23 An earlier version of Part II has been included in *Writing Taiwan: A New Literary History*, edited by Carlos Rojas and David Derwei Wang (Durham: Duke University Press, 2007).

24 See the Introductory Prefaces to *Ya-his-ya-te-ku-erh (Asia's Orphan)* and the "Short checklist of Wu Cho-liu criticism" prepared by Hsu Shu-lan at the back of *Wu-cho-liu-chi* (Short Stories by Wu cho-liu). Hereafter all references to Wu's travelogue will be in double quotation marks, serving to distinguish it from the collection of all of Wu's travel writing under the same title Nanking Journals. To avoid confusion, I use the Wade-Giles system of romanization, rather than the pinyin system, as Wade-Giles is the standard system in Taiwan. For the sake of consistency, I also cite family names first. All English translations of the passages quoted are my own, unless otherwise indicated.

of *Asia's Orphan*. For Hu T'ai-ming, the protagonist of the novel, spends some time in Nanking and except for the marriage episode, his life there comes close to what the narrator experiences in the Journals. In this section, I want to look at this short piece of travel literature, with concentration on his observations of a young woman boarding the train in relation to his notion of Taiwan's alternative modernity. I shall also make references to such works as *Travels in China* by Akutagawa Ryunosuke (1892–1927), memoirs by Ishikawa Kinichiro (1871–1945), and others to illuminate the text and context. In examining the travelogue and its implications for comparative study of societies and cultures, I shall also draw on critical remarks made by Edward Said, James Clifford, and Homi Bhabha on travel and border crossing.

To avoid confusion, we should clarify that *Nanking Journals* is also the title that the editors gave to Wu's travel writing collected after his death in one volume (1977). Made up of factual reports of journeys to other parts of the world and of nostalgic accounts of places re-visited, *Nanking Journals* is a series of travelogues ranging from objective accounts to exotic memories. The narratives vary from the minutely factual to the imaginary at the most personal level. In "Journeys to India and Africa," for example, Wu gave practically every detail regarding the itineraries; at one point, he even calculated the exact mileage that he had flown.[25] On the other hand, several of his memoirs regarding his hometown and of the school he had taught at early in his life reveal the way in which places helped constitute personal identity. In most cases, Wu as the narrator is either an insider, addressing his former friends and colleagues, or an outsider and a tourist, who passes comments on the exotic sights and sounds.

Constituting essential part of the *Journal*, "Nanking Journals" is in many ways very unique, as the author assumes an ambivalent role of neither an insider nor an outsider to a place that is both familiar and strange (or even *unheimlich*) to him. There he is a participant in and an observer of the fast changing community. But he is more often a

25 Wu Cho-liu, "Journeys to India and Africa," *Nanking tsa-kan* (Journals of Mixed Feelings toward Nanking, 1942) (Taipei: Yuen-hsing, 1977), 194–5.

comparatist of cultures and societies, recollecting and reflecting on peoples and places he encountered at different times and with different mind-sets. The style is hybrid, with the narrator appropriating the voice of both a journalist and of a cultural critic. One has difficulty, probably like Wu himself, adopting a single perspective in relation to what had been said about China in the 1930s.[26] This is more so if one considers Chinese and Japanese narratives of the time concerning the fate of modern China. This very difficulty of adjusting a proper distance and indeed angle, I shall argue, has to do with Wu's notion of an alternative modern Taiwan.

The author informs us from the very start that the journey to Nanking was partly a result of his desire to get away from Taiwan, then Japan's colony. Undertaking the job of a news reporter for *Ta-lu Hsin-pao* (Mainland News), he set out on January 12, 1941 for China, and "after staying in the big Shanghai for sometime, went on to visit Nanking and stayed there for a year and three months."[27] It is in these fifteen months – January 1941 to March 1942 – that Wu's notion of alternative modernity slowly evolved. "Before I dwell on the topic of Nanking, the capital of ancient China for over four hundred years, let me reflect on the Chinese national character, an issue seemingly so remote and indifferent. Having a long history, China appears to be permanent and unchanging," he speculated.

> Much has been said about the Chinese national character. However, I don't think any of the scholars, experts, and anthropologists have so far grasped the essence of China. For they largely make far-fetched judgments or have dangerous assumptions based on historical facts. One cannot understand China without comprehending its national character. Even the Chinese people don't have a clear picture about themselves.[28]

26 Realizing that there may be chronotopical lags between the writer and the autobiographical subject, I shall nevertheless refer to Wu as the author of and narrator in Nanking Journals. For in the Journals Wu seemed to want to give the impression that the accounts were drawn from his own personal experience and random observations.

27 Wu, *Nanking tsa-kan* (Journals of Mixed Feelings toward Nanking), 51.

28 Ibid.

As a "neither" foreigner "nor" Chinese, Wu however had a keen eye for many things in China and often came up with illuminating stories drawing on comparative studies of Chinese and Japanese societies, of ancient and modern cultures. While critical of Chinese bureaucrats and corruption in many arenas, he was fascinated by the Chinese art of survival and by its highly flexible, albeit pragmatic, sense of social existence. He commented: "Misfortune begins with one's birth, and the most unfortunate is to be born a Chinese. But, if one has a lot of money, one finds this country most carefree and enjoyable. Such is the Chinese reality."[29] Under such a reality principle, a large number of social activities – card games (mahjong), dining, theater going, public bathing, teahouse gathering, for example – gained profundity. The ways in which the system of social signification operated baffled as well as fascinated Wu:

> These people don't aim at specific targets in life, nor work for certain inherent values. They simply grasp whatever opportunities coming their way. Everything is up to the dictate of fate. Nowhere in the world have I seen a race like Chinese so leisurely waiting for chances to turn up.[30]

One could easily fault Wu for such a stereotypical representation of the Chinese and even associate a remark like this with similar condescending tones made by E.M. Forster in *A Passage to India*. For instance,

> When that strange race nears the dust and is condemned as untouchable, then nature remembers the physical perfection that she accomplished elsewhere, and throws out a god – not many, but one here and there, to prove to society how little its categories impress her.[31]

However, Wu was not trashing the commoners that he encounters in Nanking here. This is more evident if we juxtapose his account with what the Chinese intellectuals and Japanese scholars had said about the situation at the time.

29 Ibid., 61.
30 Ibid., 71.
31 E.M. Forster, *A Passage to India* (New York: Harcourt, 1924), 217.

We gather from the first few pages that Wu's journey to Nanking was overdetermined by complex factors, among them desires to escape Japan's colonialism's culture in Taiwan and to embrace the fatherland – China. It is apparent that before he left for China, he had read a number of Japanese books on the "backwardness" of the country. He was familiar with Chinese classics, particularly high T'ang poetry on lives in the ancient capitals. In a sense, the travel is a homeward bound but also something exotic. For Wu was considered to be Chinese and Japanese-Taiwanese at the same time by his fellow men. Informed by Japanese accounts of China, which unfailingly aimed to undermine the so-called "Middle Kingdom" and to substitute it with a derogatory name "Chih-na," Wu might have read a book like *Travels in China* by Akutagawa and found himself caught in the China-Japan antagonisms.

As Stephen Tanaka and Shih Shu-mei have demonstrated, a great number of Meiji intellectual leaders advocated the idea of Japan's "parting with Asia" or of its becoming the first modern Asian imperial power. To attain the goal of self-fashioning, Japan was to replace China, in order to assert its desire to be a worthy counterpart of the West in the Orient. Not only "Chih-na" was introduced as a Japanese transliteration of the Western word "China," but more scientific terms such as "toyoshi" (Oriental historiography) and "genbun itchi" (unifying writing and speech) were invented, to construct Japanese modernity and identity. In the Japan modernization processes, anti-Chinese sentiments were developed and disseminated in the form of colonial education to other parts of Asia, most notably Taiwan, Korea, Manchuria, and Shanghai. The first and most successful Japanese colony, Taiwan was for fifty years (1895–1945) considered a site for the "South Advance" Project. Japanese was designated as Taiwan's "national language" and by 1920 it is estimated that more than twenty percent of Taiwanese took up Japanese names.[32]

A book full of sneers and derision, condemning Chinese civilization in all sorts of way, *Travels in China* was a product of Akutagawa's

32 Lai Tse-han et al., *A Tragic Beginning* (Stanford: Stanford University Press, 1991), 45.

journey to China in 1921 under the aegis of Osaka mainichi shinbun. Acclaimed author of *Roshomon* and a prominent intellectual of the time, Akutagawa was very popular among Japanese audience. The travelogue was a big hit in Japan when it came out. Akutagawa's China is totally the opposite of modern Japan: dirt, urine, prostitutes on the streets, and snobbish, if not pretentious, intellectuals everywhere to betray the backwardness of the Chinese national character. The other writer in similar vent is Yokomitsu Riichi (1898–1947), who in his novel on China *(Shanghai, 1928–32)* looks upon the semi-colonial city as a "waste dump of Asia," embodying all the grotesque and filthy elements completely unthinkable to a Japanese. Scholars have indicated the ways in which Japanese writers during the 1930s used and abused China subject in very sophisticated mode of cultural translation.[33] Granted the complexity, these writers had in reality helped disseminate unfavorable images of China among Japan's common readers and in one way or another forced Chinese radicals studying in Japan to internalize such images. A notable example was Lu Hsun, who created the prototypical figure Ah Q to parody the Chinese national character. Another representative was the tortured Yu Ta-fu, whose Japan stories are packed with such expressions of despair and self-hate as: "The way the Japanese despise the Chinese is like the way we despise pigs and dogs."[34] "Oh, China, China, why can't you become rich and strong," one of his protagonists laments.[35]

In "Nanking Journals," Wu can be said to reinforce the point about China's inferiority but with a difference, as I shall argue in a later context. In several important ways, Wu deviated from the Japanese and Chinese narratives of the gaze. For Japanese intellectuals would con-

33 Naoki Sakai, *Translation and subjectivity: On "Japan" and Cultural Nationalism* (Minneapolis: University of Minnesota Press, 1997); Shih Shu-mei, *The Lure of the Modern: Writing Modernism in Semicolonial China, 1917–1937* (Berkeley: University of California Press, 2001); Lydia Liu, *Translingual Practice* (Stanford: Stanford University Press, 1995).

34 Yu Ta-fu, *Yu Ta-fu hsiao-shuo ch'uan-p'ien* (Complete Short Stories of Yu Ta-fu) (Hangchou: Che-chiang wen-yi, 1991), 46.

35 Ibid., 23.

stantly draw upon Japanese landscape to condemn or to avoid confronting things Chinese. Wu was both repulsed by and drawn to the daily event and objects he witnessed in Nanking. He mused on the discrepancies between what he had read about China and what he saw, between the gruesome destiny the Japanese had predicted for China and the unfathomable vitality of the nation in dismal. While nostalgic for the golden past, he never lost sight of what was actually happening in the everyday life. Because of his keen perception of the discrepancies, the Journal entries revealed his balanced views on the conflicts of interpretation concerning the fate of China on the part of Japanese and Chinese intellectuals. The travel to Nanking therefore enabled him to better comprehend cultural differences and to conceive Taiwan's alternative modernity as apart from Japan's developing and China's undeveloped modernity projects.

Several times, Wu compared the past with the present, citing T'ang poetry to comment on the ruinous scenes at the dark corner of Nanking. But more often is the case in which he would compare and contrast between Taiwan and Nanking in terms of clothing and gender difference. For example, he felt his shirts and trousers too narrow and shabby, put side by side with Western dress and Shanghai fashions of the time.[36] Even his friend Mr Chung's mansion with good views caused him "to lose the usual confidence."[37] Chinese women "tend to be softer and quieter," unlike Taiwanese women "who frequently raise their voice and are rather talkative, especially when there are more than three around."[38] But he found Taiwanese girls to be more passionate and dynamic, even with figures better shaped.[39] Generally, he thought that Chinese women had benefited from the climate and traditional Confucian teaching. They were more refined and elegant, as a result. However, incidents revealed otherwise. On the way to Nanking, he saw a young girl with richly decorated lace shoes, who didn't bother to wipe her own shoe

36 Wu, *Nanking tsa-kan* (Journals of Mixed Feelings toward Nanking), 54–5.
37 Ibid., 58.
38 Ibid., 79.
39 Ibid., 58.

marks on the seat clean in reaching after her suitcase on the train rack.[40] Such an ambivalent feeling toward Chinese women, especially as summed up by the image of a girl sitting on dirty shoe marks though neatly dressed, continued to haunt him and to be implicated in a peculiar process of self-fashioning. He suddenly realized that Taiwan under Japanese was more civil or at least more modernized. "Public Baths in Nanking leave a lot to be desired."[41] "As for pure water, there is not much."[42] A lot of small money had to be spent on services and tips, not to mention valuables stolen by maids. Most of elementary school education was conducted in unsafe and unhealthy buildings. Despite of poverty and depravity, Chinese could not afford to lose face. They indulged in gambling, bragging, feasting, and showing off. The most deplorable sights, however, were the beggars: they were practically everywhere.

All these come close to what the Japanese writers had said about China in the 1930s. But Wu's account was a tormented and often ambivalent narrative that tried to disclose the Chinese national character in a comparative framework. He saw not only the miserable existence in the fatherland, but also the inadequacy of Japanese vision of a collapsing "Middle Kingdom." He believed that it is by seeing "what China is and is not" that one could really appreciate the greatness of that culture. The Japanese accounts available at the time were simply superficial and self-serving. For they only wanted to emphasize China's failures and problems without understanding them. He commented:

> A great number of Japanese tourists have visited Hanshan's temple and felt much disillusioned. They don't know how to adopt Chang Chi's wondering perspective, alighting the boat by the maple bridge, in order to closely appreciate the toll of the bell.[43]

As a result, he suggested, the Japanese tended to misconstrue a "great and coherent culture" to be corrupt at the very core.

40 Ibid., 55.
41 Ibid., 60.
42 Ibid., 70.
43 Ibid., 119.

Wu was upset with the Japanese narratives regarding the prevalence of opium use, foot binding, and corruption. To him, these "uncivilized" social practices did exist but they were to be taken as representing Chinese culture. After all, Wu pointed out, Japanese and Chinese shared common written script though there were noticeable differences in the use (t'ung-wen-yi-tzu). Despite its present difficulty, China still revealed an amazing sense of totality and integrity. To negate China's achievements by singling out a small portion of its social illness was not only unfair but also misleading and absurd.[44] On the other hand, Wu was rather ambivalent about his own "Chinese" cultural identity. He constantly returned to the scene of a young girl's sitting on her own dirty shoe marks, of beggars on the street; he was baffled by the dominance of favor networks and private ties. And on top of these, he was not a Chinese native speaker: his Taiwaneseness turned out to be helplessly caught with the "double and split time" of psychic and national identification, to rephrase Homi Bhabha.[45] For he is both "minus" and "surplus" in relation to Chinese national representation and cultural membership. After all, Taiwan had been severed from China and ceded to Japan in 1895. However, the majority of Taiwanese population was from southern China in late Ming and the ties to Chinese culture had been strong.

Thus, in terms of "micro-sociological" or "micro-political" orientation, as defined by Etienne Balibar in his recent discussion of Franco-Algerian relations, Wu had problem seeing himself as a member of Chinese society. To make the situation more complicated, Japanese colonialism's culture in Taiwan left the Taiwanese in a neither-nor category – neither belonging to the universalist category of culturally Chinese, nor of a Taiwanese particularism which colonization attempted to repress. To claim oneself a Taiwanese in China during the 1930s was to put oneself in a dangerous position of a spy and traitor, a position Wu later on elaborated in the novel *Asia's Orphan*. With all these complexities in mind, Wu never let his nostalgic feeling for China get in the way of confronting China and of directing the gaze inward, to

44 Ibid.

45 Homi Bhabha, *The Location of Culture* (New York: Routledge, 1994) 144.

reflect on Taiwan's alternative modernity in response to Japan and China. In this aspect, he differed from several Japan travelers in early twentieth century Asia. To illustrate this, let us briefly return to a passage by Akutagawa. The words reveal Akutagawa's pride in and nostalgia for Japanese landscape:

> When I went to the East Asia Common Culture Academy, walking on the second floor of the dormitory, we saw a sea of blue young barley through a window at the end of the hallway. Here and there in that barley field, we saw a cluster of ordinary rape blossoms. Far beyond them we saw a huge carp streamer over a number of connected roofs. The paper carp was blowing in the wind and animatedly fluttering into the sky. This one carp streamer changed the whole scenery for me. I wasn't in China.

"I felt as though I was in Japan," he continues.

> But when I approached the window, I saw Chinese farmers working in the barley field before my eyes. I felt angered as though they weren't supposed to be there. Coming all this way to see a Japanese carp streamer in the Shanghai sky gave me a bit of joy.[46]

Akutagawa sees and fails to see Chinese farmers working in the barley field. For he shifts the sight to an imaginary center and envisions something that lies elsewhere and is out of place to the present.

In this regard, the travel experience of Ishikawa Kinichiro could be more revealing. A Japanese teacher at the Taipei Middle School (part-time 1907–1916) and Taipei Normal school (full-time, 1923–1933), Ishikawa is instrumental in introducing watercolors to Taiwan. Self-taught and dedicated to Japanese nationalism, Ishikawa was in his early stages strongly influenced by modernism, particularly English impressionistic and realistic landscape watercolors. He was not very active at home and was thought a conservative artist belonging to the rather popular school of naturalism in the Meiji period (1898–1907). In the Japanese imperial army, he was an officer and interpreter who fought bravely in a series of battles with the Chinese (1900) and the Russian

46 Akutagawa, Ryunosuke, "Travels in China", trans. Joshua Fogel, *Chinese Studies in History* 30, No. 4 (1997), 37.

(1904–1905) for a Manchuria under Japanese rule. In October 1907, Ishikawa was appointed Interpreter for the colonial Government-General in Taiwan. He also became a part-time art and language teacher at the Taipei Middle School. During those nine years in Taiwan, he was in many ways an ambivalent teacher and colonizer. In some of his watercolors done in this period, he glorified victories over the natives in colonial encounters. He toured the island widely and depicted his exotic aborigine memories in realistic detail. But he was also involved in founding the Lan-t'ing Tea Klatch to promote cultural exchanges and to interest other Japanese artists and officers in Chinese and Taiwanese art and literature. He even organized a public exhibition of his artworks in 1914, one of the first in Taiwan art history. Despite his accomplishments as an artist who made use of his impressive local knowledge, Ishikawa was still an officer and a colonizer, shown not only by the subjects of his watercolors but by the colonial Governor-General's appearance at the exhibit.

However, the situation changed when Ishikawa made his second visit to Taiwan. In September 1923, Ishikawa's Tokyo home was destroyed in a major earthquake. A one-time colleague and then principal of the Taipei Normal School sent a telegram informing the despairing Ishikawa that he would be welcome in Taipei with a full-time teaching post. Left with no family, Ishikawa accepted the offer and spent another nine years in Taiwan. The intellectual milieu in 1923 was very different than that of the previous decade. Now the colonial policy came under the charge of civilians – rather than admirals or generals – as Hara Kei, Den Kenjiro and others came to power as Prime Minister or Cabinet members. The death of the seventh governor-general Liutenant-General Akashi Motojiro in October 1919 finally gave Prime Minister Hara Kei the opportunity to make the kind of reforms in the governing structures of Taiwan and Korea that he had long favored but found it difficult during the reign of Goto Shimpei. Hara Kei was finally able to appoint Den Kenjiro (1919–1923) as Taiwan's first civilian governor-general and to charge him with reforming the colony.[47]

47 Peter Duus et al., *The Japanese Wartime Empire, 1931–1945* (Princeton: Princeton University Press, 1996), 289.

These men managed to survive political struggles, first by doing remarkably well in the colonies, particularly in Taiwan, and then by turning out domestic opponents when the latter misjudged riots in the colonies. Under the policy of integration and equal treatment, of making the colonized useful subjects to the Japanese Emperor, the arts and humanities were increasingly encouraged as means to tame the Taiwanese. (Before his departure for Shanghai, Wu Cho-liu was employed as Japanese teacher devoted to such a cause.)

As a result, when Ishikawa returned to Taipei in 1923, the painter found himself in a different ambiance and his approach to art education had moved from British and Japanese modes to a more French orientation emphasizing direct outdoor interactions with the environment. To facilitate his teaching, he translated Japanese art textbooks into Chinese and supplied local equivalent wherever necessary. As Taipei Normal School was a major college for future teachers, Ishikawa's influence on local artists was understandably strong, even though his ties with Japanese politicians were undercut by his civilian and teacher status. Several students later became outstanding watercolorists – Lan Yin-ting (1903–1979) and Hung Jui-lin (1912–1997), for instance. A number of transnational factors contributed to the ambivalent and benevolent roles Ishikawa played in the second nine years. Firstly, the unexpected earthquake which shook his house and his livelihood. Secondly, his recent tour around Europe and his exposure to modern French painting. Thirdly, the warm welcome he received from his friends in Taiwan and his position as a civilian and an art teacher. Fourthly, the emergence of Taiwanese artists and a cultural elite that was beginning to win recognition in Japan. Finally, new developments in Korea and Manchuria forced Japan to readjust its colonial policy. All in all, the material culture that Ishikawa confronted in 1923 was quite different. Several of his paintings in this period reflected this sort of change, leaving behind numerous pictures of local subjects, so many that he has been claimed by some scholars to be an integral part of modern Taiwan art.

However, it is interesting to note that during these nine years (1923–1933) Ishikawa also deliberately suppressed the use of rhetorical devices – metaphor, in particular – in comparing Taiwanese landscape to that of Japan.[48] During his first visit to Taiwan, he composed lyrics on similarities between Taiwan's coast and that of Nagasaki. Metaphoric expressions abound in his articles on Taiwan and Japan art, suggesting ways to see one as and in another. But when he returned to Taiwan as a full-time teacher, the perspective changed: he deliberately tried to set Japan apart from Taiwan. If Taiwan's mountain and hills impressed him as spectacular, they were but derivative to the more sublime Fuiji. To Ishikawa (and many Japanese artists or scholars), Chinese or Taiwanese landscape was much cruder and hence inferior. Every scene during the tour abroad served to remind them of the essentially inimitable and uncontested beautiful or sublime Japanese landscape. Any signs can only gain significance on the condition that they are so construed in relation to their originary forms in the metropolitan center.

This is where Wu departed from such artists as Akutagawa, Ishikawa, and even Lu Hsun. For the paradox is that his hermeneutic codes are given by two metropolitan centers – Japan and China – of which he had no part. And it is with the rift between the two centers that his sense of an alternative selfhood developed. When Wu left for Nanking, Japan was waging wars against China and South Asia. Japan's control of Taiwan was tightened, with military staffs regaining power in the colony. So the political situation was different from that of Ishikawa's second visit to Taiwan. The psychic structure of identification with either China or Japan was therefore very mixed. Unlike Lu Hsun or Yu Ta-fu, who readily rejected China in a desire to embrace Japanese modernity, Wu regarded his visit to Nanking as a homeward bound, a spiritual quest and an eternal return. However, like both writers he felt appalled and was greatly disillusioned by what he witnessed in the fatherland. On the other hand, he hated to be called a Taiwanese or a Japanese colonial subject. That was the primary cause for the trip to Nanking to begin with. Yet, a sense of moral luck was self-evident when he contrasted China with Taiwan. For the latter seemed to him more advanced as a beneficiary of Japan's modernity projects. The ambivalent

48 Yen, "Ishikawa on taiwan feng-ch'ing yu shui-ts'ai hua," (Ishikawa on Taiwan Landscapes and Watercolors), May 14, 1999.

sentiments toward China and Japan are but unnatural outcome of, according to Wu, Taiwan's unfortunate, albeit marginal, geographic and cultural location in between the two great nations.

A great number of his remarks on cultural difference indicate that he was deeply troubled by the identity split and a sense of loss. The athletics meeting at the National Central University was illuminating in this regard. "In Japan all activities of the meeting would be in order and follow the program to every detail. Even though the Central University did prepare its program, nothing matched it. One had difficulty identifying the beginning and, for that matter, the end," he wondered.[49]

> Students, observers, and the athletics rushed to the sports arena in a confusing commotion. Even the judges were having problems telling them apart. [...] In spite of the tumult, however, they seemed to be able to run things according to the program one way or another. I stood in awe, in great admiration of the ways in which the Chinese always managed to come up with Chinese solutions to their problems in most amazing manner.[50]

In great amazement, Wu found that everybody seemed to take it easy and in no hurry to get the right things done. "If the events should run unsmoothly, time would resolve them. There are always order in the midst of chaos."[51]

In many places, Wu commented on the "favor" and relationship *(kuan-hsi)* networks that were crucial to Chinese everyday life in no less than ambivalent terms. People often build their relations over and across all sorts of network, to gain favors or to extend favors to other members of the network.

> Nannies, servants, wards, and waiters at tea houses are integral part of Chinese society. They have forces behind them. Seemingly powerless, they can easily accomplish what would be tremendous tasks, once their network put to use. We shouldn't forget that under the shadows of social disorder, these people help get things done in vital ways.[52]

49 Wu, *Nanking tsa-kan* (Journals of Mixed Feelings toward Nanking), 84.
50 Ibid.
51 Ibid.
52 Ibid., 75.

Even the servants and maids would have to be tipped, to get things done properly. Compared to the Chinese, the Japanese were extremely neat and immaculate, to the degree of being mysophobic. The Chinese left their ancient buildings and national treasures in ruins, whereas the Japanese kept the temples of Kyoto and Nara in good shapes, even though the latter had learned a lot from the Chinese. In spite of their poverty, the Chinese spent a great of energy maintaining their looks, to keep their faces. To Wu, two features immediately distinguish a Chinese person from a Japanese: shoes and hairs. The Chinese like to polish their shoes, to make them shine, and they "put so much oil on their hairs that even flies would skip on the surface and fall."[53] But it is the geographic immensity and undecipherable mystic elements in the national character that help differentiate the Chinese from the rest. The inscrutability is in part a result from Chinese's long history of social suffering that people had got so used to war, famine, suppression, disease, torture and a whole assemblage of human problems. They had become indifferent to collective catastrophe, contingent misfortune, or structure violence. "They have no expressions and it would not be easy to hear any comments on current affairs."[54] The lack of a public sphere, however, should not obscure the fact that the Chinese way of evasion was an art of survival and a tactics of improvisation developed out of a specific cultural context in which political persecutions were imposed on the discovery of circumstantial evidences. "In other parts of the world, there may be laws instated to protect individual freedom and to seek happiness without fear or uncertainty. From foreign perspectives, Chinese people may seem indifferent, but things are more complex than that," Wu went on to explain.[55]

In his succinct comparative account of two Asian cities – Nanking and Osaka, ancient capital of Japan – Wu found Nanking to be much grander in scale and better protected with its innumerable fortresses.[56]

53 Ibid., 85.
54 Ibid., 84.
55 Ibid., 85.
56 Ibid., 106.

The most remarkable feature of the Chinese national character, according to him, is the ability to sustain all historical changes and to maintain its integrity. Foreigners would always find it very hard to be integrated into Japanese society, but Wu did meet several Japanese girls dressed in Han Chinese clothing and readily taking up Chinese forms of life. This in part owes to Confucian ethics of great harmony and the people's art of adaptability after witnessing so many uncertainties and casualties in the past five thousand years. The flexibility is manifested by China's ability to entertain opportunities to all in total freedom and that based on most simple forms of life.[57] Opportunism in various forms had pushed people of different classes to soar, but on the other hand, it also helped shape the habitus of gambling and opium use to the dismay of most radical intellectuals of the time.

As quite a few critics have pointed out, clothing or fashion is a site displaying cultural difference. On his arrival in Nanking, Wu discovered that his dress was simply too narrow and short; "compared to the Shanghai robe of grand style, it seems so out of place and almost unpresentable."[58] He was constantly attracted to the ways in which Chinese young women – in particular, high school and college students – blended traditional (or Confucian) spirituality with Western modern cultural expressions.[59] However, he also found a lot of them to be artificially fashionable, swayed by the most recent trends. In contrast, Taiwanese women were healthier and more straightforward. This is a point that would come out more explicitly in the novel *Asia's Orphan*. But the most traumatic encounter was at the Cock-crow Temple (Chi-ming ssu), where he met a great number of beggars. "From the main office, all the way up to the hill top, beggars with varying deformities line up."[60] The horrifying sight reminded Wu of pictures on torture chambers in Hell that he saw during a visit to temple in his childhood. The follow-up to such

57 Ibid., 115.

58 Ibid., 55.

59 Ibid., 79.

60 Wu Cho-liu, *Ya-his-ya-te ku-erh* (*Asia's Orphan*, 1945) (Taipei: Ts'ao-ken, 1995), 91.

a traumatic encounter with a beggar coming after him for alms in heart-breaking sobs proved even more aggravating and embittering. Throughout the Journals, Wu kept referring to the beggar episode and that of a Shanghai girl's shoe marks on the seat as traumatic scenes which eventually enlightened him as to Taiwan's radical difference to China and its alternative path to modernity.

Travel, as Clifford suggests, tends to bring about diasporic mediations between places and cultures. He thinks of such cases of displacement and transplantation "inseparable from specific, often violent, histories of economic, political, and cultural interaction – histories that generate what might be called *discrepant cosmopolitanisms*."[61] That is to say, one inevitably finds in elsewhere something discomforting or unsettling, putting into question one's world view or sense of cultural belonging. In the Journals, Wu revealed his "mixed feelings" (tsa-kan) in relation to his stay in Nanking. His experience in the metropolitan city served to tie and untie him to the imaginary homeland – China. On the one hand, he realized that the accounts put forth by Japanese intellectuals about China were misleading. A traveler and a dweller, he might well have appreciated China and its modernity in a number of ways. On the other, he had always already been mediated by his exposure to Japan's colonialism and modernity project in Taiwan, a situation that put him in a different mode, if not of a more progressive, temporality. In such a way, he could not be coeval with the Japanese and Chinese times. For he inevitably found himself defined by the two contesting modernity projects launched by China and Japan. The abundance of beggars in Nanking only functions to foreground the more advanced state of socio-economic situation in Taiwan, compared with that of China. However, as a colonial subject and a traveler, Wu could belong neither to Japan nor to China. It is in relation to Taiwan's ambivalent roles in-between China and Japan and the time lags – behind or ahead of either – that his sense of alterity developed.

61 James Clifford, *Routes: Travel and Translation in the Late Twentieth Century* (Cambridge: Harvard University Press, 1997), 36.

In this regard, Edward Said's notion of the traveler vs. the potentate and James Clifford's notion of everyday practices of dwelling and traveling should be rethought and made more complex. In spite of their usefulness, the travel theories as advocated by these two critics tend to build on center vs. periphery, the West vs. the Rest models. Our examination of Wu's travel narratives suggests that narrative identities are formed and unformed in the process of debunking cosmopolitan myths about the cultural Other. In his reply to Homi Bhabha's query regarding the economy of non-movement or the tension between movement and fixity, Clifford adumbrates that "A focus on comparative travel raises the question of dwelling, seen not as a ground or starting place but as an artificial, constrained practice of fixation."[62] One should add that the ground be seen as a contested site in its specific historical trajectories in which several forces meet and negotiate with each other. With the recognition of discrepant cosmopolitanisms, one may adopt the discursive strategy of nostalgia and exotic memories as in the case of Ishikawa. But Wu Cho-liu's narrative seems to suggest that he traveled in the time frame of an alternative modernity. The more he looked close in on to China and Japan, the more alienated he was from the two. That was the starting point of his journey into the homeless land of Asian orphan consciousness.

As a consequence, Wu uses the analogy of a fig (wu-hua-kuo) or Taiwan forsythia (lien-ch'iao) to describe the socio-cultural situation of Taiwan in relation to its fatherland and colonizers – the Japanese and then the KMT as manifested in Wu's *Wu-hua-kuo* (1970) and his posthumous *Taiwan Lien-ch'iao* (1986). A passage in *Asia's Orphan* succinctly illustrates his nuanced observation regarding Taiwan's alternative modernity: "One day, as T'ai-ming stands in front of the garden meditating, he suddenly discovers the fig already bearing fruit, ripen and plump, although only here and there behind the hugh leaves."[63] The protagonist reasons: "All existents have two forms of life, either as

62 Wu, *Nanking tsa-kan* (Journals of Mixed Feelings toward Nanking), 43.
63 Wu, *Ya-his-ya-te ku-erh (Asia's Orphan)*, 274.

Fo-sang flowers, which bloom beautifully without producing seeds, or as a fig, which takes no pride in providing pretty blossoms except bearing fruit in silence, unknown to the outside world."[64] The picture of a branch of Taiwan *lien-ch'iao* cutting across the fence and freely reaching out seems to be even more suggestive: "Those branches motioning upward or extending in all directions have been trimmed, leaving only this branch, which is lucky enough to develop according to her own will."[65] The absolute freedom may be a wishful thinking on the part of Hu T'ai-ming (and Wu Cho-liu), but the image of a *lien-ch'iao* branch soaring and of a fig bearing fruit is certainly illuminating and auspicious.

Civility and Electricity: Virtual Reality of the Genesis of Genesis

The *lien-ch'iao* (interconnectedness) trope can be extended in a most recent work by Dung Kai-cheung, entitled *T'ien-kung-k'ai-wu hsu-hsu-ju-chen* (Heavenly work in the genesis, in simulated reality, 2005), as *lien-hsien* (staying connected on the internet). The novel puts one teenager, Hsu-hsu, side by side with the narrator in front of their computer screens, disclosing their inner feelings and life worlds through the telecommunication device of on-line instant messengers. Hsu-hsu is a lonely girl eager to chat with a stranger about her day-to-day distresses and traumas, while the narrator is an autistic and tormented writer who not only suffers from claustrophobia but also from a sense of inadequacy. To both, recalling the past and writing in response to differential temporalities between sending and receiving, between the virtual cyberspace and the real world around them, provide the opportunity

64 Ibid., 274–5.
65 Wu Cho Liu, *Taiwan Lien-ch'iao* (Taipei: Ts'ao-ken, 1995), 275.

to develop a peculiar politics of friendship and even comradeship in an imagined community. The narrator tells Hsu-hsu:

> letters and words, indirect and slow as they are, actually enable one to imagine a common space, a space not subject to the binary logic of being vs. non-being, of the real vs. unreal. So I consider the impossibility of accessing you by phone or via face-to-face communication to be an advantage, to some extent. For this virtual writing process offers me extra values, to work through words, while in more leisurely fashion, to confide and to be with you.[66]

On the surface, no two persons could be more different from each other than Hsu-hsu and the narrator. Hsu-hsu likes to be the object of attention and doesn't want to be viewed as different or even eccentric;[67] in many ways, she sums up the stereotypical images of a contemporary and postmodern Hong Kong high school girl student, while the narrator is an introverted, speculative writer and intellectual constantly reflecting on his own family history and its implications for Chinese modernity. Putting them side by side, chapter by chapter, and sometimes in interface on the internet, the narrative epitomizes the critical and by no means stable path of Chinese civilization moving from the pre-modern to post-modern, from nostalgia and despair of a defeated Ch'ing empire to incessant albeit tortured desires for Western science and democracy to the post-1997 specially administrated region with its exorbitant lifestyles but politically powerless stifles. The email messages sent by the narrator tell of his grandfather's contributions to the development of electricity and telegrams in China, of his father's innovative engineering projects that helped modernize the republic. Grandpa Dong met a pretty girl in the countryside while building telephone infrastructure, he proposed and got married to her as if illuminated by divine lights generated by electricity and the setting sun. Though very much inspired by the Western technology, he in fact learned from a minor text entitled *T'ien-kung-k'ai-wu* (Heavenly Work

66 Dung Kai-cheung, *T'ien-kung-k'ai-wu hsu-hsu-ju-chen* (Heavenly work in the genesis, 2005), 51.

67 Ibid., 50.

in the Genesis, 1637) by a late Ming scholar. Through him and his son, Chinese texts of technological imaginations are resuscitated and incorporated into modernization projects which might have seemed to be largely indebted to the West.

Unlike the patriarchal figures in the family, who helped promote telecommunication and give new lives to Chinese tradition, the narrator has been less fortunate since his hand touched a Brother typewriter. He met Ju-chen, a pretty girl at a Christmas party, but she soon left him without any explanation. And from then on, feeling, emotion, and memory have become easily erasable as if on a typewriter and even more conveniently computer. However, from time to time, the repressed desire for Ju-chen and love sonnets or songs used to call her attention would return in the form of typescripts or of repetition with Hsu-hsu substituting Ju-chen in both virtual and real encounters. Readers won't miss the puns in such names as Hsu-hsu (vividly real) and Ju-chen (simulated verisimilitude), and in fact would find them interchangeable though much of the novel is on Hsu-hsu. Drawing on the new techniques of expression and of personal internet communities formation, the novel not only elaborates on the impact of electricity and long-distance communication on present-day Hong Kong, but provides snapshots of school, office, family, as well as private life in traumatic intensity. Hsu-hsu is often bullied by her classmates and confronts with threatening and grotesque images of narcotic pleasures and of social evils. According to the narrator, a large proportion of Hong Kong teenagers are loners who seek friends in bad company and journey from youthful hope to the dark abyss of the everyday banality. Sometimes mercilessly beaten up by the elders and gangsters (often both), teenagers are forced to submit or to retaliate. In many aspects, Hong Kong teenagers are very much like other Asian or American students, as globally popular ways of life and information technology are made available. The novel provides nuanced, revealing, and often self-reflexive psycho-social sketches of the ways in which civility fails in contemporary Hong Kong public culture while electronic mails and internet messages manage to bring strangers together to write to the moment as well as to trade the secrecies of survival.

It seems that the three texts in question deploy female figures from far and near to highlight the needs to reflect on the issues of Chinese civility and modernity across time and space. They show that these women play significant roles in urging us to engage in cultural criticism from within, so as to rethink what might have inspired Chinese modernity or Asian alternative modernities. In this regard, it doesn't necessarily require Canadian journalists to inform us about the various symptoms of the unfinished and also uneven Chinese modernity projects.

Part 2

Interculturality

MAN-KONG WONG

Biculturality as Modernity: A Hypothesis about the Origins of Modern Hong Kong

Throughout its different stages of development, be it the official discourse as a British colony or as China's special administrative region, Hong Kong's vitality as an example of modernity in Asia is not in question. However, questions about why and how Hong Kong acquired its modernity are not fully addressed. True, colonial rule brought the notion of free trade and commercial initiatives to nineteenth-century Hong Kong, which had turned out as a forceful momentum for a long period of growth in economy. These days, China trade remains a significant factor. As prosperity in trade does not necessarily translate into social development, trade (or free trade) is not a sufficient explanation for why Hong Kong became an exemplary modernity in Asia. The making of the bicultural character of Hong Kong, as I shall argue in this chapter, can be taken as a useful vantage point to appreciate the origin of modern Hong Kong.

While Hong Kong was generally taken as an ample representation of Asian modernity, its position seemed to be taken for granted without any serious academic deliberation. An explanation is still needed. I propose that the origin of modern Hong Kong was about to emerge during the late 1880s. For example, Patrick Mansion, later known as the father of tropical medicine, was actually active in Hong Kong from 1883 to 1889, during which he had his private practices, taught modern medicine at the newly founded Hong Kong College of Medicine for Chinese, and helped establish a dairy farm.[1] Promoting medical

1 Douglas M. Haynes, *Imperial Medicine: Patrick Manson and the Conquest of Tropical Disease* (Philadelphia: University of Pennsylvania Press, 2001).

education was self-evidently significant in paving the way for the pursuit of modernity. The founding of a dairy farm marked a change in the dietary habits of the community.[2] It was of great significance that both the medical college and the farm were made possible through the moral support and investment of businessmen of different ethnic and cultural backgrounds in the Hong Kong community, indicating that it was more than merely a result of domination from colonial rule over the silent passivity of the public. From lived experiences of the people of Hong Kong, the notion of modernity came into being as a result of active involvement from the public, regardless of their ethnic origins – Parsees, Jewish, Chinese or British, to make possible significant modern projects, such as school, medical college, university, clinic, dispensary and hospital.

Such a hybrid reality in history reminds me of a relevant perspective – biculturality in modern China as suggested by Phillip Huang. For this reason, the first part of this chapter would discuss Huang's notion of biculturality. This chapter will also discuss public education and Western medicine as the keys to understanding the making of modern Hong Kong at the turn of the century.

Philip Huang's Ideas about Biculturality in Modern China

Philip Huang suggests that students of modern Chinese history should consider "dual-cultural influences" – biculturality – as a relevant perspective to replace the politically correct teaching – a dichotomy of "imperialism/colonialism versus national independence."[3] His arguments base on his observations about the eventful lives of a group of

2 Nigel Cameron, *The Milky Way: The History of Dairy Farm* (Hong Kong: Dairy Farm, 1986).

3 Philip Huang, "Biculturality in modern China and in Chinese studies," in *Modern China* 26: 1 (January, 2000): 3–31.

eminent Chinese who were bilingual, political figures in China and Chinese scholars in America. These individuals personify the validity of being bicultural in the modern Chinese mind that is more embracing than what the mere nationalist/ideological notions of modern mind was usually thought of. I consider it most interesting to find out that Hong Kong (more as a cultural identity than a geographical terminology) seems to be one of the most convincing examples that Philip Huang has while constructing his notions of biculturality in modern China.

According to Huang, "patterns of bilingual use of Chinese and English" can be taken as "illustrations of biculturality." For this reason, he reflects on a few possibilities of being bilingual. One likely situation is that a bilingual person may separate the two languages and use them in different states of mind. He thus considers such category of "bilinguality (and biculturality)" that reveals that two languages co-exist in additive fashion.[4] Furthermore, he points out the other possibility – in a bilingual person's mind, the two languages and accordingly the two cultures may lead to "a mixing of the two." In this way, a bilingual person "may in a single sentence call on the second language because a word or an expression from that language comes to mind or perhaps because it presents precisely that intended object, image, idea or nuance." Here, Hong Kong captured his imagination as he takes it as an example by stating that people of Hong Kong "habitually switch back and forth between Chinese and English within a sentence." He thus comes to a point that such bilingual practice can be taken as a mixture, be it more as a physical mixture than a chemical compound, of both languages and culture within one's mind. A bilingual (bicultural) person has the potential capability to stand apart from each language by comparing the two and thinking about each from the perspective of the other." Huang points out that a bilingual (bicultural) person "enjoys at least the possibilities of being aware of different usage and conceptions of the equivalent or near-equivalent words in a different cultural system," which might "lead to creative impulses."[5]

4 Huang, "Biculturality in modern China and in Chinese studies," 6.
5 Ibid.

Huang also discusses biculturality in modern China. While coming to the historical situations confronting a group of bicultural persons, Huang is particularly sympathetic toward them because they were not fairly treated by their contemporaries who were swayed by the "ideologically charged environment of imperialism and anti-imperialism/nationalism."[6] Yet, Huang points out that a considerably large pool of significant figures were bicultural, such names as Sun Yat-sen, the Soong sisters (Soong Ai-ling, Soong Ch'ing-ling and Soong May-ling), Soong Tse-ven, K'ung Hsiang-hsi, Eugene Chen, Wellington Koo, Ng Ting-fang, Fu Bingchang and many others.[7] Besides individuals, Huang is of the view that biculturality in modern China can be understood through the lens of the May Fourth Movement, the introduction of German legal system in China, and a highly visible Western impact on the modern Chinese education structure. Yet, when coming to the larger picture of seeing China as a whole, Huang is of a peculiar view about Hong Kong. He writes:

> I do not to want to suggest that dual cultural influences must of necessity end in the bilingual type of cultural identity (i.e. biculturality). Not all of China is going to end up like Hong Kong, where the double linguistics and cultural heritages coexist in almost equal parts. I do want to suggest, however, is that we need to employ the same kind of perspective outlined for biculturality to think about the co-presence of Western and non-Western cultures in the modern non-Western world.[8]

Furthermore, Huang argues his case from another dimension – "the level of lived experience among individuals" where he rightly points out that "dual-cultural influences can usually coexist quite easily in the manner of two languages." He then remarks: "Ideologies might require either/or choices between tradition/modernity, Chinese/Western, autonomy/domination, or sinicization/Westernization, but the people in their life experience usually do not." I consider it with great validity

6 Ibid., 12.
7 Ibid., 12–14.
8 Ibid., 17.

of his assertion that "what the concept biculturality urges us to do is to acknowledge the on-the-ground reality of dual-cultural influences in the modern non-Western world. ... [we need] to emphasize the coexistential over the conflictual side of biculturality."[9] A quotation from his conclusion would do full justice to sum up his major points:

> I wish most of all to emphasize that the history of biculturality shows us that the copresence of two cultures does not have to lead to dichotomized choices between imperialism and nationalism or subordination and autonomy, in the manner of the histories of nations or of the constructions of Western-centric modernism or post-modernist relativism. Rather, cultural contacts at the level of everyday lived experience of the people can result in ready accommodation, without aggression or domination and victimization or subjugation. Biculturality and bilinguality of individuals in modern China and in American China studies show us in concentrated form how two cultures can coexist, intermingle, and even fuse into something new. They offer a glimpse at the possibilities for a cosmopolitanism that can come with intercultural understanding and transnational visions.[10]

It seems useful to discuss the extent to which Philip Huang's ideas of biculturality can be relevant for us to ponder over the origin of modern Hong Kong, a place recognized as bicultural. Specifically, I am interested in examining if the copresence of two cultures could lead to dichotomized choices between subordination and autonomy in Hong Kong. Equally important is to discuss the extent to which cultural contacts at the level of everyday lived experience of the people of Hong Kong during the decades between 1890s and 1910s could result in ready accommodation. If we take seriously the exploration of the everyday lived experiences of the people of Hong Kong at the turn of the century, I would imagine education and medicine to be the two most telling aspects to enable an in-depth discussion of the notions of biculturality.

9 Ibid., 22.
10 Ibid., 28–9.

Education and Biculturality

As Philip Huang repeatedly mentions the significance of bilingual ability of a bicultural identity, modern Hong Kong as an ideal example of bilingual/bicultural character, it seems useful to look at the ways in which Hong Kong acquired its bilingual ability through its public education. During the first decade of British rule in Hong Kong, there were schools that provided bilingual education, notably those schools run by missionaries. Yet, the decades between 1890s and 1910s in the development of public education were so significant that it saw the real and substantial growth of bilingual education that would contribute to the emergence of biculturality in Hong Kong. In order to understand how and why it happened, it seems useful to begin with some brief notes about the prior decades as the background.

During the first three decades of colonial rule in Hong Kong, there were already three types of schools, subsidized schools, missionary schools and the only government school. Subsidized schools came into being as a result of a grant scheme from the government since 1847 to provide small grants for those qualified village schools. The amount of funding was so little that it was impossible to hire any English teachers. As a remedy, the government paid a visiting master to teach English a few hours a week in such schools since 1853.[11] It marked the beginning of the subsidized scheme in education in Hong Kong, and it could be seen as an infant stage of modern education for the scheme had imposed certain standards and requirements in the curriculum in order to qualify a school for subsidies. Missionary schools were at first designed to be preparatory schools for theological studies. Understandably, missionaries wanted to train more local clergymen. Students were taught to achieve a high standard of English language and some modern knowledge so that they would be ready for theological training. However, they did not stay long at these schools because they were

11 Ng Lun Ngai Ha, *Interactions of East and West: Development of Public Education in Early Hong Kong* (Hong Kong: Chinese University Press, 1984), 65.

keenly sought after in the commercial and business sector. Many of them turned out to be successful Chinese merchants and social leaders. Ho A-mei, for example, became the first Chinese merchant to be admitted to the Hong Kong General Chamber of Commerce, a prominent social institution that played a key part in Hong Kong's political structure.[12] As a result, seminaries and their attached preparatory schools were closed altogether. Interestingly enough such a development led to the inception of the Central School, the only government school in Hong Kong; a leading missionary, James Legge, convinced the government and helped establish it in 1862. Not only did the school follow a modern curriculum of humanities and sciences, but it also taught Chinese language. On the other hand, subsidized schools did not make any desirable progress and thus new terms for subsidies were introduced in 1867, upon which a new grant-in-aid scheme was first introduced in 1873 and subsequently revised in 1879. After repeated efforts in improving the performance of the existing village schools proved unsuccessful, the grant-in-aid scheme now became a device for inviting partnership with voluntary bodies in the society. Missionaries began to expand their educational activities for the Chinese and to establish themselves as benefactors and accordingly reinforced their social standing. Take the London Missionary Society (LMS) as an example, the number of its schools grew from two in 1873 to thirty-three in 1893 and the number of students from eighty-seven to 2250.[13] Of course, missionaries were not able to manage all these schools by themselves and had to establish some Chinese Christians as headmasters and headmistresses. Most of these grant schools were given adequate support to hire some young educated Chinese to become English teachers. These grant schools provided modern education of which the cur-

12 Carl T. Smith, "Ho Amei: A 19th century community leader," in *A Sense of History: Studies in the Social and Urban History of Hong Kong* (Hong Kong: Hong Kong Educational Publishing Company, 1995), 50–63.

13 Wong Man Kong, "Christian missions, Chinese culture, and colonial administration: A study of the activities of James Legge and Ernest John Eitel in nineteenth century Hong Kong" (Ph.D. thesis, The Chinese University of Hong Kong, 1996), 288.

riculum was specified by the grant scheme. Despite the progress of the grant schools and the rather impressive achievement of the Central School, the government regarded students' standard of English was low and demanded improvement.[14]

The 1890s saw the beginning of real and substantial growth in English education. After the expansion of the number of schools in the 1880s, it was thought to be time to revise the grant-in-aid scheme. The number of grant schools was six in 1873, forty-eight in 1883 and 102 in 1893 while the number of students was 442 in 1873, 3,517 in 1883 and 6,250 in 1893.[15] The growth rate was staggering. The government paid close attention to the quality of education delivered in grant schools. Not only were there regular visits and examinations to ensure the quality of education in grant schools, but also the Cambridge Local Examination was introduced in Hong Kong in 1886 and it was replaced by Oxford Local Examination in 1889. Not surprisingly, these examinations became standards by which grant schools aspire to excellence.

For obvious reasons, the government would demand a higher standard of English from students. The important issue was to prefer the use of English as the language of instruction. Besides, the demand for competent English speakers in Hong Kong had become so great since the 1880s and early 1890s. It should be understood that the port of Hong Kong gradually played a very significant role in regional and international trade, specifically Hong Kong was handling about forty percent of China's foreign trade and the figure rose to about fifty percent by the early 1890s. Besides, it was always the government's standpoint that the more competent Chinese users of the English language, the better it served the multiple levels of operation needed for the more effective and smooth maintenance of the colonial rule in Hong Kong. Moreover, English language was the most important device for pursuing modern education at a higher level. Records show that the teaching staff of the Hong Kong College of Medicine for Chinese complained about students' lower standard of English which was considered a great ob-

14 Ng, *Interactions of East and West*, 65–77.
15 Ibid., 163–4.

stacle. During the early years, the top two students who managed their studies well were Sun Yat-sen and Kong Ying-wah, both of them shared one similarity – highly competent in the English language as they had their boyhood abroad in an English-speaking environment. Medical missionary John Kenneth Mackenzie of Tianjin also made a similar complaint about these lower standards of Hong Kong graduates from government and grant schools as they became medical apprentices under his supervision.

The revision of the grant-in-aid scheme in 1893 rendered new opportunities for both Protestant and Catholic missionaries, the two major stakeholders in public education. The 1880s saw the trend that missionaries were making use of the grant-in-aids scheme to establish more churches and more local Chinese Christians through the delegation of power in the management of grant schools.[16] With the revision in the terms of the grant scheme in 1893, missionaries re-orientated their plans for schools. In view of a great difference in the amount of grants received between schools that operated in "Chinese education" and "European education," which was around seventy-five percent to one hundred percent more, missionaries thought of no reason for not starting English-medium schools.[17] Not only did they therefore receive more money to run the schools, but they also kept their duties in ministering the students at schools and extending their contacts with students' families. In the two subsequent revisions of the scheme in 1903 and 1914 respectively, the use of English as the language of instruction was repeatedly stressed and highly preferred. Throughout these revisions, it should, however, be stressed that the six hours of training in the Chinese language per week that the grant scheme required remained unchanged. As a consequence, the newly established grant schools by missionaries were able to offer high quality of bilingual education and they became the preferred partners of the government to promote modern education.

16 Wong, "Christian missions, Chinese culture, and colonial administration," 164–74.

17 Ibid., 162–3.

Moreover, the introduction of English public examinations became a mechanism that ensured quality modern educations delivered at the government and grant schools. From the 1890s to 1907, there were more than 1,400 qualified Hong Kong students who took part in the Oxford Local Examinations which was thought to be of "inestimable value" because they were "of great service to Hong Kong boys in procuring for them admission to English and American schools and universities, and in obtaining exemption from professional preliminary examinations," according to G.H. Bateson Wright, headmaster of Queen's College (whose term of office: 1881–1909).[18] Similarly, the 1914 revision of the grant-in-aid scheme encouraged students of grant schools to "take the Matriculation and Junior Examination of the University of Hong Kong."[19]

Another major component in the provision of modern education in Hong Kong was the University of Hong Kong (HKU), of which its first campus was officially opened in March 1912. The early history of HKU has been well studied and needs not to be repeated here.[20] Rather, I think it is important to stress two issues. Firstly, like the provision of public education at primary and secondary level, it was a very strong spirit of local voluntarism that made possible the founding of HKU. In other words, neither the Hong Kong government nor the Colonial Office provided any substantial amount of funding to start it. The construction cost of HK$ 300,000, for example, was fully covered by an eminent Parsee merchant – H.N. Moody. The other major initial fund

18 G.H. Bateson Wright, "Education" in Arnold Wright (ed.), *Twentieth Century Impressions of Hong Kong, Shanghai, and Other Treaty Ports of China* (London, 1908) cited in Anthony Sweeting, *Education in Hong Kong, pre-1841 to 1941: Fact and Opinion: Materials for a History of Education in Hong Kong* (Hong Kong: Hong Kong University Press, 1990), 331.

19 Sweeting, *Education in Hong Kong, pre-1841 to 1941*, 345–6.

20 Brian Harrison (ed.), *University of Hong Kong: The First 50 Years, 1911–1961* (Hong Kong: Hong Kong University Press, 1961); Ng, *Interactions of East and West*; and Chan Lau Kit Ching and Peter Cunich (ed.), *An Impossible Dream: Hong Kong University from Foundation to Re-establishment, 1910–1950* (New York: Oxford University Press, 2002).

to cover the expenses was raised by a committee of leading Chinese merchants. With great skill and enthusiasm, Frederick Lugard, Governor of Hong Kong (whose term of office: 1907–1912), managed to raise a handsome amount from the British companies who had extensive business interest in Hong Kong to support the project, such as Swire Company, Hong Kong and Shanghai Bank, Jardine and Matheson, and so on. True, its founding chancellor, Governor Lugard, was very eager to lend his full support to it. However, not a single successor in the government House before World War II did the same. On the other hand, the support given by the Colonial Office was too modest, merely an annual grant of 300 and an addition of some scholarship opportunities funded by the Boxer indemnity for the Chinese government to send students to study at HKU.[21] Of the latter, it became a true blessing to some dozens of individuals and some turned out to be of great contribution to modern China. For example, Liu Xianzhou who received training in engineering and later became the vice-president of the Tsing-hua University in Beijing.[22]

Secondly, HKU specialized in professional education programs, ably conveying to the public that HKU was more of a pragmatic spirit than a colonial ideology of domination and control. For a long period of time, HKU operated only three faculties, namely Arts, Engineering and Medicine. Evidently, the Faculty of Engineering and the Faculty of Medicine were of clear professional identities in their respective fields. They were able to establish their recognitions in Britain and across the British Empire. HKU graduates would easily move to other parts of the Empire. For this reason, it was able to attract a sizable overseas Chinese from British Malay to purse university education in Hong Kong. Besides, the Faculty of Arts was taking a similar path in equipping students along vocational and professional lines: specifically normal training and business studies. Zhu Guangqian was sent to Hong

21 Norman Miners, *Hong Kong under Imperial Rule* (Hong Kong: Oxford University Press, 1991), 29.

22 Wang Gungwu, *Anglo-Chinese Encounters since 1800: War, Trade, Science and Governance* (Cambridge: Cambridge University Press, 2003), 125–6.

Kong for normal training at HKU where he was deeply attracted by the beauty of literature and paved his way for the postgraduate education at the University of Glasgow.[23] Li Tze-fong, later a key founder of the East Asia Bank, entered HKU as a student of Faculty of Arts where he studied economics and "commercial subjects were given special emphasis."[24] It should also be noted that the faculty of arts paid certain attention to the preservation of Chinese classical scholarship at its Chinese department. It may seem that such an effort did not match the pragmatic spirit *per se*. Yet, it was of a true blessing to HKU because many Chinese merchants were of genuine respect for classical scholarship, which was regarded an end in itself and the orientation for value and life. In short, HKU became a modern and bilingual educational institution that was fitting into the public anticipation of what a university should be. Prior to World War II, when the civil service did not support localization, there was no opportunity for Chinese graduate from HKU to climb up to the top post in the government. The business sector became a more popular choice.[25] In other words, the honor and prestige of HKU did not come as a result of colonial hegemony but a very useful and pragmatic spirit that satisfied its sponsors whose appreciation was revealed in their continual donation to it.

Popularizing Western Medicine

Chinese medicine was popular among the Chinese in nineteenth-century Hong Kong probably because of being a more economic option for treating an illness on the one hand and a strong sense of attachment to the commonly shared cultural tradition on the other. As an opposite

23 Ibid., 88–9.

24 Frank Ching, *The Li Dynasty: Hong Kong Aristocrats* (New York: Oxford University Press, 1999), 41.

25 David Faure, *Colonialism and the Hong Kong Mentality* (Hong Kong: Centre of Asian Studies, University of Hong Kong, 2003), 47–51.

to the seemingly dichotomy, Western medicine and its history in Hong Kong can be an important lens through which we can see the lived experience of the people of Hong Kong for their choice of bicultural and modern living. Just like what happened in education, the history of medicine in Hong Kong similarly revealed a strong spirit of local voluntarism. Western medicine began to take its real and substantial growth since the 1890s where we can see the momentum from the public was in full sway.

Subsequent to the founding of the British rule, Western medicine came to Hong Kong. But it did not turn out to be a popular choice. The government maintained hospitals and clinics of its own. Yet, only a handful of Chinese would seek treatment from them. During the 1840s and 1850s, there were medical missionaries who operated hospitals and clinics offering treatment in Western medicines. The famous medical missionary Benjamin Hobson had spent a few years in Hong Kong before he moved to Guangdong. There was even a plan for establishing a medical college. But the effort evaporated.[26] Of the reasons for their failure, the inability of attracting a community-wide support for medical projects was the key. Perhaps, it was because the timing was bad – the 1840s when the performance of Hong Kong economy was so disappointing that Western and Chinese merchants were not ready to make any contribution for philanthropy. It was only in the late 1860s when a sizeable number of affluent Chinese merchants were ready to make the founding of the Tung Wah Hospital possible.

During the 1880s, things began to change while there were signs for a growing interest in the formation of local voluntarism for medical projects. In 1881, Kwong Yat-sau, a returned Chinese Christian from Australia,[27] had taken the initiative in establishing a dispensary at the LMS Taipingshan Chapel, which lasted for only a year. But it left an

26 For a general background about the work of Benjamin Hobson, see Gerald Choa, *To Heal the Sick*.

27 For a brief outline of Kwong's life in Australia, see Ian Welch, "Alien son: the life and times of Cheok Hong Cheong (Zhang Zhouxiong), 1851–1928" (Ph.D. thesis, Australian National University, 2003), 109–11.

impression of the true blessings of Western medicine among the Chinese public. Besides, this clinic involved an affluent merchant, Henry William Davis, who turned out to be another key support for hospital project a few years later. Also in 1881, E. P. Belilios offered $ 5,000 as a matching grant for any hospital project. LMS missionaries in Hong Kong discussed it and applied for, and were granted, approval from the home base in London. But the question of insufficient funding blocked the way. The foreign secretary of the LMS visited Hong Kong in April 1883 and agreed that the hospital should be established in an area of low property prices while a missionary property was approved to be sold to cash for that purpose. Later, local missionaries were able to form a powerful committee in February 1884, with several eminent social leaders including current members of the Legislative Council. For out of the six unofficial members of the Legislative Council were involved, namely, Francis Bulkeley Johnson, Thomas Jackson, Wong Shing, and Frederick Stewart. Other committee members included: E. P. Belilios, Ho Kai, Patrick Manson, Wei Yuk, Wong Wing-Sheung, John Chalmers, and a few others. During the initial discussions, there were reservations from different sides. Yet, the most important problem was the lack of funding, although the sale of a missionary property on the Queen's Road had raised HK$ 8,000. Ho Kai helped solve the problem by covering the cost for the construction of the hospital if it was named after his recently deceased wife, Alice Walken. Besides, a pious Chinese Christian, Ko Chan-shi, agreed to sell some of her land for the hospital site. Although the plot was worth in her estimation some $ 70,000, she asked for only $ 14,000 for it from the LMS: and project now became a viable one.[28]

The hospital project received extensive public attention that made it a success. There was a high-profile public fundraising campaign, with a two-night alfresco fete that attracted 12,000 participants. The two-time acting Governor of Hong Kong, William H. Marsh (whose two terms of office: from March 1882 to March 1883 and from December

28 For a general account of the founding of the Alice Memorial Hospital, see Edward H. Paterson, *A Hospital for Hong Kong* (Hong Kong: Alice Ho Miu Ling Nethersole Hospital, 1987); and Choa, *The Life and Times of Sir Kai Ho Kai.*

1885 to April 1887), laid the foundation stone in June 1886, providing more publicity for the project. As missionary John Chalmers noted:

> With very few exceptions, the community of Hong Kong, from the Governor downwards, have always been heartily in their support of the Hospital, and it has never had any lack of funds. Sometimes, the local papers were inclined to throw cold water on it, but that was before or success was established.[29]

Even after its opening, the hospital could attract sustained public attention. One of the reasons was the founding of the Hong Kong College of Medicine for Chinese, which was attached to the hospital. Ho Kai, Patrick Manson and James Cantlie provided the driving force behind this college.[30] The medical college used the premises of the Alice Memorial Hospital for its teaching and some doctors in the hospital were at the same time teachers in the medical college. Meanwhile, the famous Manson had given H.W. Davis sufficient confidence in the project and to take a fresh interest to reopen the Nethersole Dispensary that resulted in a donation of HK$ 7,000. In this way, the voluntary service of such public figures could be a critical component in the building up and consolidation of the medical mission of the LMS in Hong Kong. It was seen above all as a matter of general public interest. As it was, the greater part of the money for these projects came from the public rather than from the LMS. Whereas the LMS contributed $ 14,000 for the Alice Memorial Hospital project, the public donated HK$ 34,500.[31] The Nethersole dispensary later attracted a donation of HK$ 12,000 as designated in the will of Richard Young, brother of William Young; the doctor who had worked there in 1881–

29 John Chalmers, "The decennial report for Hong Kong, 1880–1890." Reports, South China, LMS Archives.

30 Dafydd E. Evans, *Constancy of Purpose: An Account of the Foundation and History of the Hong Kong College of Medicine and the Faculty of Medicine of the University of Hong Kong, 1887–1987* (Hong Kong: Hong Kong University Press, 1987), 29.

31 John Chalmers, report on Hong Kong Station for 1886. Reports, South China, LMS Archives. See also, Carl T. Smith, *A Sense of History: Studies in the Social and Urban History of Hong Kong* (Hong Kong: Hong Kong Educational Publishing Company, 1994), 328.

1882.[32] By such means, the LMS medical mission picked up a new momentum during the 1880s, providing a firm base for its notable success in the ensuing decades.

The success of this revival of medical mission work was made possible through a combination of religious commitment and secular philanthropy. The missionaries were prepared to accept help from all quarters, even from non-Christians, such as E. P. Belilios. People such as Belilios, in turn, had no objection to their donations being used for work that was partly evangelical.

Not surprisingly, Belilios and other public figures enhanced their reputation in the colony and gained public honor through such philanthropic work. In return, they were instrumental in popularizing Western medicine through the strengthening of the public confidence through the endorsement of these social leaders. Ho Kai was a fine example. His work in bringing the Alice Memorial Hospital into being revealed him a diligent organizer and able mediator between the different parties, including the medical professionals, who were often in disagreement. As a Hong Kong Chinese who had received both medical and legal training in Britain, he was able to relate to and bring together a wide range of people. In particular, he was connected with the network of graduates from Aberdeen University, a prestigious identity shared by a few top colonial elites, such as Patrick Mansion, James Cantlie, John Chalmers and Frederick Stewart. Being eminent physicians, Mansion and Cantlie taught medical knowledge at the college. Chalmers, the senior missionary taking charge of LMS stations in Hong Kong and Guangzhou, taught chemistry at the college. A colonial elite since the early 1860s when he served as the founding headmaster of the Central School who was eventually appointed the Colonial Secretary of the Hong Kong government, Stewart was the college rector. Of these figures, Ho Kai was generally considered the single most important figure behind the inauguration of the Alice Memorial Hospital.[33] The

32 Smith, *A Sense of History*, 322–3.

33 Nelson Bitton, *Our Heritage in China* (London: London Missionary Society, 1913), 53.

fact that such figures as Belilios, an Indian business magnate, and Ho Kai, a Chinese Christian, were able to play such important roles in the public life of Hong Kong also indicates that it was a more liberal and in certain respects less racist society than it had been during the 1840s. This was probably critical in providing the space within which the bicultural character could have its place to be nurtured in Hong Kong.

By 1911, a LMS report was able to claim that: "[t]he medical work of the L.M.S. in Hong Kong is one of the most important and well developed branches of its endeavor in the South of China."[34] By the 1900s, there were two new LMS hospitals. Again, this was all due to a flourishing local voluntarism. The Alice Memorial Maternity Hospital came into being because of new ideas about midwifery. The government had repeatedly criticized the Chinese practice of childbirth contributing to the high infant mortality rate. By the turn of the century, many Chinese social leaders and affluent merchants were coming round to this view and were seeking means to change the situation.[35] The new maternity hospital was founded in 1904 as a result of generous support from the public. The Chinese sponsors placed a condition on their provision of $ 2,000 annually to cover the salary of a female medical missionary, namely that she was required "to treat the women of subscriber's family in their own houses … [and] to mix with the Chinese ladies and introduce to them Western hygiene and health care."[36] This condition sheds a revealing light on some of their motives for providing the funding. The Ho Miu Ling Hospital was established by the LMS in 1906 on a piece of land that was provided by the government adjacent to the Alice Memorial Hospital. Ho Miu Ling, Ho Kai's sister, financed this project. She was, like her brother, a Christian with strong connections to the LMS. Her husband was Ng Ting-fang, the

34 *London Missionary Society Decennial Report 1901–1911; Hongkong, Canton & Poklo* (Hong Kong: Hong Kong Printing Press, 1911), 20.

35 For details, see Janet George, "Moving with Chinese opinions: Hong Kong's maternity service, 1881–1941" (Ph.D. thesis, University of Sydney, 1992), 98–130.

36 George, "Moving with Chinese Opinions," 103.

first Chinese member of the Legislative Council in Hong Kong and later a prominent politician in China.

As the reputation of the Hong Kong College of Medicine for Chinese spread beyond Hong Kong, students began to be attracted from other regions of Southeast Asia, and even from India. Due to this new demand, it was decided in 1907 to drop the two words 'for Chinese' from the name of the medical college. In 1909, the government complemented the college for its work in the following terms: "Most of the licentiates have settled in the Colony, and are exerting a most useful influence in the direction of displacing the native medical methods and popularizing Western medical and sanitary knowledge."[37] In popularizing and raising demand for Western medicine in the colony, the college reinforced the LMS hospitals.

On another frontier, there was a sizeable group of Chinese pastors and Chinese church leaders who played an important role in this endeavor of popularizing Western medicine in Hong Kong. As mentioned earlier, Kwong Yat-sau played a key role in opening the Nethersole dispensary at the Taipingshan Chapel. Two other church leaders, Wong Uen Sham and Lai Fuk-chi, were instrumental in establishing dispensaries in 1884 in Tai Ping Shan and Sai Ying Poon. William Young worked in these two dispensaries after his return to Hong Kong in 1884. Both Wong and Lai had had experience in medical work. Wong had been an assistant to some German medical missionaries in the Guangdong area before he was ordained as a Rhenish pastor. Lai, his son-in-law, was hired by the LMS as a local preacher and he had received training in Western medicine while he had been assisting John Glasgow Kerr, an American medical missionary in Canton. Lai's work was highly regarded within the LMS, and he was even allowed to run the dispensary he had established when the medical missionary was absent. After the LMS hospitals were founded, they kept their preaching work on regular basis at the hospitals. On the other frontier, the LMS hospitals trained and hired a considerable number of Christian

37 "Institutions not supported by the government," *Hong Kong Administrative Report for 1909*, 18.

nurses. The midwives training program at the Alice Memorial Maternity hospital also established a good reputation, as was recognized by the government.[38] The nurses at the mission hospitals were all Christians, and it was expected that they would be actively involved in evangelical work.[39] Bible classes were held for the nurses, run by Chinese pastors such as Cheung Chuk Ling of the To Tsai Church.[40] A stronger Christian involvement in preaching at hospitals contributed to a richer notion of Western medicine which connected with this new religious identity – Christianity.

Furthermore, LMS hospitals employed some talented Chinese doctors and surgeons who gained a high reputation for their capabilities in curing and healing amongst the general public. It publicized the work of these Chinese doctors in newspapers during its fundraising drives, which raised their public profile and helped to establish confidence in them.[41] For example, Chung King Ue, alias Chung Boon Chor, the first Chinese House Surgeon at the Alice Memorial Hospital was of a great reputation. After a severe outbreak of plague in Hong Kong, he was appointed by the government in 1898 to take charge of the Tung Wah Hospital. His remit was to introduce Western medicine in this hospital for the Chinese. Chung's successor as the house surgeon at the Alice Memorial Hospital was Wan Man Kai. Later, he performed surgical operations along with Chung at the Tung Wah Hospital. Another Chinese doctor was To Ying Fan, alias Coxion To, who served at the

38 Midwives trained in the Alice Maternity Hospital were exempted from taking the written examination and some clauses that were required for those who wanted to obtain a government certificate. Details, see, "Rules framed by the Midwives Board under Section 4 of the Midwives Ordinance, 1910," *Hong Kong Government Gazette* (September 22, 1911): 400–3.

39 Jane Stewart, "Report of Hong Kong mission for the year of 1910," [n.d.]. See also, Jane Stewart, "Report of Hong Kong mission for the year of 1909," June 26, 1910. Both are available at the LMS Archives, South China, Reports.

40 Rayner, "Report for 1917 [on the nurses]" Reports, South China, LMS Archives. See also, Report for 1921, Reports, South China, LMS Archives.

41 The meeting with Dr. Chung, Medical Committee meeting, January 29, 1895, in "Medical committee report," *Sessional Papers of Hong Kong, 1895.*

Alice Memorial Hospital for twenty-three years. His wife and son were also employed in this hospital in different capacities.[42] Other Chinese doctors who worked for the LMS for some time before then, establishing themselves in private practice were Wan Man Kai, Kwan King-leung, Ho Ko Tsun, Lee Ying Yau, and Benjamin Cheonglam Wong. While their prior affiliation with the LMS hospitals was one of their cherished assets, their success in private practice in return helped boost public confidence in the LMS hospitals.

There was continuing voluntary support for the medical work of the LMS during the first two decades of the twentieth century, and if anything it became more extensive. Several prominent social leaders served on the finance committee of the LMS hospitals, and thus became involved in their management. Notable in this respect were Francis Henry May and Arthur Wimbolt Brewin. Both held important government positions, the former the Captain Superintendent of Police while the latter the Registrar-General. Their duties required them to keep close contact with the Chinese population of Hong Kong, and one way in which they managed to do this was through their connection with the LMS hospitals. Both were promoted to the rank of Colonial Secretary and both served as members of Legislative and Executive Councils. May became Governor of Hong Kong in 1912, serving to 1919. Some of the other committee members were at one stage or other also members of the Legislative Council, such as Wei Yuk, Chau Siu Ki, Ho Fook, Lau Chu Pak, Tso Seen Wan, and Ng Hon Tsz. Others had their extensive reputation in Hong Kong, such as Au Tak, and Sin Tak Fun. In all cases, these Chinese leaders were leading professionals or affluent merchants who were involved in property development, banking, trading, and other forms of business enterprise. In brief, they were symbols of wealth and power. Given their status and power in the society, their participation in the management of the hospitals helped establish themselves as well-received social institution.

42 Paterson, *A Hospital for Hong Kong*, 58, 70.

Conclusion

This essay does not give a full account of the parameters of either Western or Chinese (or Asian) cultures in Hong Kong. In fact, there is not much coverage on the history of Chinese education in Hong Kong. Nor is there any substantial description about the history of Chinese medicine. It is because the significance of the notion of biculturality is not based on any type of Western-Chinese symmetry. Rather, it is of great interest here to examine why and how the co-presence of two cultures became possible. In Hong Kong, English education and Western medicine did not come into being as a result of any dichotomized choice between subordination and autonomy in Hong Kong. Moreover, it is intended to illuminate that cultural contacts at the level of everyday lived experience of the people of Hong Kong during the decades between 1890s and 1910s could reveal ready accommodation.

True, Hong Kong was a colony under absolute British control. Yet, it does not mean everything that happened in Hong Kong was because of colonial or anti-colonial issues. In Hong Kong, the momentum for bicultural and modern projects came from a strong spirit of local voluntarism in the community. It seems to indicate that the lived experiences of the people (or the choice of the people) showed that modernity came more out of pragmatic needs.

Last but not least, the Hong Kong case can be of great use in examining two more issues that chart out possibility for future research. Firstly, the local voluntarism that made possible biculturality did not draw along the ethnic lines. Secondly, the dynamics of Christian missions intertwined with the quest for modernity rendered the Christian identity with a richer impression for this new religious, cultural and social identity at the turn of the century.

Allen Chun

Hong Kong "Identity" after the End of History

> History is what hurts, it is what refuses desire and sets inexorable limits to individual as well as collective praxis, which its "ruses" turn into grisly and ironic reversals of their overt intention. But this History can be apprehended only through its effects, and never directly as some reified force.
>
> Frederic Jameson, *The Political Unconscious: Narrative as Socially Symbolic Act*

1997: A Year of No Significance

The renowned sociologist Wong Siu-lun began his essay, "Changing Hong Kong Identities," by declaring, "the year 1997 is a year of significance for Hong Kong."[1] The long anticipated rite of passage is over. With the change of flags at the handover ceremony on July 1 of that year, Hong Kong ceased to be a British colony. It acquired the new status of a Special Administrative Region [SAR] of China. As if to point to the subjective complexity underlying an objective reality, he cited remarks made by Chief Secretary Anson Chan, who, in reflecting on personal experiences in the first year after the handover, said, "[the] real transition has been much more complex, subtle and profound [...] That is because the real transition is about identity and not sovereign-

1 Wong Siu-lun, "Changing Hong Kong identities," in Wang Gungwu and John Wong (eds), *Hong Kong in China: The Challenges of Transition* (Singapore: Times Academic Press, 1999), 181.

ty."[2] In other words, real identities lurk beneath. One might then wonder what is so fictive about sovereignty that makes identity so real.

I argue on the contrary that history is in the first instance more about fictions than about realities. The historical irony of Hong Kong's official handover to China on July 1, 1997 (or "return to the motherland," depending on one's point of view) was that the future of Hong Kong, which had been a cession in perpetuity, was made to coincide with the end of the ninety-nine-year lease of the New Territories. Few people remember anymore that the New Territories was supposed to be administered as an extension of Hong Kong, with due respect to native (presumably unchanging) tradition, even though the reality of modern expansion effectively incorporated it later into the larger colonial history of Hong Kong. One might add to this the mystery of why the Chinese government on the other hand continued to play along with the official reality of the lease, denying all the while the validity of Hong Kong's status as a ceded colony (being the result of a treaty signed under duress). It not only made Handover Day a Chinese national holiday, whose media hype became an industry in itself, but the coincidence of Hong Kong's celebration of Queen Elizabeth's birthday on the eve of the handover also canonized the five-day weekend into an event of unreal proportions many times over. Thus, the reality of Hong Kong's colonial existence, already mystified by its official disappearance, was suddenly resurrected by the fiction of a lease that had without doubt been meaningless, if not long dead. If sovereignty is rooted in such a fiction, then how unreal can identity be?

Most people who write about identity speak as though we are *ipso facto* supposed to have one; if not one, then many. Life is thus a process through which we negotiate on the basis of our identity(ies). Yet fewer people can systematically say precisely when and why we should invoke our identity(ies), *if at all*. Identity is, strictly speaking, a conscious articulation of one's cultural positionality (among other things), which may in turn be rooted in real ethnic traits or lifestyles. Yet despite our

2 For a report on Chan's talk, see the essay by Chris Yeung entitled "Role of civil servants comes under scrutiny" (*South China Morning Post*, July 1, 1998).

uncertainty as to whether we are really invoking facts or fictions, we are, if anything, almost certainly dealing with selective meanings and purposive strategies. The fact that identities have changed and continue to change suggests then that they are either a response to changing realities or the basis on which we actively shape and, in the process of it, change our world. I think there is much truth in both positions, but I argue that the role of facts and fictions is grossly misunderstood, and this is the reason why the very process of identity formation (as imagination and practice) is in essence a struggle to define, while it is at the same time subverted by inherent conflicts of interests and interpretations. To this confusion of what is fact and fiction, one should add the ongoing dialectic between the conscious articulation of identity (however grounded in fact or fiction) and those unconscious sociopolitical processes that make possible and demarcate the boundaries of identity. We *think* we know who we are, when in fact our situatedness within the larger geopolitical order of things limits our scope of choices and strategies rather than vice versa. Unlike history, in Jameson's formulation, we can consciously apprehend identity only through its reified forces, while we are at the same time being transformed unconsciously by its effects.

Identities can easily be driven by illusions, and postwar Hong Kong is an ideal example of how identities have been constantly made and remade. With ties to a culture industry and other institutions of author-ity, the history of Hong Kong identity(ies) can be seen in some instances more fittingly as a history of hype. As we all know, public sentiment in Hong Kong has always been prone to what Gustav Le Bon once called "the psychology of the crowd" *(la psychologie de la foule)*, which can perhaps be deliberately misread as a crude pun on mass mentality. The stock market has been known to plunge drastically during moments of mass hysteria, and the slightest rumors of scandal have been known to cause a run on local banks, with nervous clients lining up for days to empty their savings accounts. Sentiments can swing from one extreme to another. Anti-PRC sentiment was, of course, strongest in reaction to the June 4 Tiananmen Incident of 1989, but it has been countered also by waves of nationalistic fervor, judging at least from the euphoria created by Beijing's almost successful bid, in 1994, for the (Sydney) Olympics. In the long run, these moments are precisely that; that is, they come and go. But more importantly, the volatile and fragile nature that seems to characterize Hong Kong public sentiment (of which identity is a specific politicized manifestation) is as much a reflection of its arbitrariness or unpredictability on the surface as a function of an institutional system that appears to make real the collective ramifications of individual desires and fears.

The market has made what Hong Kong is today, where utilitarian rationality is not only an economic logic that drives the value of commodities and property but also a kind of ethos that dictates entire lifestyles, even though we tend to forget that global politics of the 1960s was what really transformed Hong Kong into a market society. In this sense, the fear of capital flight that often epitomizes the seeming fragility or ephemerality of Hong Kong's economy is really a function of the absence of a place based rural or industrial infrastructure that is the basis of economies elsewhere. In other respects, microeconomic laissez-faire is tempered by macroeconomic state intervention. The volatility of the HK dollar in 1984 led eventually to its currency peg to the US dollar, while the colonial government's regulation of land policy was an important aspect of Hong Kong's planned urban and industrial modernization.

In short, the more one has been led to believe that identity in Hong Kong is a product of inherently individual desires and rational intents, the more it tends to take on to the contrary a fictive character. In the pre-1997 era, one has been led to believe that a concrete Hong Kong identity exists or is important in some respect, even though we all know that this identity is an invention that is less than fifty years old. Its distinctiveness is in effect less a product of its unique inventive quality than, in the first instance, of a changing socio-political landscape that has defined its parameters and shaped its possibilities of meaning. Moreover, in order to ask what post-1997 identity is or whether it exists at all, one must first ask whether 1997 marks a significant change in socio-political terms. This remains a matter of debate and interpretation.

1997 is a year of no significance, it can be argued. Or to put it in another way, it is one that marks a potentially significant transition but at an underlying level masks socio-political processes whose nature is still unclear or in the midst of being played out, in my opinion. In actuality, the hype of 1997 did not begin in 1997 or in the carnival atmosphere that led up to its ritual handover on July 1. It had been thirteen years in the making. Some of the changes in mindset that predicated this new identity had been put into place during the "transitional" years and to some extent have simply continued into the post-1997 era. But the socio-political circumstances of the transition itself in the larger flow of things have been unpredictable and are worth careful scrutiny. They are the end point of analysis instead of its point of departure.

Not surprisingly, the most heated debates and crises over identity took place in the mid-1980s then in the year leading up to the handover itself. Nonetheless, in the entire transitional era, one can detect a subtle shift of sentiment with regard to definitions of the self that have been cultivated and reproduced in different regimes of subjective identification and cultural representation. This has already been the subject of many surveys as well as semiotic analysis of various kinds. It is not my intention to review the literature in this regard, except to say that all of these discourses and analyses focus too much upon deconstructing in a literal sense the superficial definitions of Hong Kongness vis-à-vis China and the West in order to uncover the underlying substance of these identities. In the final analysis, the existence of colonialism and nationalism is always inferred but never directly confronted as an institution of practice. In what senses do the facts of colonialism depend on its fictions, and vice versa? In what senses is nationalism dualistically opposed to colonialism, and in what senses is it a neo-colonialism? The transition signified by the year "1997" invokes many possible political processes, but in order to understand colonialism and nationalism it is necessary to unpack the relationship between their ongoing discourses and practices in a Hong Kong context.

The ethos of utilitarian familism and the myth of apolitical man tend to be the most often cited metaphors (myths) to characterize the culture and lifestyle of people living in postwar Hong Kong. Their "actuality" is a function of the degree to which people behave or think they behave in such ways, superficially speaking.[3] Stereotypes are less useful here for being generally recognized matters of fact than for underscoring the historical peculiarity of socio-political processes that give rise to such phenomena. In this case, discursive fictions serve conveniently to mask the real relations of power that are constitutive of the socio-political system. Without doubt, the utilitarian lifestyle for which Hong Kong is so famous is largely the product of the 1970s. However, the free market economy that gave rise to this lifestyle was itself the consequence of a complex political struggle to transcend the nationalist strife that enveloped Hong Kong as well as a moment in the evolution of the modern world system. The fact that we view this utilitarian ethos largely as a progressive manifestation of the modern lifestyle is at the same time a fiction that has neatly disguised the exploitative aspects of the capitalist system. Eugene Cooper perhaps phrased it best, when he said that free market development in Hong Kong was "a veritable proving ground for Marxist theory, where the enterprising student of Marxist political economy can literally watch chapters of *Capital* unfold before his eyes."[4] The notion of the typical Hong Konger as apolitical is also without doubt a product of that same modern, materialistic era, but few people note that this apolitical façade was strictly enforced by a colonial government bent on deflecting nationalist conflict from the territory to the extent of suppressing all forms of political dissent. It was also during this period that the Hong Kong government officially disavowed use of the word colony to describe Hong Kong, while preferring instead to call it a territory, an undoubtedly more value-free term. Names in themselves may not mean much, but the mainte-

3 In this regard, the most representative works are Hugh Baker, "Social change in Hong Kong: Hong Kong man in search of majority," *The China Quarterly* 136 (1993): 864–77 and Lau Siu-kai, "Utilitarian familism" in A.Y.C. King and R.P.L. Lee (eds), *Social Life and Development in Hong Kong* (Hong Kong: The Chinese University Press, 1981).

4 Eugene Cooper, "Karl Marx's other island: the evolution of peripheral capitalism in Hong Kong," *Bulletin of Concerned Asian Scholars* 14, No. 1 (1982): 25.

nance of an apolitical façade has more than just a matter-of-fact tone to it. The institutionalization of an apolitical mentality and lifestyle ultimately has the goal of deflecting the essential violence of colonial power that maintains the system, like the way the virtues of modernization have obscured the exploitative dimensions of capitalism. Whether Hong Kong's political system or social lifestyle has remained colonial, despite names to the contrary, is perhaps a matter of interpretation, but discursive fictions are an important factor in understanding the underlying institutional reality. In this regard, one cannot neatly separate the regime of colonialism from nationalism, or even modernity. I submit that their mutually collusive relationships form in essence the socio-political ground, which in the final analysis engenders "identity."[5]

"Post-Colonial" Hong Kong: What's Culture Got to Do with It?

In the year preceding the handover, after years of official disavowal by the government of Hong Kong's colonial existence, a large stream of publications in both the English and Chinese scholarly literature appeared, dealing precisely with topics in relation to colonialism. Whether this explosion of interest was an attempt to cash in on a trendy topic in the wake of colonialism's demise or the result of other more serious intellectual concerns is anyone's speculation, but it was also without doubt fueled to some extent by corresponding realizations of cultural difference. I hesitate to say that such discoveries of difference are sentiments of nationalism, but it is clear that the appearance of an explicit positionality about colonialism as a real (or discursive) other marks a

5 I have made this basic argument more systematically in a previous publication: Allen Chun, "Discourses of identity in the changing spaces of public culture in Taiwan, Hong Kong and Singapore," *Theory Culture & Society* 13, No. 2 (1996): 51–75.

subjective distance or removal from its object, as though the latter can now be "gazed," both in light of impending transition and people's attachment or identification to it. It is as if one said, "colonialism has now become history." Thus, the end of history marked (if not championed) the arrival of a different future while at the same time relegating colonialism to its destined fate in the sociopolitical evolution of things.

The plethora of retrospective publications on colonialism that appeared in anticipation of the handover actually covers a wide range of critical perspectives. In addition to books that dealt with issues of sovereignty, the "one-country, two-systems" framework, Hong Kong Basic Law and calls for democracy, there was no shortage of publications in English alone ruminating on the historical legacy of colonialism in Hong Kong, both positive and negative.[6]

Colonial difference aside, it is important to note that the inevitability of 1997 in the years leading up to the handover did indeed invoke attempts by China, at least rhetorically, to cultivate nationalist sentiment at a local level as well as attempts by institutions in Hong Kong to

6 Writings by Western authors can be divided into two camps, those largely sympathetic to the British legacy, such as Robert Adley, *All Change Hong Kong* (Poole, Dorset: Blandford Press, 1984); H.K. Lamb, *A Date with Fate: Hong Kong 1997* (Hong Kong: Lincoln Green, 1984); Graham Johnson, *1997 and After: Will Hong Kong Survive?* (Toronto: Joint Center on Modern East Asia, 1985); and Alvin Rabushka, *Freedom's Fall in Hong Kong* (Stanford: Hoover Institution, 1997); and those critical of the colonial sellout of Hong Kong, such as Brian Nicholson, *A Conspiracy to Destroy Hong Kong* (Essex: Bear Books, 1992); L. Erwin Atwood and Anne-Marie Major, *Goodbye, Gweilo: Public Opinion and the 1997 Problem in Hong Kong* (Cresskill: Hampton Press, 1996); Ted Thomas, *What's Going to Happen in 1997 in Hong Kong* (Hong Kong: Simon and Schuster, 1996); and Richard Ingham, *Hong Kong: City on the Edge* (Hong Kong: Agence France-Presse, 1997). Local writers have on the other hand tended to be more concerned with the ability of Hong Kong to remain autonomous and threats of Chinese hegemony: Michelangelo Wong, *1997 and All That: A Tremulous Look into the Future* (Hong Kong: Lincoln Green, 1984); Liang Fu-lin, *Jiuqi hou xianggang qianzhan* (The future of Hong Kong after 1997) (Hong Kong: Wide Angle Press, 1995); Kwok Nai-wang, *1997: Hong Kong's Struggle for Selfhood* (Hong Kong: Daga Press, 1996); and Emily Lau (Liu Huiqing), *Xianggang keyi shuo bu* (Hong Kong can say no) (Hong Kong: Hongye Bookstore, 1998).

cultivate favor with its Chinese counterparts, in the interest of future constructive engagement. Needless to say, the resurgence of cultural nationalism in China in the past decade had often become the source of the government's appeal to popular support among its masses. While sometimes seen as a heavy-handed tactic in a Hong Kong context, the rhetoric of nationalism also had to be viewed in the way it overlapped with the discourse of democracy and the collusion of capitalist interests. As constructive engagement, conformity to nationalist pressures (imagined or real) had not just taken the form of positive initiatives, as evidenced by the fast-growing numbers of PRC scholars invited to and students enrolled by universities in Hong Kong prior to the handover, but had also taken the form of negative sanctions, evidenced by the increasing prevalence of self-censorship that was imposed during the same period within media, political and intellectual circles. In this sense, increasing pressure to conform, whether one called this explicit or implicit nationalism or not, already began to be rooted in pre-handover Hong Kong, and this trend corresponded simultaneously with a phase of overt anti-colonialism or impending post-colonialism.

Thus, nationalizing sentiments in the transitional era leading up to 1997 had as its goal the objectification of colonialism as a real other and the inculcation of a different kind of identity. In effect, some sense of identity had to be heightened, not only in reference to a newly objectified other but also in contrast to an apolitical other of the prior era, which became a source of cultural ambiguity during the transitional era.[7] But more importantly, with these nationalizing sentiments came the *fiction* that identity was somehow necessary for survival in the

7 Much has been said about the search for an unknown Chineseness that dominated Hong Kong films in the transitional era as well as the sense of ambiguity that a generation of youth brought up in colonial Hong Kong felt in being forced to identify with an alien culture. On handover night, it is reported a fifteen-year-old girl's dream where "she is on stage about to sing the Chinese national anthem. She is holding a flag and the audience is muttering in *putonghua*. Suddenly she realizes that she knows neither the melody nor the words"; Rozanna Lilley, "The Hong Kong Handover," *Communal Plural: Journal of Transnational and Crosscultural Studies* 8, No. 2 (2000): 179.

inevitable future. There are no hard and fast rules that dictate that identity is necessary for the survival of anything; it is a function of "the system" per se. Western identity was not necessary for people's survival under a colonial system that tried in fact to maintain the separations of social hierarchy. Similarly, the absence of a higher abstract identity in the apolitical 1970s may have been a cause of what some saw was the source of Hong Kong's cultural and intellectual desert, but in another sense it served as an ideal vehicle for institutionalizing another kind of social system driven by divisions of class and differential access to cultural resources. Impending nationalism played on the resurrection of a colonial other and deprivations of cultural identity, not because political change was inevitable but rather because it *viewed* shared identity as a necessary foundation for that new political order.

Yet the question is not why or if identity is *really* necessary, but rather *what is it for*? One might also add, who is it for and to what extent do alternative notions of culture provide the basis of effective counter-identities? I think the developmental trends leading up to 1997 that invoked a nationalistic mindset were enough to presage the order of things to come. In the waning years of the transition, different rhetorical contests were played out on different levels that continued well into the post-1997 era. Aside from the debate over how and to what extent the one-country, two-systems rule would be implemented, the other debate that invoked much discussion involved the rule of democracy. The notion of identity impinged on both debates but in different ways. Seen from the perspective of "one-country, two-systems," culture appeared to enjoy some kind of autonomy, in the sense that it only seemed to be a matter of political affiliation and not a matter of social and economic lifestyle. However, in the context of democracy debates, culture seemed to be an irrelevant factor, secondary to the criterion of political participation, which was seen as the defining characteristic in relation to the perceived importance and continued maintenance of local autonomy.

One can debate at great length as to whether the principle of "one-country, two-systems" actually guarantees autonomy of the political sphere from the economic. However, the great tide of nationalism that continued to swell in the waning years leading up to 1997, manifested in overt discourse as well as in implicit action (through constructive engagement of various kinds and the imposition of self-censorship), should have indicated that, if anything, the post-1997 years would see more of the same. In light of the resurrected anti-colonialism, the label "Royal" had already begun to be deleted from all government and other affiliated institutions, sometimes amidst the clamor of protest to replace all icons of colonial legacy with Chinese ones. In the aftermath of the "glorious restoration" *(guangfu)* of Taiwan by China, the KMT government renamed all the major streets there with names extolling Confucian virtues, such as *Renai* (benevolence) and *Zhongxiao* (loyalty) Road, or with names memorializing Chinese places and people. Nationalist revolutions everywhere else caused streets to be renamed, routinely, one might add. This systematic swelling of nationalist fervor that was being cultivated in the transition years should have easily spilled into the educational sphere, with increased emphasis on learning Chinese language and history.[8] Given popular acceptance of the handover's inevitability and the change of political sovereignty, the mood should have been ripe for the imposition of a new, if not different, "identity." Indeed, several writers have gone further by predicting the radical penetration of Party, military and other bureaucratic institutions after the

8 As a result of the Sino-British Declaration of 1984, the Hong Kong Education Department drew up guidelines on civic education, one in 1985 and another in 1996. The priority of more recent guidelines was clearly the inculcation of values pertaining to the national community. As a PRC educator, Li Yixian, put it, the curriculum should be refocused to accent "love of the country and nation, as well as education in the proper social behavior"; Li Yixian, "On the characteristics, strong points, and shortcomings of education in Hong Kong: a mainland educator's view of education in Hong Kong" in G. Postiglione (ed.), *Education and Society in Hong Kong* (Hong Kong: Hong Kong University Press, 1996), 254. Hughes and Stone note interesting parallels in the relationship between nation-building and curriculum reforms in Hong Kong and Taiwan, despite their concrete differences; Christopher Hughes and Robert Stone, "Nation-building and curriculum reform in Hong Kong and Taiwan," *The China Quarterly* 159 (1999): 977–91. The implementation of the actual guidelines in Hong Kong during the post-1997 era remains unclear and unexplored, however.

handover.[9] Jamie Allen perhaps put forward the most pessimistic view, when he predicted that, after the Party sets up shop, the party would be over.[10]

Despite the inevitability of the handover and presumed public acceptance of the change of sovereignty, if not identity as well, one might wonder why, to the contrary, little has changed in post-1997 Hong Kong. The People's Liberation Army, under the intense scrutiny of the handover media, entered Hong Kong, but little else to signal the advent of military or Party domination materialized.[11] Despite the fears of political oppression that prompted the media to adopt self-censorship, the relative freedom of the press in airing critical views of official government policy after the establishment of the SAR regime ran counter to the trends anticipated by heightened nationalism, which was supposed to be the point of departure for all institutional changes.[12] If all these changes predicated by the end of colonial history and advent of a new cultural identity failed to materialize, then one might ask, what does culture have to do with "post-colonial" Hong Kong, if anything? Even the nationalizing rhetoric seemed to diminish accordingly.

Culture is rarely a politically neutral entity; identity is even less so. Rising nationalist sentiment in mainland China has often served an

9 Chinese dissidents represented the harshest critics of China's intentions, citing political motives of various sorts. See, for instance, Yao Biyang, *China's Secrets and Hong Kong's Future* (New York: Vintage Press, 1995); and He Pin and Gao Xin, *Beijing ruhe kongzhi xianggang* (How Beijing Controls Hong Kong) (Ontario, Mississanga: Mirror Books, 1998).

10 Jamie Allen, *Seeing Red: China's Uncompromising Takeover of Hong Kong* (Singapore: Heinemann, 1997).

11 Even Martin Lee, leader of the democratic movement in Hong Kong was surprised. In late July, he noted that Chinese government officials had been quiet on Hong Kong issues and "we no longer hear intimidatory remarks from Beijing as we did when the last governor was here."

12 As Frank Ching has noted, the preparatory committee created in 1996 to oversee the handover was abolished, as were other bodies that had been seen as potential instruments for interfering in Hong Kong affairs; Frank Ching, "The Hong Kong press: Will it remain free after 1997?" *Asian Affairs, an American Review* 24, No. 4 (1998): 218.

important function, especially in recent decades, in providing necessary popular support for the government's actions and policies. In the case of Hong Kong, it could have effectively served to facilitate political integration.[13]

The Public Sphere in Search of a "Structural" Transformation

One can easily speculate on the possible reasons why so little has changed in the socio-political order of things, especially in light of various indicators to the contrary. The Chinese government made several official proclamations, perhaps in countering fears of anticipated suppression of press freedom, that it would adopt a position of non-interference in local affairs. In light of assorted events that have taken place in Hong Kong after 1997, there will always be disagreement on the degree to which Beijing is perceived to have or has actually interfered in the running of Hong Kong. It is not my intention to offer any interpretation of these events; instead I merely wish to point out that things could have radically changed just on the basis of the critical mass that had accumulated to disassemble the legacy of colonial culture, install new beginnings by gradually reorienting Hong Kong back to its political roots and institutionalizing the means by which a newly emerging identity could be fostered and put into practice. All of these things had already been successfully inculcated into individual thought and behavior long in advance of the handover. Why did the government then kill the momentum that would have facilitated such (presumably desirable) integration?

13 In this sense, Law Wing-sang's assessment of northbound colonialism seems correct, in that the project of nationalist integration is in essence no different from a colonialist hegemony; Law Wing-sang, "Northbound colonialism: a politics of post-PC Hong Kong," *Positions: East Asia Critique* 8, No. 1 (2000): 229–64.

In support of Beijing's non-interference policy, many observers had also hinted that the insistence on keeping a good face on the "one-country, two-systems" rule had to do instead with the PRC's attempt to woo the confidence of people in Taiwan to return to the motherland under the same kind of setup. This is rather dubious, as Hong Kong was the not the first or only example where the PRC has claimed to guarantee local "autonomy" (Tibet being the other) and because its hard line tactics, which threatened Taiwan militarily in the event of independence, were largely inconsistent with its soft-sell pitch. Besides, political priorities can always change China's view of or policy on anything, as has already been demonstrated on many occasions during the past few decades.

In all of this, the democratization movement in Hong Kong government seemed to have an uncertain future. Thanks to the colonial legacy of autocratic rule in Hong Kong, the post-1997 administration found it more convenient to maintain the status quo, while championing the rule of Hong Kong by Hong Kongers. Efforts to demand increased direct democratic participation in the election of legislators and running of government continued to be fought for and frustrated, and such efforts have mostly been pursued without regard to culture and identity issues. In other words, unlike Taiwan, where the national independence movement had derived its energy from efforts to demonstrate the existence of a separate Taiwanese ethnic-*cum*-cultural consciousness vis-à-vis Chinese ethnicity, the democracy campaign in Hong Kong had largely been a political or legal issue, devoid of cultural content. This also colored the way in which issues regarding the public sphere have developed, in contrast to Taiwan. In Hong Kong, there was a sharper contrast between the state (and its functional interests) and elements of a public effectively excluded from democratic participation. In Taiwan, ethnic coloration of political issues was largely a survival of a cultural nationalist policy of the former KMT regime that can mutate, if ideological difference between various parties becomes articulated in increasingly political terms. Moreover, in Hong Kong, there is no firm indication that local identity can or will ever have useful political leverage.

I deliberately point to the question of identity, the principle of local autonomy and issues of democratization to show that, in discussions of the Hong Kong public sphere, they are and have been seen largely as mutually distinct factors. They tend to represent different struggles and were not mobilized to influence each other, whereas in other venues, such as Taiwan, it can be argued that these factors have always been mutually intertwined (if not hopelessly entangled). Moreover, I would argue that the cultural arbitrariness of Hong Kong's situation is a discursive *fiction* that obscures other facets of institutional reality that are relevant to the emergence of a very different kind of structural transformation in the public sphere.

First of all, whatever role a "new" national identity was meant to play or could have played after 1997 was effectively undermined by the Asian financial crisis in late 1997, which continued well into 1998. At least in a political arena, identity issues receded far into the background with the onset and deepening of economic recession that made societal survival the prime substance of public discourse. In the face of international attacks on the Hong Kong dollar, which threatened to destabilize the Asian economy, Beijing allied with the Hong Kong government, but primarily to present a unified political front that was based solely on economic considerations (defending the currency peg). The pivotal position of Hong Kong in insulating mainland China from the Asian recession strengthened, if anything, the autonomy of the Hong Kong government in establishing policy and controlling the fiscal crisis. The Tung Chee-hwa administration suffered a sharp loss of confidence during this crisis, but it probably had more to do with his performance in handling political affairs than attacks on the nature of his autocratic rule. In effect, issues of identity, local autonomy and democratic rule would appear to be distinct, discursively speaking, but their significance in any political context can and does *in fact* change vis-à-vis other issues.

Official non-interference in the media had also appeared to enhance the existence of Hong Kong autonomy, but this was actually only a partial reality that disguised the changing nature of Hong Kong's "public" sphere. The fiction that contributed to the notion that Hong Kong was an autonomous "region" was reflective to some extent of the

PRC's position that, at least in some functional respects, Hong Kong could be seen as separate from China. Economically, China was linked integrally to the global economy through Hong Kong, and the most recent fiscal crisis had demonstrated that Hong Kong still played a major role in this regard. In social and local political matters, Hong Kong's autonomy impacted less on developments on the mainland. As long as the political scheme of things favored the appointment of Beijing-sympathetic cliques in power, media opposition was a matter for local government to handle and did not directly impact upon Beijing. However, freedom of the press was curiously enough restricted only to "local" affairs. As Frank Ching keenly noted, the Hong Kong media tread more cautiously in news pertaining to China, or, to be more precise, news and information requiring the cooperation of Chinese agencies and China-backed companies.[15] Some topics were too sensitive or were seen as totally taboo, such as the activities of official agencies that fronted for the Communist Party. As Michael Curtin had also noted, the boundaries of media openness and closeness was a function of the fact that the Hong Kong media was not a local entity but one whose market depended on expansion into China.[15] As he put it, "this strategy of expansion into the mainland market thus requires the cooperation of government officials, if the industry is going to reap the benefits of its popularity." The principle of media freedom was thus compromised to satisfy the reality of market access and control. This reinforced the necessity of self-censorship as well.

In short, business interests have in fact always been intertwined with politics in ways that influenced *at an underlying level* support for or compromising of certain ideological principles (whether it be identity or democracy). This realization then solidified "the rules of the game." This complicit relation of power (and *guanxi*) is in the end the largest threat to the emergence of a true democratic public sphere. This is the *real* face of post-1997 Hong Kong.

14 Ching, "The Hong Kong press: Will it remain free after 1997?" 217–25.

15 Michael Curtin, "Images of trust, economies of suspicion: Hong Kong media after 1997," *Historical Journal of Film, Radio and Television* 18, No. 2 (1998): 288.

Apprehending History through its "Effects"

One of the strange surprises of a short visit I made to Hong Kong in November 1994 during the intense bidding for the 2000 Olympics (which was eventually won by Sydney, Australia) was not so much the fact that once "apolitical" Hong Kongers now seemed to be awash in a euphoric patriotic fervor but rather how all this came about. It surprised me even more that a politically neutral Hong Kong friend, who was a long term Australian resident, was also swept up by the prevailing current of opinion and media hype to admit as well that Beijing would almost surely win the Olympic bid. Of course, the intensity of "nationalistic" sentiments had its roots in a rising and ongoing renaissance of Chinese consciousness that covered the transitional era, which ranged from a quiet resurgence of interest in lost historical and intellectual roots to overt expressions of political solidarity. Yet, one should also not lose track of the fact that this sudden outpour of nationalist sentiment was as much the product of an inherent Chinese consciousness that Hong Kongers have *always* had (even during the colonial era) as it was the machination of sophisticated media hype. Hong Kong business interests had the most to gain from a successful bid by Beijing to hold the Olympics, and it was essentially the same interest that drove them to seek *guanxi* alliances with important officials and entrepreneurs in the PRC. In other words, they were not simply motivated more by profit motives than nationalistic feelings per se, but more importantly they were quite able and often willing to manipulate such sentiments (up and down) purely for the sake of self-interested commercial gain. Hence, the economy's new tie to culture.

Thus, it is not really surprising, in retrospect, that the first people who ardently supported reunification of Hong Kong with China or at least expressed confidence in the future of a post-colonial Hong Kong were rich capitalists. At the same time, these same people were most likely to steer clear away from any overt conflict with Beijing, especially in the face of democratization movements and campaigns for increased local autonomy. In this context, unlike the "apolitical" capitalism that was characteristic of the 1970s, capitalist interests of the post-colonial era may have been driven by the same purely self-interested profit motives of capitalists found elsewhere, but in a Hong Kong context specifically it was clear that such capitalists would knowingly, if not willingly, subordinate democratic ideals and manipulate nationalist sentiments in order to protect their own vested interests, if necessary. This *unholy* alliance between business and the new regime was not only designed to be the foundation of the new order. More importantly, its success was dependent largely on suppressing those (democratizing) forces that represented a challenge to this power relationship.

Quite clearly, the kind of structural transformation that was required in order to give rise to a democratic public sphere in post-1997 Hong Kong involved not only the advent of open, rational communication but more importantly a challenge to the various forces that had resulted in the institutional collusion of big business and political bureaucratic interests. The predominance of commercial interests in government was nothing new to Hong Kong, given its founding in the history of global trade and the strong representation of major corporate interests in the colonial government, but the policy of the SAR government to divide legislative representation according to functional constituencies at the expense of direct democracy thus insured corporate interests a direct and omnipresent role. In the era leading up to 1997, nationalistic fervor was a useful mode of representation to promote their own interests as well as to curry favor with counterparts within the PRC. In the ensuing Asian recession, the mood of societal survivalism forced the government to prioritize purely economic interests at the expense of other values but in a way that made identity, among other things, secondary concerns. Moreover, not unlike the market sensibilities that had forced the media to mute its criticism when transcending local boundaries, the expansion of Hong Kong corporate interests into China that had co-opted them into toeing the line in Hong Kong also showed that the domain of the public sphere had effectively transcended a local Hong Kong context. Despite its fictional autonomy (under the one-country, two systems scheme), the reality of its post-1997 existence thus thrust Hong Kong society into a mutually dependent economic and political relationship with the PRC. The Hong Kong media (and film industry) now had to expand its market into the PRC just to survive locally, and Hong Kong corporate interests viewed control of the PRC market in turn as a larger priority than the local Hong Kong one. In short, the reality of this larger sphere of economic and political interaction was eventually the bottom line that in turn forced compromises made at a local level. In the final analysis, who cared about identity, as long as everyone could make ends meet and got what he/she sought, despite the various façades?

At one level, the appearance of official autonomy does not prevent Beijing from trying to impose laws to repress acts of dissent or seditious behavior. Pro-democracy forces can also counter by rallying in the streets, especially if they remain stifled in efforts to make changes in the system, but strategies of collusion have inculcated a new mode of dependency relations.

To call this newly evolving system of relations *guanxi* capitalism would be overly simplistic. As a mode of capitalism, it is driven by a utilitarian logic that understands the dominant power of the market in controlling the flow of capital. China is consciously aware that it is at the center of an expanding global market, both in terms of outsource production for the developed nations and the consumption of global products, and this awareness has in turn allowed it to use its pivotal role to control people's access to desired resources or benefits of the system by making people conform to the rules of the game in all other respects. Thus, the media has learned that it is free to print whatever it pleases in matters pertaining to Hong Kong (hence is autonomous), but that in matters involving China or cooperation with Chinese agencies it is forced accordingly to toe the proper ideological line as one's price of admission. Increasingly, they toe the line, especially when they discover that the economic survival of their own enterprise is dependent on expansion into the China market. The willingness of Western global media, such as STAR-TV, to censor BBC news and other programs, when they comment unfavorably on China, as a condition of their continued access, demonstrates that it is not just a local policy specific to Hong Kong. Taiwanese businessmen, entertainers and professionals of all sorts have learned to mute any expressions of or sympathy for Taiwanese independence so as not to jeopardize their own prospects for cashing in on the lucrative China market, especially when it has become obvious that this market is much richer than their own. Most recently, PRC authorities also revoked a tourist visa to Hong Kong for Taipei Mayor Ma Ying-jeou for making politically incorrect remarks. Such sanctions seem superficial and frivolous, but they underscore the point that, while the market is in principle open, people are free to make money, and there is no attempt by the government to control the redistribution of income, as has been the case of old socialist economies, access to the market is in practice a privilege that can be politically controlled, if deemed desirable or necessary. Hence, the economy's new tie to political ideology. To say the least, it is clearly anti-democratic as well.

More fundamentally, the subjective positioning behind this new capitalism is hardly the kind one would expect from a poor third world nation. China is supremely confident in its ability to pull the strings behind the system and in the process protect its own sense of ideological purity. The continued flow of global investment attests in part to their faith in this regard. Driving this subjective centrality is an imminently real nationalistic fervor (or deep-seated cultural arrogance), which matches the size of its ambitions to rectify centuries of imperialism and political shame. Ultimately, the biggest fiction is that of "one-country, two-systems." The ritual façade of the handover has marked the fictive significance of 1997, and the fiction of Hong Kong's autonomy in a meaningless ideological framework has reset the clock again on its eventual integration with the mainland. In the PRC, it is ironic to note that so-called "socialism with Chinese characteristics" has in fact led, among other things, to the abolition of the term for social class *(shehui jieji).* In Hong Kong, embrace of the motherland has instead refined institutional capitalism to new heights.

What is (Post) Colonial "Modernity"?

The history of Hong Kong, both in its evolution as a colonial city-state and its post-1997 transformation as special administrative region of China, should have relevant and significant things to say about the nature and operation of colonial modernity. It should lead one above all to question what coloniality and modernity is as well as the collusive relationship between the two. Coloniality should be questioned not only for how it exists in fact (as a mode of political practice) but also how it portrays itself as representation (through cultural discourse, subjective narrative, (re)writings of history, ritual or other codifications of memory and fictive denials). These same forms of coloniality can also be used to legitimate the existence of other forms of political institutions not termed colonial, strictly speaking. If so, then the continued existence of colonialism can easily transcend its explicit change of political status, because it is in effect a matter of interpretation. Modernity deserves to be questioned in the same way. Far from being an autonomous and value-free entity, it is on the contrary something that is put into practice in the service of that same political evolution. Global capitalism is in this regard not only the abstract operation of a market society, as though a realization of utilitarian ideals, but also the end product of its own ongoing, mutating historical process. In the context of the colonial development of Hong Kong into the post-1997 era, one can witness its subtle and complex transformations. More importantly, these transformations are part and parcel of its necessarily collusive relationships to changing policies and governmentality in the abstract.

The work of Bernard Cohn on late colonial India offers a useful parallel into the collusive relationship between the cultural sociology of the state, structurations of modernity and constructions of identity.[16] His observations about cultural and social objectification that he

16 Bernard S. Cohn, "The census, social structure and objectification in South Asia," *Folk* 26 (1984): 25–49.

argued were fundamental to British colonial rule in India has proved to be broadly endemic to diverse forms of modern govern-"mentality" throughout the world. These processes have been the source of unending discourses and struggles over "identity." More than just castes of mind or imagined communities in the making, identities have always been cultural fictions predicated upon the assumption of real roots and the need to reaffirm them. The tendency to objectify "ethnic" identity in particular has been in effect symptomatic of attempts to define the illusory nature and form of such an *ethnos*, but it is also perhaps characteristic of society's need to inculcate the *ethos* of its own modernity, whether it is encoded in the rule of law, civilizing imperatives, moral regulation, personhood or the etiquette of everyday interaction. These changing discourses of identity supplement (rather than conflict with) the extraordinary extent to which state apparatuses have labored to compel people into "becoming their I. D." Taken as an entire cartography of power, they freeze us, as Corrigan and Sayer phrased it, through these programs of power, "into mythic statuses of sedimented language."[17] *Why identify?* I do not personally believe that it is necessary to identify with anything. Yet, people elsewhere go to great lengths to prove that identities are real, even worth dying for.

If identity, like Cohn's colonial impositions of caste and social structure, are fictions or inventions, then history must be seen as the ongoing institutional and political embodiment of fiction as fact and the constant interaction of discourse and practice. Fictions can run deep, and it is in the process of institutionalization that its political violence becomes "normalized." Hong Kong's Colonial Secretary of State, Sir Philip Haddon-Cave once joked, in 1985:

> When Sir John Bremridge [the Finance Minister] came to see me about the [Chinese] banks he was in a rage.
> "I've told them", he spluttered, "they've got to toe the line, otherwise … otherwise, we'll *nationalise* them"!
> "Oh, no Sir John", I said, "you *can't* say 'nationalise' – we're not a nation".

17 Philip Corrigan and Derek Sayer, *The Great Arch: English State Formation as Cultural Revolution*, 2nd edn. (Oxford: Blackwell, 1991), 211.

> "Well, we're a colony, aren't we"? he said, "so we'll *colonise* them"!
> "Oh *no*, Sir John", I explained, "you *can't* say that, we *never* refer to Hong Kong as a 'colony' these days".
> "Well then", he replied, "what *are* we called now"?
> "Well", I explained, "these days we call ourselves a 'territory'".
> "Right then", said Sir John, "we'll *terrorise* them"!

Statements about what is or supposed to be, when Hong Kong was literally a colony, should raise similar questions about what post 1997 Hong Kong is or is supposed to be after the end of colonialism. Names are only part of the story, but they are an important preamble to how people construct their identities then in turn tie them into the practices and politics of a deeper struggle to define and regulate a particular ethos of life or mode of survival.

In light of such events, history is an ongoing process whose underlying forces and rules cannot be predetermined but instead must be seen in its specific context of making and on its own terms, not unlike Durkheim's *sui generis* social facts. One can see a complex interaction between culture (as discourse, representations or ideologies) on the one hand and institutions (i.e., its politics and social practices) on the other. Colonialism has been in this regard *above all* a regime of political practice that depended to some extent on the efficacy of modernity as culture, however defined. Colonialism's mutations in time and place, despite various name changes, are constant reminders of its groundedness, ultimately in practice and not in theory.

Underlying these complex interactions between culture and politics, facts and fictions, and strategic intents of agents located within this geometry of power, I would still argue that there is much room for new theorizing. In this regard, the question of whether and how colonialism constitutes an "-ism" or system of any sort is probably less important than how different interacting -isms manifest themselves in practice and endeavor to institutionalize their existence and underlying values within a context of power that is constantly mutating. Within this framework, it is clearly not enough to read culture and politics as text but as entities that are in fact intrinsically intertwined and whose particular meanings and intents are produced in conscious relation to the interaction of various agents or actors. What requires more clarification is this ongoing context of power that situates this interaction of cultural strategies and intents. The dynamics of this power geometry requires a critical epistemology that can transcend the rhetoric of colonialism, nationalism, capitalism and the ends of history.

Yiu-wai Chu

The Donaldization of Hong Kong Society

Introduction

"Strong Governance for the People," reads the title of Donald Yam-kuen Tsang's first Chief Executive's Policy Address (2005–2006). Donald Tsang formally succeeded Tung Chee-hwa as the Chief Executive of Hong Kong Special Administrative Region on June 21, 2005, and he won the third-term Chief Executive election, with 649 votes (eighty-four percent of the total valid votes) on March 25, 2007. According to the figures released by the Public Opinion Program of the University of Hong Kong, the rating of Donald Tsang when he first assumed duty in June 2005 was 72.3, remarkably high when compared to the rating of Tung (47.4 in March 2005).[1] Besides the difficulty during the Tung administration and the steady economic revival during Tsang's in Hong Kong, the "Hong Kongness" of Donald Tsang also contributes, at least in part, to his popularity. "Tsang is popular because he is not Tung. He was born and raised in Hong Kong and is a Hong Kong person, Cantonese speaker, to the core," says Michael DeGolyer, director of the Hong Kong Transition Project at Hong Kong Baptist University.[2] On a number of occasions Tsang claimed himself to be a native "Hong Kong boy." What constitutes the "Hong Kongness" here? Unlike Tung who was born to a rich and famous family, Tsang climbed up the social

1 HKU POP Site, "Rating of Chief Executive Donald Tsang Yam-kuen"; http://hkupop.hku.hk/chinese/popexpress/ce2005/donald_new/poll/chart_new/poll4.gif; last accessed: March 1, 2008.

2 Gary LaMoshi, "Hong Kong's (un)happy anniversary," *Asia Times*, http://www.atimes.com/atimes/China /GF29Ad01.html; last accessed: March 1, 2008.

ladder from grassroots to elite, from a salesman to the Chief Executive. This is considered by many a legend of Hong Kong. But Mainland officials seem to have less interest in legend than political reality. As early as November 25, 1997 when Tsang was still the Financial Secretary of Hong Kong Special Administration Region, he said in a seminar at St. Anthony's College of Oxford University something evincing Hong Kong's role in the opening up of China to the world:

> The commitment of the Chinese Government to deepening of market based reform has been demonstrated by the plans set out at the 15th Party Congress. Gone is the old focus on physical and numerical targets. In their place are policies and strategies to tackle the real problems of the state owned enterprises – social security, housing and health care; ownership; profitability. Growth is to be sought through upgrading of technology, skills training and productivity increases, not by increasing inputs. Opening up to international markets is to be extended by reducing import tariffs, expanding foreign trading rights of enterprises, gradual opening of the services sector and through strengthening of legal processes. This portrays a powerful and confident nation *on the move to modernity while focusing on the well-being of her people*. In this process, the Hong Kong SAR will play its part (my emphasis).[3]

Interestingly enough, "the move to modernity while focusing on the well-being of her people" here has a strange resemblance to the title of Tsang's first Chief Executive's Policy Address. Notoriously indecisive and weak in governance, Tung was widely criticized as making Hong Kong a less liberal modern city than Mainland cities such as Shanghai. In China's move to modernity, if it is real, Hong Kong can no longer function as a gateway to the world if it loses its "modernity." Richard Boucher, former American Consulate General in Hong Kong, reinstated the five mainstays in a lunch seminar shortly before his departure from Hong Kong in July 1999. He first mentioned these mainstays in 1996 when he assumed duty in Hong Kong: the legal system, free information flow, the responsible legislative structure, the sound

3 "Speech by the Financial Secretary, Mr Donald Tsang, at a seminar at St. Anthony's College, Oxford University (November 25, 1997)," http://www.info.gov.hk/isd/speech/25fs-ox.htm; last accessed: March 1, 2008.

civil servant system and Hong Kong's independent participation in international organization.[4] When he was still the Financial Secretary, Donald Tsang gave a paperweight to Jiang Zemin, the former President of PRC, on which are inscribed what he believes to be the four pillars for the success of Hong Kong: observance of the rule of law, free flow of information, non-corrupt government, a level-playing field. Tsang and Boucher are obviously using the same language that Tung Chee-hwa did not speak well. So what Donald Tsang has been striving after being appointed as the Chief Executive has very much to do with strong governance with an eye to these factors which assure Hong Kong's modernity when compared to China.

Whether modernity is singular or plural has been under heated debates. The following questions related to modernity are worthwhile noting here: "How is modernity configured – and contested – in different cultural and regional contexts? How do people in different world areas construct notions of progress vis-à-vis those of tradition or history?" These questions

> […] force us to confront the cultural diversity of the contemporary world while considering a larger issue: how it is that people in different world areas are coming to have more in common at the same time that they are becoming increasingly diverse, for instance, through new forms of cultural elaboration and differentiation.[5]

The recent Donaldization of Hong Kong society might shed light on this issue and provide us with another angle to examine Hong Kong modernity/modernities. In what follows I will go into an analysis of what I mean by Donaldization before I come back to the important question related to Hong Kong modernity.

4 Cited from "Five mainstays of prosperity" (in Chinese) *Apple Daily*, June 24, 1999.

5 Bruce M. Knauft, "Vernacular modernities," http://www.anthropology.emory.edu/FACULTY/ANTBK/ vernacularModernities/vernacularModernities.html; last accessed: March 1, 2008.

What Donaldization Is: Strong Governance

What does it mean by "strong governance" hailed by Donald Tsang? Tsang made it very clear in his opening remarks at the Question and Answer Session of Legislative Council on March 30, 2006, "Policies should not only be made decisively, but should also respond effectively to public aspirations."[6] With the hindsight of Tung's failure due to his weak governance, Donald Tsang uses "strong governance" to mark a culture of governance based on public views and effective execution. In fact he had successfully proved his strong governance when he was campaigning for Chief Executive in June 2005. Just a month after he expressed his discontents with horse racing coverage and the Ten Gold Songs Awards program of the Radio Television of Hong Kong (RTHK), a public broadcaster, the RTHK decided to drop horse racing which it had covered for more than 30 years.[7] This subsequently stirred up heated debates over RTHK's independence as a public broadcaster.

Donald Tsang's strong governance proved to be welcomed by Hong Kong people. He has enjoyed high public opinion ratings when compared to his predecessor. The Donaldization of Hong Kong society, interestingly enough, has a strange echo with the controversial McDonaldization in the field of social and cultural studies. The golden arch of McDonalds' is a symbol of Western modernity in non-western societies. While rationalization is equated with modernization in standard interpretations of Max Weber, McDonaldization can be seen as a kind of incarnation of capitalist modernity; it is in essence the process of rationalization. According to George Ritzer's controversial *The McDonaldization of Society*, the four main dimensions of McDonaldization are efficiency,

6 Cited from "Opening remarks by CE at question and answer session of legislative council," Government Information Centre of the Hong Kong Special Administrative Region, http://www.info.gov.hk/gia/general/200603/30/P200603300203.htm; last accessed: March 1, 2008.

7 Jimmy Cheung and Ambrose Leung, "Tsang knew of racing axe when speaking out," *South China Morning Post*, July 12, 2005.

calculability, predictability and control. "Efficiency" is generally considered one of the magic words of the success of Hong Kong. Not only Hong Kong people themselves but also Mainland officials think so. Donald Tsang regards "efficiency" as part of the so-called "Hong Kong spirit" by saying,

> During almost 40 years of public service, I have, together with the people of Hong Kong, experienced many ups and downs. We have grown up with Hong Kong and, collectively with our 'Hong Kong spirit', endured many trials. With their bare hands, Hong Kong people have built a vibrant world city that is caring and just, without compromising its efficiency.[8]

Meanwhile, *China Daily* reported Donald Tsang's formal appointment as Hong Kong's new chief executive in the following manner,

> The resolution and efficiency he demonstrated during his term of acting CE won general acclaim [...] Such a lofty degree of support has bolstered his mandate and laid a solid foundation for his rule as well as his mission of strengthening governance, enhancing government efficiency and establishing a true executive-led regime.[9]

"Efficiency" – the rational determination of the best mode of production in Ritzer's sense – can be put alongside with the Chief Executive's well-known flying dragon pin and bow-ties. In his maiden Policy Address on October 12, 2005, the word "efficiency" is repeatedly mentioned. At the outset, the Chief Executive defines a strong government by noting that it "heeds public opinion, adopting the public interest as the guiding principle and accepting wide public participation in policy formulation," and the important point is that such a government will have "a clear direction, consistency in policy making, forceful and deci-

8 Cited from "Policy address by Chief Executive 2005–6," Government Information Centre of the Hong Kong Special Administrative Region, http://www.info.gov.hk/gia/general/200510/12/ P200510120136.htm; last accessed: March 1, 2008.

9 Cited from "Challenges, chances in sight for Tsang," *People Daily's Online*, June 22, 2005, http://english1.peopledaily.com.cn/200506/22/eng20050622_191692.html; last accessed: March 1, 2008.

sive leadership that is efficient and effective."[10] He also claims he would focus on institutional and operational efficiency, and in order to improve operational efficiency, three panels would be set up under the Commission on Strategic Development to study political, economic and social development while the Central Policy Unit will provide research and secretariat support to the Commission.

Donald Tsang did not forget the contribution of the civil service of Hong Kong, of which he has been a part for many years. He considers the civil service "the backbone of the SAR Government, and of effective governance," applauding it as "clean, efficient and accountable with outstanding professionalism and prestige." This is apparently a complement not only to the civil service but also himself. The outstanding professionalism here underscores efficiency as well as calculability and predictability. Civil servants trained by the former British government would act in a rational way which is calculable and predictable. In Ritzer's sense, calculability means assessing outcomes based on quantifiable rather than subjective criteria (i.e. quantity over quality), and predictability refers to the uniformity of product and standardized outcomes. Big Macs sold all over the world are the same; they might not be good, but they are big. In the eyes of both Donald and McDonalds', such a substitution of more predictable non-human for human civil servants/labor is good for control. It is thus not surprising that the government issued the "Consultation Document on Further Development of the Political Appointment System" on July 26, 2006 "to canvass views from the community on how best to further develop the political appointment system."[11] The Government proposes to create new positions to support Principal Officials, namely Deputy Directors of Bureau and Assistants to Directors of Bureau. This can well be seen as a move to further enhance the Chief Executive's control in the process of Donaldization.

10 Cited from "Policy address by Chief Executive 2005–6".

11 Cited from "Government publishes consultation document on further development of the political appointment system," Government Information Centre of the Hong Kong SAR, http://www.info.gov.hk/gia/general/200607/26/P200607260143.htm; last accessed: March 1, 2008.

I do not intend to dwell upon a detailed discussion of Ritzer's argument here. I would just like to raise Douglas Kellner's point to further my own argument: beside instrumental rationality and efficiency McDonaldization also encompasses a postmodern realm of hyperreality, simulation, implosion, and hybridity.[12] The appointment of spin doctors has showed Donald Tsang's concern of his own public image. Having learned from mistakes, Tung Chee-hwa at long last appointed a "spin doctor," Stephen Sui-lung Lam, to fill the new post of Information Coordinator in 1998. Ironically though, the appointment of Stephen Lam was widely criticized as Lam's rank and salary are unexpectedly high, much higher than his counterparts in the United States or the United Kingdom. It proved to be a nightmare for both, as Lam had to "spin" for himself much more than for Tung. Donald Tsang, trained by the British, is of course smart enough to choose the model of Tony Blair, but not Tung Chee-hwa. Taking the successful model of "spin doctor" of Alastair Campbell, Tsang appointed Andy On-tat Ho, former journalist and public relations man, as Chief Executive's Information Coordinator. Together with the naming of Wong Yan-lung, a young barrister, to assume the post of Secretary for Justice, it gives an impression of the government's "open-minded-ness":

> That is why Tsang is prepared to enlist a spin doctor such as Andy Ho, who is on record as being sympathetic to democratic ideas far beyond those which the administration plans to implement, and it also explains why Wong Yan-lung, a well respected barrister, occupies the seat once kept lukewarm by Elsie Leung, an old-style leftist whose ideological qualifications outshone her legal competence. The presence of such people suggests a more open-minded administration, not, as many insist a government obsessed with spin and presentation.[13]

The "open-minded" impression here made a merciless contrast to the "close-minded" incompetent Tung administration widely criticized as using officials according to kinship more than ability. This further strengthens the rational strong governance of the new Tsang adminis-

12 Douglas Kellner, "Theorizing McDonaldization: a multiperspectivist approach," in Barry Smart (ed.), *Resisting McDonaldization* (London: Sage, 1999), 186–206.

13 Stephen Vines, "He's always on the run," *The Standard*, February 24, 2006.

tration. A veteran bureaucrat, Donald Tsang proves Max Weber's saying that bureaucracy is the most modern form of social organization.

Besides, Tung Chee-hwa, unlike his predecessor Chris Patten, was not interested in showmanship. Hong Kong people still remember very well how Patten tried a bowl of herbal tea in a crowded street in Mong Kok not long after he assumed the duty of the last governor of Hong Kong. The way he unabashedly swallowed his favorite "Tai-cheong" egg tarts in front of cameras is perhaps more memorable to Hong Kong people than his political career. Donald Tsang took a tip from his former boss, knowing that the secret of Patten's popularity was due, at least in part, to his high-profile image. He did not hesitate to perform political shows to "meet-and-greet" different walks of life and grab media attention. He did not even mind to pick up rubbish in the street in front of cameras during his "meet-and-greet" activities on June 1, 2006. It is not surprising that he easily grabbed the headline of Hong Kong newspapers. This episode echoes well with another important dimension of (Mc)Donaldization: public image. It seems to me what McDonalds' does, Donald does it better. While McDonald's increased the number of its 24-hour restaurants in Hong Kong, Tsang openly declared himself as a 24-hour Chief Executive when he was criticized by legislators after his visit to his election office during working hours. In terms of image, while the bow-ties of Donald Tsang might be less flamboyant than Uncle McDonald's, they exert a similar function of branding. When he was still Chief Secretary for Administration, Donald Tsang launched a "Brand Hong Kong" program to promote Hong Kong on the global stage as "Asia's world city." The program chose a flying dragon which is, in its own words, "[a] modern interpretation of a dragon incorporating the letters HK and the Chinese characters for Hong Kong":

> The flowing lines of the Dragon also mirror Chinese calligraphy. This dual expression symbolizes a fusion of East and West that characterizes Hong Kong. The Dragon's smooth, fluid shape imparts a sense of movement and speed, communicating that Hong Kong is forever changing.[14]

14 "Background to Our Brand," *Brand Hong Kong*, http://www.brandhk.gov.hk/brandhk/eview.htm last accessed March 1, 2008.

The well-known bow-ties are always worn with a flying dragon pin on the lapel of the Chief Executive's suits.

The flying dragon soars high across the border to the Pearl River Delta. To link pan-Pearl River Delta Region to the world through Hong Kong was a project started back in the Tung Chee-hwa era.

> The pan-Pearl River Delta region is Hong Kong's next stage in development – it is another base outside the Pearl River Delta region. We have just started to realize its great potential. It might even be more efficient than the Pearl River Delta region in terms of mutual assistance,

Donald Tsang remarked in Chengdu during a visit to Sichuan to meet nine provincial leaders in July 2005.[15] The concept of "megacity" has further expanded before it is properly developed. On the basis of extensive research conducted in this region, Manuel Castells predicts that

> [...] this Southern China Metropolis [includes the ports of Hong Kong and Macao, and the rapidly expanding Chinese industrial centers of Guangzhou, Huizhou, and Zhaoqing], only vaguely perceived in most of the world at this time, is likely to become the most representative urban face of the 21st century.

But what is more important seems to be another defining characteristic of the next millennium's megacities:

> [...] while they are globally connected to the world economy, they are locally disconnected, or split along economic lines, with luxury high-rise commercial and residential districts located cheek-by-jowl beside festering inner-city slums.

Unfortunately, this is of course something Donaldization does not care to consider.

15 Ambrose Leung, "Closer links the next stage for HK, says Tsang," *South China Morning Post*, July 25, 2005.

De-McDonaldization

While Tsang's governance is strong in regard to those sectors related to the administration of a global city, it is not in other aspects of modernities. The Donaldization of Hong Kong society has arguably been targeting upon selected modernities. Talking about multiple modernitites, S.N. Eisenstadt notes, problems relating to the environment and gender are two of the most important new problems today.[16] These two problems have not been left untouched by the Tsang administration. But the responses are far from convincing. With respect to gender let me focus on an issue concerning criminalizing buggery. In this case Tsang is criticized for the privatization of not only public business but also morals. When being asked about a High Court ruling in August 2005 which overturned a law that criminalized buggery for men under the age of twenty-one on the grounds that it was discriminatory during a question-and-answer session with more than 1,000 young people, Tsang claimed that while everyone has his or her own moral values, he opined that the privatization of morals has become a danger in Hong Kong society. In other words, he had reservations about sayings like "since what I do does not affect others and it has nothing to do with other people, why should I be constrained?" Jake van der Kamp from the *South China Morning Post* responded to this issue,

> It may be true, as Mr Tsang says, that moral values in any society are shared by that entire society. It may be equally true that government is common to that entire society. This does not, however, automatically mean that moral values are a government matter.[17]

16 Shmuel N. Eisenstadt, *Multiple Modernities* (New Brunswick and London: Transaction, 2002), 24.

17 Jake van der Kamp, "Donald should stick to his day job and stop trying to play God," *South China Morning Post*, October 18, 2005. http://simonworld.mu.nu/archives/126603.php (accessed: May 10, 2007).

Apparently enough, no distinction in the age of consent should be made between homosexual and heterosexual sexes. Kamp goes on to ask a very important question,

> Do his reservations about the 'privatization of morals' mean that he would like to adopt a Singapore-style Big Daddy government in which matters of personal and private conduct are subject to government scrutiny for common codes of moral rectitude?

I guess Donald Tsang must feel uncomfortable being criticized as adopting a Singapore-style as the Singapore Big Daddy Lee Kuan Yew is widely known to be the idol of Tung Chee-hwa.

To another set of important new problems today, those relating to the environment, Tsang's governance seems to be less helplessly weak. Vehement charges have been made to his policy on environment protection. Mei Ng, the Director of Friends of the Earth (HK), complains, "Shortsighted economical gains based on ecological destruction, cultural erosion and over consumption have been a trademark of Hong Kong's legacy in the past fifty years of governance."[18] Edwin Lau, Assistant Director of Friends of the Earth (HK), grumbles this way,

> Chief Executive Mr Donald Tsang has vowed on various occasions to pursue strong governance. But when it comes to environmental issues, our government chokes on its frailty in demanding the power companies to develop renewable energy, to retrofit their pollution abatement installations and practicing Demand Side Management, and in regulating smog-forming emissions from cars, franchised buses, coaches and transborder lorries.[19]

In the face of harsh criticisms, Donaldization is determined to treat modernity seriously. On July 25, 2006, Donald Tsang launched the Action Blue Sky Campaign which uses "Clean Air for a Cool Hong

18 Mei Ng, "Unfinished business of the disney theme park," *Friends of the Earth* (2005) http://www.foe.org.hk/welcome/geten.asp?language=en&id_path=1,%207,%2028,%20152,%202908,%203096; last accessed: March 1, 2008.

19 Edwin Lau, "Running in the dark," *Friends of the Earth* (Febuary 22, 2006) http://www.foe.org.hk/welcome/geten.asp?id_path=1,%207,%2028,%20151,%203154,%203196; last accessed: March 1, 2008.

Kong!" as its slogan. Publicity and educational activities will be rolled out "to encourage the community and the business sector to do their part to clean up the air."[20] Tsang repeatedly reminded Hong Kong people to set their air-conditioners to 25.5 degrees Celsius in order to save electricity. He also urged the private sector to dress down in summer, and to show his commitment he did not even mind taking off his famous bow-ties. It is a bit surprising, however, for Tsang to start his "Letter to Hong Kong People" on air pollution with Marshall McLuhan who put forward the notion of global village back in the 1960s.[21] Whether the Blue Sky Campaign is targeted upon environmental protection or branding Hong Kong as a global city we still have to wait to see.

As apparent in the "Blue Sky Campaign," Donald Tsang pays close attention to channeling public discontents. This can be considered as a move of "de-McDonaldization" in the sense of George Ritzer and Todd Stillman. Ritzer and Stillman argue that in order to attract larger crowds, ballparks in the United States have recently undergone a process of reenchantment "whereby the magical allure of the ballpark is simulated to increase the consumer appeal in a rationalized setting."[22] Their conclusion is that although a kind of de-McDonaldization accompanies the reenchantment, the process is in fact artificial and superficial: "it is simulated de-McDonaldization, which remains rational at the core." It is in this light we can further examine the government's recent emphasis on "collective memories" in Hong Kong. Famous for its swiftly changing cityscape, Hong Kong is not interested in preserving collective memory until the Star Ferry Pier and Queen's Pier episodes. The furor over the

20 Cited from "CE launches Action Blue Sky Campaign," Information Services Department of Hong Kong Special Administration Region, July 25, 2006, http://news.gov.hk/en/category/environment/ 060725/html/060725en04001.htm#; last accessed: March 1, 2008.

21 Donald Tsang, "Choosing fresh air "(in Chinese), Letter to Hong Kong People, July 23, 2006, http://www.ceo.gov.hk/chi/letter/23-07-2006.htm; last accessed: March 1, 2008.

22 George Ritzer and Todd Stillman, "The postmodern ballpark as a leisure setting: enchantment and simulated De-McDonaldization," *Leisure Sciences* 23 (2001): 99–113.

demolition of Star Ferry has forced the Chief Executive to address the importance of collective memory. "The growing interest in what we call collective memory," he said in his "Letter to Hong Kong," "has sparked something of an awakening in our community" which "enables Hong Kong to join in what is fast becoming a global momentum to preserve universal memories for the sake of the world's future generations."[23] Admitting that it is necessary to strike a balance between development and conservation, Tsang tried to prove his serious intention of addressing the public's call for heritage conservation by reforming the Culture and Heritage Commission to incorporate different voices from different walks of life. Without a radical reconsideration of the neo-liberal logic of the so-called "Asia's world city," the turn to collective memory cannot but be rational at the core: a way to absorb the *vox populi*. In this sense, bulldozers did not target only at Star Ferry and Queen's Pier, they are everywhere flattening the world according to the operational logic of a neoliberal city. What de-McDonaldization offers is simply a reenchantment whereby the magical allure of the collective memory is simulated to increase the public's appeal in a rationalized setting.

What Donaldization Is Not: For the People

The Donaldization of Hong Kong society has brought as many problems as solutions. Critics argue that modernity is in fact singular: the global winning of capitalism (such as Fredric Jameson's *A Singular Modernity*). This is particularly true to Hong Kong, a place famous for its "compensatory logic," i.e. "because the people in Hong Kong are lacking in something essential – political power – that they have to turn their energy elsewhere, economics."[24] This "logic" is inherently built

23 Donald Tsang, "Choosing fresh air."

24 Rey Chow, *Ethics after Idealism: Theory, Culture, Ethnicity, Reading* (Bloomington: Indiana University Press, 1998), 171.

in what Tsang claims to be "Hong Kong-ness." The neo-liberal "big market, small government" is perhaps one of the most frequently heard slogans in Hong Kong. Small but strong: a small government that has been insisting to occupy the very expensive Tamar site with spectacular view of the Victoria Harbor. When it comes to social welfares, they are redefined as wastes of resources with an eye to efficiency. In a speech delivered in a conference on how to strengthen Hong Kong families, the Chief Executive sounded the alarm of the aging of Hong Kong population, admitting that more and more families need government's assistance. But at the same time he also stressed that assistance should not be put on a par with resources allocation; the point is how to use existing resources to tackle the problem.[25] It is apparent here that the "big market, small government" is mistaken to be the only operational logic of a global city, and that social welfare provided to the minorities are seen as wasting resources.[26] But when it comes to government headquarter, despite repeated criticisms Donald Tsang defended government plans to build its grand new headquarters on the Tamar site – 4.2 hectare site on the shores of Victoria Harbor in the Admiralty district. At last thanks to Donald Tsang's political maneuvering the government got enough ballots in the Legislative Council to start the Tamar project rolling. Behind the Tamar site project is a desire for landmark,

25 "Chief Executive's speech on how to strengthen Hong Kong families" (in Chinese), *Government Information Centre of Hong Kong Special Administrative Region*, September 5, 2006, http://www.info.gov.hk/gia/general/200609/05/P200609050086.htm; last accessed on March 1, 2008.

26 In fact, Hong Kong is famous for its "positive non-intervention." In September 2006, Donald Tsang declared the end of "positive non-intervention," a policy previously hailed as a pillar of Hong Kong's economic success. This invited criticisms not only by lawmakers but also the Nobel laureate Milton Friedman. In his "Hong Kong wrong" published shortly before he passed away, Milton Friedman argues the ending of positive non- intervention would make Hong Kong move into China's direction; Milton Friedman, "Hong Kong wrong," *The Wall Street Journal* (October 2006). The difference between "positive non-intervention" and "big market, small government" might not be significant to a leftist, but in Hong Kong it is a very sensitive matter. As this paper does not focus on economic policy, I have no intention of going into the debate in details.

which is related to the branding of Hong Kong. It has been mentioned above the Hong Kong government places heavy emphasis on building a brand of its own, and landmark is arguably an efficient means to highlight the brand of Hong Kong. The now abandoned controversial design of canopy covering almost the whole of West Kowloon Cultural District is another landmark project of the government. This is not the right place to stir up another round of debates on West Kowloon or the Tamar Site. My intention here rests with bringing forth the operational logic of a global city and its relation to Donaldization.

In the name of efficiency the Chief Executive pledged to downsize the civil service establishment to about 160,000 posts by the end of March 2007, which is a common strategy of a global enterprise. The means to achieve such a reduction are infamously controversial in the debate of globalization: privatization of public enterprises, outsourcing, and the like. While Thomas Friedman sees them as flatteners of the world that create a new playing field,[27] Castells has sounded the alarm of inequality, polarization, poverty, and misery and the rise of the Fourth World in the global economy, which is aggravated by privatization and outsourcing.[28] The Link REIT can be cited as a typical example of privatization. It is one of the world's largest real estate investment trusts, comprising 180 properties formerly owned by the Hong Kong Housing Authority, a Hong Kong Government agency. Lo Siu Lan, a sixty-seven-year-old public housing tenant, challenged the legitimacy of Link REIT shortly before it was to offer its listing to the public in December 2004, which forced the government to put off its plan. The derailment of Link REIT turned into the biggest joke of the year, and the long legal battle did not end until the Court of Final Appeal ruled that the sale can go forward in July 2005. "It violates the regulations on public property. The Housing Authority is cheating on the judge and the people," said Albert Wai-yip Chan, a democratic legislator who backed Lo from the beginning of the legal battle. "Privatizing the assets is only

27 Thomas Friedman, *The World Is Flat: A Brief History of the Twenty-first Century* (New York: Farrar, Straus and Giroux, 2005).

28 Manuel Castells, *End of Millennium* (Oxford: Blackwell, 1998).

beneficial to the rich and thus widens the rich-poor gap," added Chan, and "the selling of public housing assets doesn't serve the people but rather private business."[29] The case was not simply against selling public housing assets, as democratic legislator Lee Cheuk-yan put it clearly, "it is more about opposition to 'big market, small government'." It is perhaps sheer coincidence that within a month after Donald Tsang formally became the chief executive, the Link Reit case was settled, at least legally. The case that started to stir up discussions during Tung administration underlined, besides Tsang's strong governance, one important point: Tung or Tsang, privatization is the direction to follow in a global city like Hong Kong.

Another aspect of what Donaldization is not is related to strong governance but goes beyond it by including a dimension of Mainland influence. It is rather unfortunate that beside "strong governance," the most widely discussed issue related to Tsang has been favoritism but not "for the people." On one occasion Tsang openly admitted it is necessary to distinguish close and distant relatives, "Some politicians have chosen to be in the opposition and will oppose every policy raised by the government whether or not the policy is reasonable." He went on to add,

> Their sole intention appears to be to shatter the government's popularity and prestige while at the same time satisfying their personal and political will, and while seeking media exposure. They are not concerned as to whether the proposal is rational [...] As such, I don't see how I can persuade them [to support government policies]. No matter how I go about trying to appease them, or be friendly with them, I will fail.[30]

Although Tsang blatantly denied it is a kind of favoritism by saying "[t]his is not a question of my personal preference," he has been widely criticized as alienating the opposition parties. Lawmaker Kwok Ka-ki, among others, criticized Tsang as being responsible for creating new

29 Wendy Leung, "Fighting talk goes on or defiant old campaigner," *The Standard*, July 21, 2005.

30 Michael Ng, "Tsang alienates opposition," *The Standard*, May 19, 2006.

kind of political climate of "side-lining the unfriendly Legco members from the pan-democratic camp," which would create "a 'deadlock' in the legislature that ultimately hurt Hong Kong's citizens."[31] Ma Ngok, a Hong Kong political scientist, claims that strong governance is in fact a kind of consensus politics widely practiced in the days of being a British colony, which he thinks is a reasonably good choice when compared with the unskillful use of force during the Tung administration.[32] Consensus has to be built upon communicative rationality, which stroke a seeming balance in Hong Kong society under the British rule before 1997. During the days of Tung, the balance, should there be any, became horrible, and Tsang was trying to use strong governance to restore that. But he later knew it was a mission impossible. And so he put forward the point that close and distant relatives are different, which looks contradictory to modernitites. Lawmaker Lee Cheuk-yan even charged this as a kind of dictatorship. Looking at this from another angle, it can be said to be another kind of alternative modernities similar to *guanxi* capitalism. Scholars have used the term *guanxi* (personal relationship) to account for "practices in Chinese culture that may serve as the functional substitute for rational law for the purpose of reducing transaction costs and facilitating economic growth." Albert Chen's analysis of *guanxi* (personal relationship) according to Weber's theory can shed light on our discussion here. Albert Chen borrows Weber's point that a "logically formal and rational legal system" is almost a necessary condition for the operation of capitalism as a similarly "rational" economic system,[33] and examines its applicability to China. China's economy has been market-driven since its opening to the world in the last three decades or so, but its legal system is far from "rational" in the sense of Weber, and Albert Chen ponders why it is so. Carol Jones's

31 Jonathan Cheng, "Lawmaker Kwok blasts Government 'arrogance'," *The Standard*, May 29, 2006.

32 Ma Ngok, "Strong governance or consensus politics?" (in Chinese) *Ming Pao*, April 13, 2006.

33 Refer to Max Rheinstein (ed.), *Max Weber on Law in Economy and Society* (Cambridge: Harvard University Press, 1954).

essay on "Capitalism, globalization and Rule of Law: an alternative trajectory of legal change in China" has noted lucidly that

> [...] business practices in China rely on *guanxi* (personal relationships or connections) rather than on law and legal institutions as the basis of security of expectations;[34] China's economy depends on 'the Rule of Relationships *(guanxi)*' rather than the Rule of Law.

In other words, the rule of law as form of modernity has less urgency to develop in China due to the practice of *guanxi* capitalism, which can reduce transaction costs and facilitate economic growth, a kind of alternative but incomplete modernity. Chen concludes his essay by saying that:

> In the course of time, it may well evolve new forms of the market economy and of democracy that are quite different from those in the West. Similarly, the species of legal rationality that ultimately emerges in China may also differ from the kind of Western legal rationality that we are familiar with today.[35]

Ai-hwa Ong has also examined the practices of family businesses and their reliance on *guanxi* (personal and kinship networks) across borders, arguing that *guanxi* is "basically a structure of limits and inequality for the many and of flexibility and mobility for the few."[36] While *guanxi* is about the lack of rational legal system in the Mainland, we need another concept to elaborate the lack of people-base democracy and concern for justice in the age of globalization. Eisenstadt has pinpointed the appropriation of modernity in non-western societies must entail "the continuous selection, reinterpretation, and reformation of these imported ideas."[37] I would argue if strong governance and for the people are being considered at once, Ong's worry might in a way be

34 Carol A. G. Jones, "Capitalism, globalization and rule of law: an alternative trajectory of legal change in China," *Social and Legal Studies* 3 (1994): 195–221.

35 Albert H. Y. Chen, "Rational law, economic development and the case of China," *Social and Legal Studies* 8 (1999): 97–120.

36 Ai-hwa Ong, *Neoliberalism as Exception: Mutations in Citizenship and Sovereignty* (Durham: Duke University Press, 2006), 117

37 Eisenstadt, *Multiple Modernities*, 15.

soothed. Unfortunately, by far, the Donaldization of Hong Kong society tends to place the sole emphasis on using a variety of neo-liberal strategies in order to compete in the global economy, and these strategies of governing, to borrow Ong's words, are "re-engineering political spaces and populations".

Concluding Remarks

Dilip Gaonkar concludes her introduction to *Alternative Modernities* by saying that "everywhere, at every national/cultural site, modernity is not one but many; modernity is not new but old and familiar; modernity is incomplete and necessarily so."[38] While I agree to this, I would also add, as reflected from the above analysis of Donaldization, the important question is that modernity is incomplete for different reasons in different places. Situated between China and the world, Hong Kong modernities are alternative, hybrid and multiple. In this sense Eisenstadt's point is applicable to Hong Kong:

> Not only do multiple modernities continue to emerge – by now going beyond the premises of the nation-state – but within all societies, new questionings and reinterpretations of different dimensions of modernity are emerging.[39]

The Donaldization of Hong Kong society evinces Hong Kong modernities in a different way. It has to be stressed that the alternative modernities of Hong Kong are limited by its famous hot commerce and cool politics character. It is shaped by its role as a neo-liberal global city on the one hand (as Dirlik succinctly points out, "The world of Global Modernity insists on the reconfiguration of relationships of power and culture as they were constituted in a modernity dominated by Euro/

38 Dilip Parameshwar Gaonkar, *Alternative Modernities* (Durham: Duke University Press, 2001), 23.
39 Eisenstadt, *Multiple Modernities*, 24.

America"[40]), and its lack of political autonomy on the other. While Donald Tsang foregrounds efficiency and effectiveness, under its strong governance shell is a hopeless lack of political power, which gives rise to a kind of "mosaic" modernities in Hong Kong. By "mosaic" I am not referring to what Jenny Lau claims in her edited volume *Multiple Modernities* which uses different studies to form "a mosaic of Asian modernities."[41] The "mosaic" here is borrowed from Lau Sai-leung, now a member of the Central Policy Unit, who takes charge of specific studies and research projects. Before becoming a think-tank of Donald Tsang, Lau was a columnist who made acute criticisms of the politics in Hong Kong. In an essay entitled "Mosaic democracy" he uses the mosaic in Japanese AV pornograph (used to block the genital organs) to refer to the political situations of Hong Kong.[42] In Lau Sai-leung's view, without universal suffrage and a government elected by the people, Hong Kong's democracy, the most important parts of Hong Kong politics, seems to be covered by mosaics, and people find it hard to view the political reality masked by the mosaics. If we consider democracy the pillar of a modern society, the modernities in Hong Kong cannot but look "mosaic" in the sense that some appealing parts are being covered up. Michael Hardt and Antonio Negri argue in their *Multitude: War and Democracy in the Age of Empire* that "[t]he creation of the multitude, its innovation in networks, and its decision-making ability in common makes democracy possible for the first time today" and "[w]hen the multitude is finally able to rule itself, democracy becomes possible."[43] This seems less possible, however, in the shadow of Donaldization of Hong Kong society.

40 Arif Dirlik, "Asian studies/transdisciplinarity," *Asia Source* (September 5, 2006); cited from http://www.asiasource.org/asip/dirlik.cfm; last accessed: March 1, 2008.

41 Jenny Kwok-Wah Lau, *Multiple Modernities: Cinemas and Popular Media in Transcultural East Asia* (Philadelphia: Temple University Press, 2003).

42 Lau Sai-leung et al., *One Hundred Days of Reform* (in Chinese) (Hong Kong: Cup, 2005), 32–41.

43 Michael Hardt and Antonio Negri, *Multitude: War and Democracy in the Age of Empire* (London: Penguin, 2004), 340.

Donaldization cannot but be incomplete: on the one hand it has to present a global outlook and on the other it cannot but be local in terms of politics. Arif Dirlik's point can be borrowed to account for the Donaldization of Hong Kong society:

> If we are to speak of alternative or multiple modernities, which presently valorize the persistence of traditions and 'civilizational' legacies, we need to recognize that the very language of alternatives and multiplicity is enabled historically by the presupposition of a common modernity shaped by a globalizing capitalism.[44]

As long as the Mainland wants to keep Hong Kong as a free-wheeling capital of capital, Hong Kong has to remain modern as a global city dominated by neo-liberal operational logic. Strong governance is undoubtedly effective in shaping Hong Kong into a global city, and this is welcomed by Mainland officials and some Hong Kong people. Between "strong governance" and "for the people," however, is a gap too wide to be bridged by neo-liberal logic alone. If we agree to Nilüfer Göle's point that one of the most important characteristics of modernity is simply its potential capacity for continual self-correction,[45] the thing that matters is how to continuously work towards bridging that gap. Whether this is what Donaldization can or cannot do I am not able to tell, but it is clear that the gap will widen if Donaldization is nothing more than McDonaldization.

44 Arif Dirlik, "Global modernity? Modernity in an age of global capitalism," *European Journal of Social Theory* 6 (2003): 275–92.

45 Nilüfer Göle, "Snapshots of Islamic Modernities," in, Shmuel N. Eisenstadt (ed.), *Multiple Modernities* (New Brunswick and London: Transaction, 2002), 91–117.

AMY LEE

Frozen Motion: Nostalgia and Wang Anyi's Shanghai

Oscar Wilde, the Irish playwright, famous for his wit and his daring, once said, "There is only one thing in life worse than being talked about, and that is not being talked about." Although this famous observation from *The Picture of Dorian Gray* (1891) was really about the specific human condition in his novel, many would agree that this observation also describes vividly a mentality in our twenty-first century world of intense consumerism and visual hegemony. To be talked about may represent a special value, an ability to capture attention, the capacity to engage others' time and energy. Advertising may seem the most obvious exploiter of the "being talked about-ness" in carrying out its business, and so is the media, as we can see in the increasingly outrageous magazine covers, newspaper headlines, and the proliferation of user participation in the discussion of "scandalous" events on the internet. In publishing, autobiography – involving the revelation of personal secrets of the rich and famous – assumes an ever-expanding market. Whether authentic or not, these so-called never revealed personal secrets command a lot of attention and readers rush to buy the latest autobiographies of celebrities to consume bits and pieces of their recorded life and memories.

While Foucault claims that Western men and women have been created to be modern "confessing animals," this urge to talk about one's own life can be found in contemporary Chinese societies too. Autobiographical narratives written by Chinese writers have become quite an important presence since the 1980s and have become part of the popular culture. Wei Hui's *Shanghai Baby* (1999) and its translations (2001) seem to bring Chinese daring and desire to reveal to the level of Western culture. Mu Zimei's blog which claims to be a record of her sex life, and her later publication of these entries into paperback[1] also seem to expose a daring not usually perceived as a Chinese quality. Besides the increasing "individual" nature in many of the popular fiction, in the so-called "more serious writing," the individual has also taken up an increasingly important position. Commenting on the development of modern Chinese fiction, Zhou Xinmin[2] notes that Chinese writers' works during the 1950s through to the 1970s do not show an important individual voice/subject, as the individual very often was used as the channel to express the development of history. Into the 1980s, with the Scar literature, the individual becomes more of a focus while still maintaining very much a parallel relationship with history – suffering, thoughts and feelings of the individuals still play an important role in reflecting the general thought of the historical times. But in the 1990s, a new type of fiction seems to prevail – while the historical aspect might still be an important component in the narrative, it has become one of the aspects of the individual life. In the more recent works by Wang Anyi, we can find this new interaction between the collective story and the individual story.

Wang Anyi has been hailed as one of the most important Chinese writers since the 1980s, probably due not only to the variety of narratives she has created, but also her dedication to engage with the complexity of real life in the contemporary Chinese society, as well as her daring to provoke responses to some conventional images of some of the most long-standing icons of the Chinese culture. Her group of Shanghai fictions also earns her the reputation of being the "successor" to the Shanghai School of writing after Ailing Zhang. And it is the intention of this essay to examine two examples from this group of novels featuring Shanghai as an important component, to explore Wang's presentations

1 Her work has been published into two paperbacks. The revealing blog entries causing an outcry was published as *Yi Qing Shu* by a Hong Kong publisher, Cosmos, in 2004; and another collection, titled *Rong Qi*, also came out in 2004 by the same publisher.

2 Xinmin Zhou, "Writing the individual in the historical dimension: The 'Individual' in recent novels by Wang Anyi," *Xiao Shuo Ping Lun* 3 (2003): 40–5.

of Shanghai, as setting, as character, as a prevailing mood, and also as a statement of identity. While Shanghai the city certainly does not suffer from anonymity in the Wildean sense, her appearance in Wang's narratives does not simply repeat its traditional and cultural meanings.

This essay will thus discuss the much acclaimed prize-winning novel *The Everlasting Regret*[3] (1995) and *Reality and Fiction: A Shanghai Story* (1993), both of which carry a heavy Shanghai component, and both a nostalgic rendering of the now by-gone Shanghai. And of course the old Shanghai is ironically what is in vogue now. As described by Dai in the discussion entitled "Imagined Nostalgia":

> Shanghai becomes today's important "immigration" city and yesterday's "Primer Port of the East," "Ten Miles of Foreign Goods," and "Adventurer's Paradise." It becomes the unconscious of contemporary Chinese history – a place in history that must gain its writing through forgetting, that must transform itself into an appropriate and necessary discovery. As a specific historical and existing real space, Shanghai reflects the historical period that includes the beginning of China's belonging to the world. In addition, with its success in the past (or perhaps today or in the future) in setting trends, finding opportunities, and witnessing miracles, Shanghai provides a somewhat infectiously decadent, but alluring, background and setting.[4]

Indeed the attraction of Shanghai, as an object of a narrative, comes from its both traditional and unconventional identity. She has a past of being a highly Westernized city in the same rank as the major metropolitan cities in the world. This "glorious" past of the city of Shanghai is felt to be her rightful past, especially seen side by side with her status today. Shanghai, with a population of more than 13.5 million, is one

3 The original Chinese title of the novel is *Chang Hen Ge*, a borrowing from a Tang poem by famous poet Bai Juyi. The poem tells the sad story of the love affair between the Tang Emperor and his concubine. The Emperor was forced to kill his beloved concubine when his country was on the verge of collapse. The sad poem is thus a long ("chang" in Chinese) song ("ge" in Chinese) of sorrow ("hen" in Chinese). Interestingly, although Wang Anyi's novel is also about a woman who sadly cannot enjoy fulfilled romantic love in her life, the meaning of the story is not quite the same as the Tang poem.

4 Jinhua Dai, "Imagined nostalgia," *Boundary 2* 24, No. 3 (1997), 158.

of the five super cities of the world, and one of ten world's largest seaports. Shanghai today is of course a perfect example of how evident globalization as a universal force is, but compared to other big cities in the world there is an added sense of nostalgia when her past is evoked.

This added sense of nostalgia is most apparent when the image of Shanghai is evoked. Although it is one of the five super cities in the world and is a heavily built and highly packed piece of land, the favorite visual image and probably the most quoted image of Shanghai is the Bund.[5] No tourist visiting Shanghai would leave without taking at least one daytime and one night-time photo of the area, using the western buildings lining the Huangpu River as the background. While the skyscrapers which are a common feature of the city and the Oriental Pearl TV Tower[6] are more modern additions to the landscape of the city and may be more representative of its present status, the Bund with the western buildings remains the signature of this city because of the nostalgia value of that phase of Shanghai history. The overwhelming prevalence of the Bund on postcards representing Shanghai bears witness to the uniquely structured identity of the city.

Yet at the same time when the nostalgic picture of the old glamorous Shanghai is evoked, one sees also the other side of this nostalgia

5 The Bund is an area of Huangpu District in Shanghai. It was the former Shanghai International Settlement. Today the historical colonial-typed buildings still line the Huangpu River, although their functions have changed over the century with the change of Chinese government during the period. These western-style buildings used to house banks and trading houses from numerous overseas countries as well as the consulates of Russia and Britain. At the end of the nineteenth and the beginning of the twentieth century, it was a major financial hub of East Asia, and during the 1940s it housed the major financial institutions in China. With the establishment of the People's Republic of China in 1949, these foreign institutions were moved, but beginning from the 1980s with the Open Door Policy, financial institutions and hotels were reestablished in these buildings.

6 The Oriental Pearl TV Tower was opened on October 1, 1994 (National Day). It was designed to be a landmark of the city and its height signatures its symbolic significance. Being 467.9 meters high, it was the tallest in Asia and the 3rd tallest tower of its kind in the world. In the 1990s, the Oriental Pearl TV Tower was claimed to be one of Shanghai's ten new spectacles.

which reveals a genuine need. Dai also points out the contradiction embodied in the rapid transformation as a country enters modernity:

> On the one hand, the ideology of progress is undergoing the materializing process of identification and verification, which consequently brings the joy and excitement of discovery; on the other hand, even a "homegrown" Chinese is suddenly stripped of hometown, homeland, and home country and abandoned to the beautiful new world. The feeling of family is no longer conveyed by a Hutong (small lane, Mongolian in origin), a courtyard, a street corner, a city, but by the increasing retreat and confinement to the sleeping quarters, which consist of an apartment's entryway and its four walls.[7]

Because of this loss of the sense of "being home," "The emergence of nostalgia answers a cultural need. It attempts to provide not only an imagined haven in the face of a reality of weariness and toil, but also, more importantly, a positive construction."[8] These constructions together "create a culture, a fashion, a cultural, psychological, and consumerist need and wish fulfillment."[9]

This fashion of a constructed image of a "Shanghai culture" has had a history of at least half a century, although the meaning of these images has changed through the decades. The Shanghai of the 1930s through to the 1940s was historically recorded as a highly westernized city, whose westernization did not only stay on the level of commodities, entertainment, style of dress, but penetrated through to the heart of everyday life such as language, education and mentality. But for this "historical" record to be transferred through to the end of the twentieth century and the beginning of the twenty-first century, the "historical document" is not so much the history books as the proliferation of visual products such as postcards, calendars and advertising posters which have become collectors' items today and which reproductions have become popular decorations symbolizing a cultured awareness of a distant but still touchable Shanghai identity.

7 Ibid., 146–7.
8 Ibid., 148.
9 Ibid., 149.

So what we have arrived at so far is an often-repeated nostalgic picture of Shanghai in all her glamour, as a backward glance to a once authentic reality, or as a much needed construction to counteract a present day weary desire for a better origin. Nostalgia has always been considered a sentiment evoked to fight against a dissatisfactory present, no matter to what degree has the nostalgic picture been true to a lived past. As Zhang Xudong suggests in "Shanghai Nostalgia: Postrevolutionary Allegories in Wang Anyi's Literary Production in the 1990s":

> This nostalgia has become a way for Shanghai residents to absorb a socioeconomic shock, culturally, as the tidal wave of commodities and consumption is seen through the misty veil of past images made vivid by an avalanche of old photos, calendars, postcards, cigarette boxes, and commercial ads beautifully reprinted and sold as "classics" *(jingpin)*.[10]

A city, captured in a particular moment, frozen in motion for the perpetuation of a cultural function, is the story of Shanghai. But is there but one kind of nostalgia? And nostalgia is only for one particular purpose?

In an essay comparing Ailing Zhang and Wang Anyi's Shanghai novels, Deng Hanmei remarks that while Ailing Zhang's nostalgia is an expression of her own very individual sentiments toward a beautiful and elegant Shanghai life which she had lived through, "Wang Anyi's nostalgia is not only an expression of sentiments, but also a revelation of the picture of the life of urban dwellers. There is a deep philosophical meaning behind this nostalgia."[11] Interestingly, Ailing Zhang's nostalgia is that of a native Shanghai woman's own remembrance and yearning for a past which she has touched with her own finger tips; Wang Anyi, born in Nanjing, constructs her nostalgia second hand through her contact with films, novels, and stories told to her by her elders. Her nostalgia is twice removed from the origin, an attempt to recapture a past which has been variously recaptured by other individual minds.

10 Xudong Zhang, "Shanghai nostalgia: postrevolutionary allegories in Wang Anyi's literary production in the 1990s," *Positions* 8, No. 2 (Fall, 2000): 355.

11 Hanmei Deng, "The nostalgic theme in Shanghai novels of Zhang Ailing and Wang Anyi," *Journal of Nantong Teachers College (Social Sciences Edition)* 20, No. 4 (November 2004): 82.

Perhaps this is why Wang Anyi's Shanghai novels are so persistent and so meticulously written. Being twice removed from the object of desire, extra effort is needed to render the picture alive. Instead of merely repeating the much loved images of Shanghai on the postcards and the calendars, Wang creates her Shanghai through clusters of daily life activities. Wang herself says in an interview:

> I am a novelist, not a historian, and not a sociologist either. I don't want to write about major historical events in novels. The artistic form of the novel should be representing the daily life.[12]

History is day in day out, drips and drops of changes in life.[13]

As suggested by the title of Li Xin's essay, the core of Shanghai in Wang's novels is the "perseverance of daily life." Ordinary people preparing their daily meals, doing their everyday washing, haggling in shops, gossiping, and going to bed at night dreaming of a favorite movie star … indeed these daily motions of the most ordinary people are the basic building blocks of Wang's Shanghai scenarios. In the following, *The Everlasting Regret* and *Reality and Fiction: The Shanghai Story* will be examined to discuss how the frozen motions of these ordinary beings and events work as Wang Anyi's special Shanghai nostalgia.

Of her novels published so far, the prize winning *The Everlasting Regret* is probably the most well-known.[14] Very briefly, *The Everlasting Regret* tells the story of Wang Qiyao, a sixteen-year-old Shanghai girl at the beginning of the story (1946). She is one of the thousands of common Shanghai girls in the city, and her unusual life begins when she participates in the Miss Shanghai Beauty Pageant and comes third. Immediately she becomes the mistress of a nationalist officer, and moves into the elegant but isolated Alice Mansion which keeps other lonely

12 Quoted in Xin Li, "The core of Shanghai: perseverance of daily life: an understanding of the theme of Wang Anyi's Shanghai fictions," *Journal of Shandong Normal University (Humanities and Social Sciences)* 49, No. 1 (2004): 50.

13 Ibid.

14 The popularity of the novel may also be due to the film made from the novel in 2005, directed by Hong Kong director Stanley Kwan, and starring prominent Hong Kong and Mainland Chinese actors and actresses.

hearts and bodies. Her man dies in an accident and she moves back to Ping-An li near her own family, living a self-sufficient and lonely life through the politically turbulent 1950s and 1960s. She has a daughter, the result of an unfulfilled affair, but the two do not get along with each other. After the Cultural Revolution, into the 1980s, Wang is already a woman in her fifties, but the economically richer China yearns for the past glamour. Wang Qiyao the ex-miss-Shanghai becomes an icon of fashion again and enjoys the younger generation's companionship. Here among the younger generation, she thinks she finds the last chance for a romance, which turns out to be an illusion, and dies the victim of robbery in her own house.

Although the duration of the fictional space is also the duration of the character Wang Qiyao's life (1946 to 1986), and her experiences, thoughts and feelings are given detailed description, the novel does not impress one as the story of Wang Qiyao, an individual. Rather, the focus is on Shanghai, which Wang the writer considers a stage where women are displayed to their best advantage. In fact, the very first section of the first chapter of the novel is a meticulous description of nongtang, a special feature of the Shanghai city. It is then followed by a section on rumors,[15] the out house ("guige"), pigeons, before Wang Qiyao is finally introduced in section five. And how is she introduced? "Wang Qiyao is a typical daughter of the Shanghai Nongtang."[16] Instead of the nongtang (the place) being an element to define the human character, it is more like the human character here is a feature of the place nongtang. For four full pages, "Wang Qiyao" is being described as a component in various disguises of the nongtang. Finally, we have "Shanghai's nongtang always has a girlie quality, the name of this quality is Wang Qiyao."[17] At this stage, it is quite clear that the subject of the novel is not Wang Qiyao as an individual human being,

15 This can be read as a tribute to another successful Shanghai writer, Ailing Zhang, who wrote a novel with exactly the same title, Liu Yan (meaning rumors, or literally, "floating words").

16 Wang, *Ballad of Eternal Remorse* (Hong Kong: Cosmos, 2004), 34.

17 Ibid., 37.

but more Wang Qiyao as a replacement of the quality of Shanghai. In fact, Wang herself says, "I am writing directly the story of the city, but this woman is the shadow of this city."[18]

The nongtang is such an important symbolic feature of the Shanghai identity that Wang published a picture book called *Wang Anyi's Shanghai* (2004). It contains a collection of photos which represent the Shanghai in Wang's eyes, and each picture is accompanied by a short personal anecdote, either a personal experience, or a reflective observation, and in many cases, old stories of Shanghai told by longtime residents. Some of these stories and experiences find their way into the writer's short story collections – as if the copious words Wang has produced over the years about Shanghai are not enough to render her identity and pictures are finally to be mobilized to do the job. In this picture book, nongtang has a primary presence, especially its physical appearance and how its structure gives rise to the unique "girlie quality" alluded to in the novel. A nongtang is an enclosed area where a number of families live and share an open community space. But a feeling of exclusiveness is ironically shattered by the presence of many of these nongtangs filling the residential area of the city, and moreover by the fact that servants working in different nongtangs form an intricate network of communication which is not visible but enormously effective. This seemingly confined area, with its overwhelmingly quick and efficient communication via gossip, is to Wang a most representative feature of the identity of Shanghai – the visual feature of the nongtang is the true embodiment of the invisible human network uniquely operating in Shanghai, and giving her her unique character.

Throughout the novel, we see Shanghai through Wang Qiyao's life. We see the ordinariness of her pre-Miss-Shanghai life, the elegance of her new role as the mistress of an important politician, the numerous daily-life practices, objects and food she spends time to take care of during the turbulent eras of modern China, and the revival of life in the post-Cultural Revolution era. At this moment of the 1950s, we see

18 Qichao Xu, "Artistic innovation in Ballad of Eternal Remorse – Wang Qiyao," *Xinan minzu daxue xuebao (renmin sheke ban)* 12 (2004): 87–8.

that Wang Qiyao has moved back to Ping-An Li, which is introduced by the narrator as, "In the Shanghai city there are at least one hundred Ping-An Li-s."[19] In this ordinary neighborhood, ordinary people such as Wang Qiyao gather and spend their days like this:

> They put the iron pan on the stove to fry the sun-dried water melon seeds, mixed with a few pieces of large gingko. The bitter fragrance of gingko has a penetrating power, which distinguishes itself from the numerous known and unknown smells, bearing with it a feeling of raising the awareness of the world. This they don't care. […] They talk about the glutinous sweetness of fried chestnuts, the fragrance of melon seeds, and quickly the bitterness of gingko. They also speak of the fine smoothness of small glutinous rice dumplings, the maturity of Amazake, and the delicate eggs in the Amazake soup.[20]

That is just one of the numerous scenes of ordinary citizens such as Wang Qiyao and her neighbor living their lives in the difficult 1950s. Wang, like many other, is already a self-dependent woman who needs to work to support herself:

> Wang Qiyao studied in a nursing school for 3 months, and got a license for giving vaccination. She hangs a placard outside Ping-An Li to advertise her service. This kind of advertising placard can be seen once in every three nongtangs, indicating the livelihood of different Wang Qiyaos.[21]

Once again Wang Qiyao is collective rather than an individual. Just like Pang-An Li, of which there are at least one hundred in Shanghai, Wang is also one of the many similar individuals found in that city. Seen in this way, the novel which spans forty years of Wang's life is actually a visual rendition of Shanghai life over the forty plus years.

Near the end of the story, at the moment of her death, we have this description:

> She then understands, that the woman on the bed is herself, death by murder. And then the lights go off, darkness descends. Another two or three hours, the

19 Wang, *Ballad of Eternal Remorse*, 61.
20 Ibid., 198.
21 Ibid., 162.

> pigeons will start their journey. When they shoot up into the sky from their nests, their agile movement leaves a shadow on the curtain of her room. The pot of Oleander on the opposite side blooms, beginning another natural round of vegetation's life and death.[22]

There are two things to note in this ending. Firstly, the last moment of her life is not the last moment of the novel. Instead, this event of her ceasing to exist is just another action in the display. Secondly, this last moment brings the novel and the action full circle back to the beginning of the novel, when the sixteen-year-old Wang visits a studio and sees a movie in the making. What she sees is exactly the scene of her own end – a woman lying dead in her own bed. Although the story of *The Everlasting Regret* goes on for four hundred pages, the beginning and the end of Wang Qiyao is the same fixated image, while decades of actions in between come to nothing. It is as if the entire novel has given us but one frozen picture of Shanghai, and this Shanghai is a woman. Wang herself says:

> Wang Qiyao's image is my impression of Shanghai. In my eyes, Shanghai is a woman's image. She is a legend born in modern shanghai, she changes from a small fishing village into "the Paris in the East", where it is dark she is murky, where it is bright she is brilliant to close your eyes. She is a wonderful woman.[23]

While *The Everlasting Regret* may be seen as a story of a city disguised as a story of a woman, *Reality and Fiction* (1995) is quite frankly a contradiction. Not only because "reality" and "fiction" are two supposedly opposite contents, the subtitle *"A Shanghai Story"* is even more confusing because the narrative starts with an autobiographical note. The book was published as an individual novel in 1993, but it was included as part two of the double volume titled *Fuxi yu muxi de shenhua*.[24] Part one of that volume was later published as *Sadness at the Pacific*, in which she describes her trip to Singapore, and tries to map her contemporary experience onto a possibly similar experience by her father about five

22 Ibid., 398.
23 Xu, "Artistic innovation in Ballad of Eternal Remorse – Wang Qiyao," 88.
24 *Patrilineal and Matrilineal Myths* (Hangzhou: Zhejiang Wenyi Chubanshe, 1994).

decades ago. While it is interesting to see the same texts going through different guises and assuming different faces, it is also important to reflect on the significance of this narrative to the author. If, as Wang Anyi says, that Shanghai is a perfect stage for the women characters in her novels, it does seem to be an equally perfect stage for Wang the author to display herself. The stage of Shanghai is particularly significant to the author because her bond to the city is post-natal.

Wang Anyi was born in Nanjing in 1954, to parents who were active pro-revolutionaries. During the Cultural Revolution she was sent to Anhui the rural areas to learn from the farmers; after the Cultural Revolution, she went to settle in Shanghai. In the preface of *Reality and Fiction*, she supplies the detail of the first time she entered Shanghai, which was her mother's hometown. Before she was one year old, her parents took her on a train and together they returned to their hometown – with Wang the baby sitting on the baby toilet throughout the journey because she was sick. Wang the narrator thus became part of an "immigrant family" ("wai-lai-hu"), although her mother was a Shanghai native, and spoke better Shanghainese than Putonghua. This immigrant status in what is literally her "mother's land" is, I think, the reason why the writing of Shanghai features so significantly in her works, especially the autobiographical pieces. These autobiographical pieces of Shanghai frozen in writing may be seen as her attempts to reconstruct the umbilical cord between herself and Shanghai that her mother had severed by escaping from the city.

Beginning with her childhood, the novel is written such that the odd chapters represent the narrator's own memory and experiences, the supposed "reality" of the narrator's life; while the even chapters carry information she obtains from research, the "fiction" bit. From the first chapter, readers are unsettled as to the narrator's relationship to Shanghai, the setting of the story. The first chapter begins: "In the city of Shanghai, we are just like an immigrant family. Mother insists in speaking Putonghua, although she knows Shanghainese, and speaks it more accurately than Putonghua."[25] Instead of providing an orienta-

25 Wang, *Reality and Fiction: A Shanghai Story* (Taipei: Mai Tian, 1996), 39.

tion for the readers, the starting point of this autobiographical novel is a rootlessness, an inability in the main character to feel that she belongs. Right from the beginning, the narrator has never stopped talking about her frustration over her inability to communicate and merge with the locals of Shanghai.

So why is this self-narrative a story of Shanghai when she cannot even feel a sense of belonging? One may even ask what right does she have to tell the story? This situation reminds us of numerous other intergenerational stories told by the daughter, or granddaughter, about the mother and the grandmother who are brought up in a completely different cultural environment. Different from many of the intergenerational writing, however, even her source of information, her mother, only has hazy memory about her own family in Shanghai. The narrator admits:

> Frankly, my mother has only very vague memory of the above mentioned people, she only has some impression about some props, for example, her great-uncle's monkey, 7-katty uncle's pipe. I then start with these props to organize the relationships of our family.[26]

And indeed the narrator goes on to re-create possible scenarios of what could have happened around the vaguely remembered people, and "props."

This daughter's reconstruction of the family history thus feels very different from those maternal linear stories told by some other writers. Here the mother seems to have no intention to hand down a treasured family story to the daughter, for the purpose of preserving something in the "mother" culture. Rather it is the daughter who is desperately trying to hold on to whatever small token she has to use as clues to reconstruct, and probably failing that, to create the story of her family. It is her mother's escape from Shanghai when she was eighteen years old that gives rise to the situation of this narrative. The narrator exclaims, "Shanghai had thus been dumped by my mother."[27] The re-

26 Ibid., 63.
27 Ibid., 69.

construction of her family story is an attempt to rescue what her mother has thrown away, especially after "my mother's family's final dissolution."[28] Wang, the narrator, having no physical root of herself in the city, creates an emotional root through the creation of a narrative for something which is irreparably lost. And Shanghai is the stage for displaying this nostalgia for a never-experienced ideal world.

The first and the odd-numbered chapters are a record of the narrator's remembered experience from her childhood and teenage years. These reverse journeys retrieve different actions, but always comes back to her fixated loneliness: her not being allowed to play with children in the neighborhood because they are of a different background, her sense of feeling herself an orphan because her mother does not have a family story to tell her. This sense of loneliness culminates in one particular scene in her self-narrative which I think is representative of the overall feeling and also reason for the construction of this story of Shanghai. For a time she had some friends who were Red Guards. They wore the smart and respected uniform and visited her every day. The young narrator was very proud of having them as frequent visitors and considered their friendship a special one. But she discovered by accident that the friendship she regarded as exclusive was nothing like that at all, and she was just one of the many acquaintances the Red Guards had. She felt depressed, and one day when she walked past a grand old house which her mother had pointed out to her as belonging to her great-aunt, she suffered a sudden attack of loneliness: "I stood in front of the house. I saw that it was already old and ruined. One question suddenly rushed to my heart, and that was: Whose child am I?!"[29] The total loss of orientation was so great that she cried in front of that old house.

The young narrator cries in front of the old house which her mother points out to her as belonging to a member of the family not because the narrator herself remembers anything about the house, or the person. She has literally nothing to do with the house at all, and that is the problem. The house (with many other objects) features as important to

28 Ibid.
29 Ibid., 173.

her because it reminds her of what she "DOES NOT HAVE". Her sense of nostalgia, if it can be called that, is of something she has never experienced before, something with which she does not even have a second hand relationship. This nostalgic relationship with the subject of her writing runs through many of her works, not only in her autobiographical writings, but also in her fictions, the most obvious example is *The Everlasting Regret*, which I have already discussed. Viewed in this way, Wang's love affair with the past, and her love affair with Shanghai are the same: this love of the absent subject makes her write again and again to materialize the absent subject. The act of writing is literally the act of creation, the writer has to write to create herself through a bond with the literary subjects.

And this act of creation is remarkably presented in the even-numbered chapters of *Reality and Fiction*. Chapter two starts with the reason for the search, as we already have guessed, an absence: "No one told us myths about our ancestors. This kind of myth in our family is a serious absence."[30] "Without family myths, we all become orphans, miserable and lonely, one end of our lives hidden in blinding darkness, and the other end hiding in hazy mist."[31] Here what catches my attention is the use of the word "orphan." By saying that "they" (meaning the family) become orphans, of course the narrator does not really mean that they have lost their parents. The image of an orphan, one who does not belong to a place, and needs to find one to attach to, is the fundamental reason for the writing. In the first chapter of the narrative, she also reveals that one of the most important events which happened to her and her family is her discovery of her mother's status as an orphan: "And then, one event which seems to me extremely important happened. This event, no matter whether in terms of our family history, or in terms of our family's social relations, is of fundamental importance."[32] Her mother had been orphaned when quite young. With this discovery, everything seems to fall into place – the inherent lack of

30 Ibid., 71.
31 Ibid., 75.
32 Ibid., 48.

a personal story starts with her orphaned mother, and this has passed on to her the narrator. She has a need to create her story (in reverse), a story so true to her mentality that it has to be filled with details and intricate turnings. By writing Shanghai, she writes herself.

She starts the investigation with her mother's surname, "Ru," which takes her to the seven meanings of the surname, and back to two thousand years of history in China. From then on, it is a literary journey of reading and re-reading, interpretation of mainstream official histories and alternative, half-fictional stories and legends about the bloodline starting with the name "Ru." The beginning of her mother's family, apparently, is nothing grand or glamorous – the first of her ancestors she could trace was a captive by the Western tribes in a battle. This captive, because of his appearance, was named "Mu Gu Lu" which means "bald head," who later escaped by reading the stars, and started his own tribe "Rou Ran" – which was referred to as stupid and humble in mainstream Chinese history books, according to the narrator. Later one of the sons also learned how to read the stars and apply that to the organization of their daily life. And the narrator goes on to tell what happened to each generation, how they defended their own state from the attack of the Chinese from the mainland, and how they established their own country with proper systems, rituals, armies and hierarchies. The narrator traces the life of a few generations of heroes in this period, until the downfall and the absence of any more heroic figures.

When she describes the heroic deeds of her ancestors, the narrator intrudes:

> It is impossible to write a family myth without heroes. With no heroes, how can we descendants build up our sense of pride? I choose She-Lun to be my heroic ancestor, because he is brave and intelligent, he has a big heart and big mind, he pushes the Rou-Ran history to its summit. He died while trying to escape.[33]

It is at this point when readers may feel that the "truth" of this family myth, though the result of an apparently serious research, may be a little less accurate than it looks on paper. While the narrator cites an-

33 Ibid., 98.

cient historical records and quotes verbatim the ancient Chinese writing when she mentions these historical personalities, the declaration concerning her choice of family hero immediately makes us aware of an individual who is willing things to happen in a certain way.

The authority of this individual voice is made even more obvious when at the end of this chapter she announces the disappearance of any traces of her ancestors:

> They had not created any civilization, only left behind an overwhelming sense of life instinct, and I, the descendant, am one of the creations of this instinct.[34]

The narrator can find no material objects, no concrete evidence of the existence and moreover the short-lived glory of her ancestors. But if there is no material evidence left by the supposed ancestors, how did the narrator come to such conclusions about her family? We may or may not be convinced by the content of her writing, but one thing is certain – she has presented to us the words on the page as her family history. When she says, "and I, the descendant, am one of the creations of this instinct," she is declaring the validity of this piece of writing through the fact that she exists and creates.

Here again, the relationship between the text and the narrator is interesting. While the text is supposed to explain the existence of the narrator, the narrator instead explains the text by simply saying SHE is a descendent. There, she is, so the story is. This journey in search of a past ends somewhat like *The Everlasting Regret*. In the epilogue of the narrative, the narrator/author talks about the naming of the novel. "Genesis" has been suggested to her, but she does not want the religious connotation of that proposed title. She says:

> Finally I decided, that I would open my way of creating this world on paper, i.e. the so-called "creation" method to the public, and that is "reality and fiction". It is only with the name that a birth turns into a reality. Now, no one can cancel or reject it. It is such a joyful and encouraging moment![35]

34 Ibid., 99.
35 Ibid., 323.

The end comes full circle back to the beginning: the loneliness, the need to have a root, the significance of freezing the action of the subject on paper. Her self-created history is rather generations of men doing their usual business to survive in a changing society, a playing out of the life instinct which in her comes out as the writing – episode after episode of containment.

Epilogue

The narrator's own story of creation is subtitled "A Shanghai Story." Shanghai is, of course, not just one story. It has been a piece of land once occupied and practically ruled by foreign powers, it has once been (and still is in many ways) the model of elegance and fashion, a city with its unique and traditional alleys (the nongtangs) which house the most ordinary and common citizens who speak the same dialect. Shanghai is a paradox with its mixture of foreign and Chinese features, elegant and basic atmosphere, the elite and ordinary qualities, and it is perhaps the perfect embodiment for the author's story because it is the converging point of so many different and conflicting pictures that it is an impossible existence.

Perhaps Oscar Wilde is right when he says that "no man is rich enough to buy back his past." But this contemporary Chinese woman writer is in need enough to create her own.

EVA K. W. MAN

The Relation of "Self" and "Others" in the Confucian Traditions and Its Implications to Global Feminisms and Public Philosophies

Introduction

Under the calls of global feminism and public philosophy, there is the common project of an utopian form of emancipation. Postmodern discourses, on the other hand, confirm that conceptualizations of difference have constituted the relations of domination, and these are the barriers to gender equality and human liberation as a whole.

If differences are originated from the construction of subjectivity and otherness, this may explain why some feminist theories are read as profoundly transgressive of the binary opposition of Self to Other, as Helen Cixous has suggested.[1] It is said that otherness as difference can be understood only if sameness and difference are seen as placed in an oppositional relation. For example, feminine sexuality is defined only in terms of its difference from masculine sexuality, when femininity and masculinity underwrite the hierarchical structuring of binary oppositional thought. This structure, it is argued, is fundamentally oppositional yet simultaneously involves a certain interdependence, only that the benefits of which are not equally distributed.[2] As Cixous said:

1 Lucy Sargisson, *Contemporary Feminist Utopianism* (London: Routledge, 1996) 169.
2 Ibid., 170–5.

> Already I knew all about the "reality" that supports History's progress: everything throughout the centuries depends upon the distinction between the Selfsame, the ownself … and that which limits it: … (that) is the "other."[3]

The further elaboration that woman is constructed as Man's other by this binary system of hierarchical opposition, leads to the facts that women internalize the hierarchy and the related values. They have a different knowledge of reality and they find themselves inferior and contemptible, while individual women are also alienated from other women, like in forms of those beauty discourses.[4]

Thus, it is claimed that in moving to the direction of global feminisms and public philosophies, one should create (or renew) other forms of self/other relation, those not being grounded in arrogant perception, or fear of difference, or other manifestations of cultural superiority. Homogenizing views of the self/other relation are thus suggested, which should promote unifying conception, and which key terms are affinity, empathy and intimacy.[5] An example is Iris Marion Young's suggestion. She has promoted the ideal of community in the form of communitarian ideal, and made the claims that it privileges unity over difference, immediacy over mediation, and sympathy over the recognization of the limits of one's understanding of others from their own points of view. The ideal seeks to "realize the unity of the general will and individual subjectivity," and aims to "end the conflicts and violence of human interaction."[6]

One will agree that these suggestions will provoke a paradigm shift, implying that the development of a sense of self is dependent on one's relations with others, and that each person's moral integrity is integrally related to the maintenance of the moral integrity of

3 Helen Cixous and Catherine Clement, *The Newly Born Woman*, trans. by Betsy Wing (Manchester: Manchester University Press, 1986) 70–1.

4 Sargisson, 181–2.

5 Ibid., 183.

6 Iris M. Young, "The ideal of community and the politics of difference," in Linda J. Nicholson (ed.) *Feminism/Postmodernism* (London: Routledge, 1990) 300–8.

others. In brief, self interest cannot be separated from the interests of others.[7] Moreover, this self relation to others is non-possessive and at the same time heterogeneous, i.e. the two subjects involved are same and different, known and strange, inclusion and exclusion. It is not threatened by the existence of an otherness, but is rather delighting to discover, to respect, to favor, and to cherish, as suggested by Helen Cixous and Catherine Clement.[8]

Elizabeth Grosz, with her reference to Levinas, has outlined four characteristics of the "other." She suggests that:[9]

1) The other is a form of exteriority, separate from and unpredicted by the subject.
2) The other is the sites of excess, an unabsorbable, indigestible residue.
3) The other is an infinite category.
4) The other is an activity, in relation to which the subject is passively positioned.

But when it means that the other summons up the subject, I was reminded of the Confucian's notions of the self and other, and the inspirations they would grant to global feminism and public philosophies on most feminists' agendas. One of these inspirations comes from Ann Ferguson's "Aspect Theory," saying:[10]

> If the self is seen as having many aspects, then it cannot be determined universally which are prior, most fundamental, or more or less authentic. Rather, aspects of our selves are developed by participating in social practices that insist on certain skills and values.

7 Caroline Whitbeck, "A different reality: feminist ontology," in Ann Garry and Marilyn Pearsall (eds), *Women, Knowledge, and Reality: Explorations in Feminist Philosophy* (London: Unwin Hyman, 1989) 66 and 67.

8 Cixous and Clement, 78.

9 Elizabeth Grosz, *Sexual Subversion: Three French Feminists* (London: Allen & Unwin) 142.

10 Ann Ferguson, "A feminist theory of the self," in Garry and Pearsall, 101–2.

In this sense, let us firstly revisit the ideals of global feminisms and public philosophies, to go along the line.

Global Feminism

Global Feminism refers to movements of women's rights on a global scale. It corresponds to "Transnational Feminism," "World Feminism," and "International Feminism." In brief, it aims to dismantle the currently predominant structures of global patriarchy.[11] One will then expect conflicts and disagreements, as communities of various situations are involved. There is the claim that even the notion of the so called "community," which assumes collectivities as homogeneous, will overlook the conflicting interests among their members. Moreover, as critics point out, in the conditions of modernity, the effects of globalization and space / time compressions have resulted in immense changes to the lives of vast numbers of people and local "communities" in highly unpredicted ways. One can immediately think of the migration and dislocation problems.[12]

There are suggestions that in order to conceptualize feminisms globally, we need to think about them organizationally, tactically as well as ideologically.[13] In doing so, we need to view feminisms and internationalism from their national, comparative, and international locations, and to engage in more comparative work before expanding our horizons to feminisms practiced at a global level. The main objective of global femi-

11 See "Global feminism," in *Wikipedia* at http://en.wikipedia.org/wiki/Global_Feminism.

12 Tijen Uguris, "Gender, ethicity and 'the community': locations with multiple identities" in Ali, Suki, Coate, Kelly, and Goro Wangui wa (eds), *Global Feminist Politics: Identities in a Changing World* (London: Taylor & Francis Ltd. 2000) 49.

13 See Leila J. Rupp, "Feminisms and internationalism: a view from the centre." *Gender & History*, Vol. 10 Issue 3 (Oxford, UK: Blackwell Publishing, November, 1998) 535–9.

nism is thus to conceptualize feminisms broadly enough to encompass a vast array of local variations displaying multiple identities, which should build on the basic common denominators of women's relationship. These commonalities include reproductive capabilities, susceptibility to gendered violence, lack of political power, fighting domestic violence, promoting women's rights, establishing rape as a war crime etc. But I agree that there should be more to envisage on the agenda.[14]

Those who work towards global feminisms raise the question of communication, especially when gender experts act as communicators and lobby with public policy-makers for the planning and monitoring the effects of policy on gender.[15] The so called "gender mainstreaming" process goes some ways to achieving a feminist consensus on common issues mentioned above, and the need to mainstream these debates in the global discussion. As the agreement is that there should be more mutual understandings, and justice is the intersection of all, referring to a shared base on which policy-making can be re-built.[16] Thus an international forum or global civil society becomes more important, and one should initiate critical self-transformation.[17]

The problem of discussion thus comes from this: How could one begin to deal meaningfully with a subject matter that runs across the global, and all of the cultural, economic, historical, and political diversity within it? If the intersection is justice, where should we start? Here I think of public philosophy and its foundational thinking, which should echo with the introduction of this paper: the notions of the "private" and "public," "self" and "others."

14 Ibid., 538.

15 Gemma Carney, "Communicating or just talking? Gender mainstreaming and the communication of global feminism," *Women & Language*. Urbana, Ill: Vol. 26, Issue 1 (Spring, 2003) 52–60.

16 Ibid., 59.

17 Ibid., 1.

Public Philosophy and the Dualism of the "Private" and "Public," "Self" and "Other"

An agreement is that public philosophy cannot be narrowly defined as political philosophy, as it concerns all the issues emerging in the public fields, be it political, economic, social, moral, religious, or communicational. It represents a certain kind of normative belief, which has become social doctrines.

It is said that when Walter Lippmann (1889–1974) first referred public philosophy to the doctrine of natural law and western civilization, its primary goal is to certify that there are higher general rules above mankind, or universal moral norms that humans should follow. Examples are some common and unchangeable values and beliefs, such as familial piety, faith to friends, ban on killing the innocent etc. These are the basis of public philosophies; they promote to pursue public welfare than private interests.[18] The tone under is different from feminist scholars like Iris Young, who are skeptical of proclamations of universality and hold the communitarian position that emphasize more on local traditions and beliefs.

Though Walter Lippman's notion of public philosophy is concerned with public rationality, public good and public justice, from the area of a state to the space of a community, the Western discourses on public philosophy have implied a dichotomous thinking. This thinking leads to the existence of separations and barriers between dualistic concepts such as self and other, private and public, home and work place, physical and social, minority and majority, male and female. The basic dichotomy that affects gender relations is the distinction between the self and other, and thus the private and public.[19]

18 Jiang Yi-Huah, "Confucianism and East Asian public philosophy: an analysis of harmonize but not conform," *National Taiwan University Journal* (2007). http://homepage.ntu.edu.tw/~jiang/PDF/D11.pdf, 2.

19 Tijen Uguris, "Gender, ethicity and 'the community': locations with multiple identities" in Ali, Suki, Coate, Kelly, and Goro Wangui wa (eds), *Global Feminist Politics: Identities in a Changing World* (London: Taylor & Francis Ltd. 2000) 58.

The traditional patriarchal and heterosexist power structures are maintained through the constant use of this kind of dichotomy, and the effects are to construct, control, discipline, confine, exclude and suppress gender and sexual differences.[20] The private, an analogy to the female gender, is traditionally associated with the domestic, the embodied, the natural, the family, property, personal life, intimacy, passion and immanence; where as the public is the domain of the disembodied, the abstract, the cultural, rationality, critical public discourse, citizenship, the market place, the state, heroism and transcendence.[21] Other references involve also the dichotomous thinking of a boundary between an inside and an outside, like a lot of women are now still leading an enclosed, indoor and private life, which is another way of constructing an imagined opposing position between the "self" and "other."[22]

The concern with women in this aspect is that philosophy has rich resources to offer to policy makers who think well about distributive justice in connection with women's inequality, and the opportunities or "capabilities," which are connected directly to the quality of life.[23] But at the same time, philosophers should also clarify issues of cultural relativism.[24] Moreover, public philosophy should search for "the origins of social order," common good and beliefs, and international order.[25] Four principles of public philosophy were discussed:

1) public philosophy is based upon the common truth;
2) public philosophy should be committed to the common good;

20 N. Duncan, "Renegotiating gender and sexuality in public and private spaces," in N. Duncan (ed.), *Body spaces: Destablishing Geographies of Gender and Sexuality* (London: Routledge, 1996) 128.

21 Ibid., 128.

22 Uguris, 61.

23 Martha C. Nussbaum, "Public philosophy and international feminism," *Ethics* 108 (Chicago: University of Chicago, July, 1998) 769–70.

24 Ibid., 792.

25 See Jinghao Zhou, *Remaking China's Public Philosophy for the Twenty-first Century* (USA: Praeger Publishers, 2003) 15.

3) but the public good is not necessarily in agreement with public opinion; and
4) public philosophy is compatible with the theological truths reflected in our public myths.

It was suggested that these commonly shared beliefs should reflect an experience of a higher order of goods.[26]

Thus, comparison was made between public philosophy and civil religion. It was concluded that:

1) both public philosophy and civil religion are important to articulate and support political order;
2) civil religion provides an ultimate meaning for public myths and ultimately articulates a political order; and
3) public philosophy accommodates both political theory and civil religion.[27]

It was agreed that civil religion has the full characteristics of recognized leadership, participation, statements of beliefs and moral codes.[28]

In this sense, is Confucianism a form of civil religion? In what ways does it promote public philosophy? And what are the inspirations it may provide to the thoughts of global feminism?

The Confucian's Reading of the "Self" and "Other"

Due to the limited space for elaboration in this paper, I choose to focus on one representative Confucian text for the above discussion. It is well known that the Confucian classical text, *The Great Learning (Da Xue)*,

26 See ibid., 15.
27 Ibid., 16.
28 Richard John Neuhaus, "From civil religion to public philosophy," in Leroy S. Rouner (ed.), *Civil Religion and Political Theology* (Fort Worth, Texas: Dryden Press, 1998) 3.

which is originally the forty-second chapter of the *Book of Rites* in the Han Dynasty, sums up the Confucian educational, moral, and political programs. It is summarized as the so-called three principles and eight items. The three principles of the first paragraph signals the ideal of inward sageness (nei-sheng), which starts from self, and is then extended to others, and refers to the ideal of outward kingliness (wai-wang). For the three principles, the text says:[29]

> The Way of the great learning consists in manifesting illustrious virtue, loving the people, and abiding (Zhi), in the highest good.

Manifesting one's illustrious virtue is said to be a subjective requirement of an educated person, loving the people is a behavioral requirement, and abiding in the highest good is a combined requirement of an educated person's psychological and behavioral attitudes. These three principles follow the main direction of ancient Confucian education, which is self-cultivation.

One should note that Song scholars Cheng Yi and Zhu Xi present another reading of the second principle: instead of reading it as "loving the people" (qin min), they have suggested "renewing the people" (xin min).[30] Zhu Xi comments that the term "renewing" means abolition of bad old orientations, and that it strongly implies public reformation and cultivation.[31]

The third paragraph introduces the eight items needed to realize Confucian ideal; first within the individual, then extending to society, and finally to the world. The text says:

> The ancients who wished to manifest their illustrious virtue to the world would first bring order to the states. Those who wished to regulate their states would first regulate their families. Those who wished to regulate their families would first cultivate their personal lives. Those who wished to cultivate their personal

29 The text's English translation refers to Chan Wing-tsit, trans. and comp. *A Source Book in Chinese Philosophy* (Princeton, N.J.: Princeton University Press, 1963) 86–87.

30 Ibid., 86.

31 Ibid., 87.

lives would first rectify their minds. Those who wished to rectify their minds would first make their wills sincere. Those who wish their wills sincere would first extend their knowledge. The extension of knowledge [zhi-zhi] consists in the investigation of things [ge-wu]. When things are investigated, knowledge is extended; when knowledge is extended, the will becomes sincere, when the will is sincere, the mind is rectified; when the mind is rectified, personal life is cultivated; when personal life is cultivated, the family will be regulated; when the family is regulated, the state will be in order; and when the state is in order, there will be peace throughout the world.

The relation of the self and other starts with *self-cultivation*. Here comes the reading that the rectification of one's mind ends with virtues, this is the ideal of "sagehood" (or sageness), where harmonization of the inner feelings and the feelings of others is achieved, and also the achievement of constant freedom and creativity of oneself.

Zhu Xi's commentary on this notion is that:[32]

[...] there are few men in the world who know what is bad in those whom they love and what is good in those whom they dislike [...] This is what is meant by saying that if the personal is not cultivated, one cannot regulate his family.

An elaboration is that a person's family will be regulated in the sense that each person in the family will behave correctly according to his or her position.[33] Here comes another syllogistic extension: one who has

32 One should note that Zhu Xi's commentaries on this Confucian Classics were made the official texts in the civil service examination from 1313, despite the fact that the debates around his reading have a significant impact on the decanonization of *The Great Learning*. One impact comes from the famous philosophical battle between Zhu Xi and Lu Xiang Shan (1139–1193), a contemporary influential Confucian in Song, on the notion of *"ge-wu."* According to analysis reviewed by neo-Confucian scholars, Zhu Xi favors an intellectual or discursive approach to the term *ge-wu*, or investigation of things, whereas Lu champions an intuitive approach. Zhu is said to stress the need to examine knowledge as much as possible, both moral and non-moral, while Lu's intuitive approach emphasizes moral effort and introspection, relegating the pursuit of discursive knowledge to secondary importance. See Chan, 90.

33 Cheng Chung-ying, *New Dimensions of Confucian and Neo-Confucian Philosophy* (New York: State University of New York Press, 1991) 229.

achieved the regulation of one's family can be a virtuous example for people outside that family. This practice of virtue for a man in the position of ruling a state is *governing the state well.*[34] Then if a state is well governed, there is no doubt that the whole world could be ordered following the state's example.

It is claimed that the important reasons why Confucianism has such a profound influence on Chinese society and culture are that the central principles of Confucianism preserve traditional Chinese family values, which conformed to the core of the patriarchal religion. The discourses reinforce the social relationship between ruled and ruler, son and father, wife and husband, female and male, and brothers and sisters, and the law of social life was in conformity with the law of nature, in this sense, it is a civil religion. The union of moral behaviors, nature, and society is accorded to the law of the universe in the traditional belief, and the first important responsibility for a self is to follow the heavenly law and promote social and universal harmony. It is thus said that filial piety is then not merely an ethical value, but has a "religion resonance."[35]

The fervor of harmony thus overrules the models of dichotomy and binary opposition, and the act of harmony is originated from the moral mind. This is illustrated more clearly in another Confucian text, *The Doctrine of the Means*, which said:[36]

> Feelings like joy, anger, sorrow and happiness are in the state of the mean when they are kept in heart; they are in the state of harmony when expressed in agreement with moral standards. The mean is the fundament of everything under heaven, and harmony is the universal way. With the mean and harmony, the universe remains orderly, and everything thereon grows and flourishes.

Yet the moral reason involved will still tell right from wrong, as the Confucius' saying:[37]

34 Cheng, 227–30.
35 See Zhou, 45.
36 See Chan Wing Tsit's translation.
37 See ibid. on *Analects*, Book XIII.

> The gentleman (or the noble-minded) harmonizes but not conforms. The small man conforms but not harmonizes.

The difference discussed here is that if we merely hide our judgment and subordinate our opinions to others in order to seek superficial agreement and peace, it is just to "conform," but not "harmonize." To harmonize proposes loyalty and forgiveness and to be good with others, it is the ideal inter-personal relationship that Confucianism pursues. These are also the moral practices motivated by the basic moral principle of *Ren*, which in turn should act in accordance to rites *(li)*.

Confucius has explicated the universality of *Ren* as "not to impose on others what you yourself do not desire," and "do not do to others what you do not want others do to you." The discourses demonstrate living interpretations and the richness of the meaning of harmony *(he)*. Harmony makes sense because there are different opinions or standpoints, and it can be established only when the differences can co-exist.[38]

The notion of harmony elaborated in *The Doctrine of the Mean* demonstrates the non-differentiated meaning of all the dualistic terms, including the "self' and "other," "private" and "public." It said:[39]

> All things exist together but never harm each other; all ways function together but never go against each other. Virtues of minor significance are like rivers nourishing things in their valleys; virtues of major significance are basics nourishing all things. That describes the mightiness of the Heaven.

The Great Learning echoes with the above Confucian texts, saying that one should be tame and docile to preserve the collective or public values. To be a *jun-zi* is the precondition to regulate the family and to serve the country, and the key to becoming a *jun-zi* is self-cultivation through moral knowledge. Though one may recall the social discourses of a woman *jun-zi*, which refer to the three obediences (to obey her

38 Jiang Yi-Huah, "Confucianism and East Asian public philosophy: an analysis of harmonize but not conform," http://homepage.ntu.edu.tw/~jiang/PDF/D11.pdf, 16.

39 See Chan's translation.

father before marriage, her husband during married life, and her sons in widowhood) and the four virtues (fidelity, physical charm, propriety in speech, and efficiency in needlework); it is said that all have worked together to maintain Chinese social order and political structure and the related "harmony."[40]

Concluding Remark

When one can read the multiplicity of public philosophy and the core of an East Asian public philosophy in the classical Confucian texts, the characters may refer to the priority of some issues in concern. Discussions of the "coexistence of loyalty and piety," "distinction between righteousness and interests," and "from inner Sageness to outward Kingliness" etc. are over the Western discussions of "division between the public and the private," "theory and practice," "means and ends," and "the universal and the particular."[41]

But this applies also to the special problems involved and the related critical reading. While it does not accord with the binary oppositions and dichotomous thoughts, it has shifted to a hierarchical authoritarianism which penetrates the five human relations, and its gender elitism has never endowed women with equal status. While the Confucian model is not horizontally oppositional or in dichotomous form, and is emphasizing on the correlation and interdependence of the self and others, its public myths and political order are still vertically hierarchical and authoritarian. It is these places where "creative transformation" and reinterpretations of the traditional philosophical resources are raised, and so are its necessary integrations with other contemporary and heterogeneous discourses.

40 Zhou, 54–5.
41 Jiang, 6.

The Confucian notion of "harmonizes but not conforms" suggests to global feminisms the respect and the praise of the co-existence of different standpoints, capacities and the needs of women in a vast variety of situations. The Confucian saying of "the Sageness within and the Kingliness without" sends its moral message to public philosophies, which are always concerned with the foundation and the practices of justice.

The following Confucius' quotation from the *Analects* may act as a summary of Confucian's reading of the "Self" and "Other":[42]

> Now the man of perfect virtue, wishing to be established himself, seeks also to establish others; wishing to be enlarged himself, he seeks also to enlarge others.
>
> To be able to judge of others by what is nigh in ourselves; [...] this may be called the art of virtue.

42 See Chan's translation of *Analects*, chapter 28.

Part 3

Hybridity

Robbie B. H. Goh

Cyberasian: Science, Hybridity, Modernity, and the Asian Body

Cyborg Romances and Ideologies of Atonement

Cyborgs are protean, endlessly productive technological and cultural entities. Haraway[1] famously argues that "we are all cyborgs," made into "theorized and fabricated hybrids of machine and organism" by a multiplicity of technologies and structures from late twentieth century society onwards. If we include the notion of "techniques of thought" – the "direct operational skills" but also the "means of appropriate thinking" corresponding to, interacting with, and in some ways shaped and caused by, technology[2] – then it certainly is true that we (at least, those fortunate enough to inhabit societal positions where educational opportunities, infrastructure, technology and information are reasonably accessible) live cyborg lives, systematically interfacing with a variety of technologies. The term "cyborg," in the positive and inclusive manner that theorists like Haraway use it, can indeed be too inclusive to allow for finer analyses: there is after all a big difference of degree (even if precise quantifications are not possible) between, say, the digital literati of the Bay Area networking socially and commercially in cyberspace or surgeons and patients interacting through fMRIs, on the one hand, and primary schoolchildren in an Indian public school reading mass-

1 Donna Haraway, "A cyborg manifesto: science, technology and socialist-feminism in the late twentieth century" in David Bell and Barbara M. Kennedy (eds), *The Cybercultures Reader* (London: Routledge, 2000), 291–324; 292.

2 Andrew Murphie and John Potts, *Culture and Technology* (Houndmills: Palgrave MacMillan, 2003), 5.

produced primers or people in Singapore gathered around a coffeeshop television set to watch the soccer World Cup on cable TV on the other. It might be helpful to return to the etymology of the cyborg ("cybernetic organism") via "cybernetic" (from the Greek "kubernetes," meaning helmsman or controller); the point about the cyborg is that there is a surrender or resignation of control to the machine, which precedes the organic and steers it through life (and past death). Classic cyborgs of the 1960s, such as Marvel Comics' Iron Man character, are as much revivified and sustained by their cybernetic systems (Tony Stark has a life-threatening heart ailment which the iron suit keeps at bay) as enhanced by them. In contrast, a number of everyday technologies, while no doubt changing aspects of lived experience, are not life-controlling and indispensable in quite the same way.

This admittedly rough but fundamental distinction immediately suggests the geopolitical differentiations which must apply to cyborg possibilities. Not only is the reach, extent and transformative power of technology much greater in "the West" (i.e. North America and Western Europe, but in particular America), but its discursive, semiotic and thus also the ideological affirmation of cyborg identities is also clear, whereas it is at best ambivalent in many Asian nations. The overwhelming expression of cyborg culture is American: from speculative fiction of the mid-twentieth century onwards, to cyborg-like advertising images, to the mass appeal of Hollywood cinema, to the lifestyle and popular image of the cyber-geek, to the culture of Silicon Valley and the dotcom billionaire, to the theorizing of sociological and media conditions of American networked urbanism. The best-known images and texts from American popular culture – from classic cyborgs like the Six Million Dollar Man, Iron Man, Dr Octopus and Wolverine, to more recent ones in *Blade Runner*, the *Terminator* series, *Robocop*, William Gibson's "Sprawl" novels, individual characters like Data and the Borg in *Star Trek: The Next Generation*, the cyber cowboys and cowgirls in the novels of Neal Stephenson and Melissa Scott, the dot.com wizards in films like *Anti-Trust* as well as those living in Seattle and Silicon Valley, the code-bending Messianic figure of Neo in the *Matrix* series – have a near-global dissemination and recognition, helping to reinforce the Americanization of the cyborg. Such cyborg figures have certainly been read in ambivalent terms in the existing scholarship, as indicating the "undecidable nature of the opposition between human [*sic*] and its technological double," revealing the human origins and projections of a "post-industrial techno-dystopian" society.[3] For Jameson,[4] cyborg texts such as cyberpunk evince a "high-tech paranoia" with "labyrinthine conspiracies of autonomous but deadly interlocking and competing information agencies" that indicates a culture grappling to "think the impossible totality of the contemporary world system."

Yet even these negative aspects ultimately serve to endorse a new techno-human future in which cyborg couplings heroically overcome older limitations and evils while nevertheless affirming select essential human qualities: in Haraway's classic formulation,[5] the cyborg indicates "the power to survive," to form new "connections," the commitment to "partiality, irony, intimacy, and perversity." Movie cyborgs, despite the inevitable dystopian elements in their portrayal and that of the human society and agents that cause them, all embody redeeming qualities that serve to assure audiences, if not of the essentially human nature of cyborg futures, then at least their accommodation and familiarization as something not too far removed from human experience. Over the course of the *Terminator* series, the protagonist cyborg (played by Arnold Schwarzenegger) goes from villain to hero, "humanized" as a figure capable of at least a modicum of affection, loyalty, and growth, so that his destruction is actually seen as a loss akin to human death.[6] The androids in *Blade Runner* display a loyalty and protectiveness to-

3 Forest Pyle, "Making cyborgs, making humans: of terminators and Blade Runners" in David Bell and Barbara M. Kennedy (eds), *The Cybercultures Reader* (London: Routledge, 2000), 124–48; 130; David Tomas, "The technophilic body: on technicity in William Gibson's cyborg culture" in David Bell and Barbara M. Kennedy (eds), *The Cybercultures Reader* (London: Routledge, 2000), 175–89; 175.

4 Fredric Jameson, *Postmodernism: Or, the Cultural Logic of Late Capitalism* (Durham: Duke University Press, 1995), 38.

5 Haraway, "Cyborg manifesto," 292–3, 311.

6 Pyle, "Making Cyborgs," 134.

ward each other, a sentimentality and clinging to life, that considerably closes the gap between machine and human, even if it does not totally override the chilling displays of their strength and ruthlessness. Heroic cyborg figures like the Terminator, Robocop, Neo in the *Matrix*, Picard-turned-Borg in *Star Trek: First Contact*, the android Bishop in *Aliens* – all savior figures who master their treacherously dehumanizing machine aspects, exerting free will in order to save mankind or a group of humans – are the apogee of our cyborg futures, reinstating human society's values into the otherwise frightening prospect of our technological trajectory.

The bulk of these cyborg narratives thus serve the main ideological purpose of undermining "the value of the distinction between real and simulation, between authentic and prosthetic," and between human and technological.[7] They might thus be read as narrative atonements for the mistakes of human society, including that of its urban-industrial-technological dystopian aspect, figuring (at least some of) the begotten children of science as truly human and thus confirming the redemptive moral project of technological development. Nightmares of machines gone wild – willful self-conscious supercomputers, unthinking killer robots, doomsday devices, mutant monsters – are not entirely exorcised, but at least palliated and controlled by narratives in which "the human" ultimately masters, controls, and asserts its defining characteristics over the coldness of the machine. In the process, ritual deaths (often in graphically violent, disfiguring and dismembering ways enabled by the fact that this is pseudo-flesh) serve as a symbolic atonement of technology's evils, and clear the moral and psychical space for cyborg evolutions to come. The narratological and symbolic unfolding of this space is most clearly seen in the archetype of the Terminator (and for that matter, Robocop): in its inhumanly stripped, metallic, vicious aspect (the Terminator in its assassination mode, Robocop programmed to abet the criminal party, both of them under-

7 Alison Landsberg, "Prosthetic memory: Total Recall and Blade Runner" in Mike Featherstone and Roger Burrows (eds), *Cyberspace/Cyberbodies/Cyberpunk: Cultures of Technological Embodiment* (London: Sage, 1995), 175–90; 186.

going ritualistic shedding of their human skins/semblances, in various stages of exposed disassembly), this figure foregrounds humanity's worst fears of the "rise of the machines" to assume life-and-death control (kubernetes) over mankind. However, the cathartic nature of this narrative becomes evident in that once this worst fear is exposed and confronted, it finally turns out to be less fearsome: the Terminator over the course of the sequels turns into an increasingly humanized, moral, protective and even paternalistic and humorous (in its use of the ironic phrase "hasta la vista, baby") figure, while Officer Murphy is able to use his human memory, will and moral instinct to override the machine's illegitimate directives. Both figures thus typify the cyborg as a combination of awesome machinery and human morality, to both cathartic and redemptive (one is tempted to say Messianic) effect.

At its most extreme form, this ideology leads to a utopianism of the machine, in which technology is fully embraced as the means to "beat the meat" and overcome a body seen as limited and flawed – a kind of "euphoria and a sense of the limitless extension of being" which Sobchack[8] reminds us is a "false consciousness." By and large, however, these texts serve the less euphoric but no less ideological purpose of both displaying and exorcising technology's threats, and in so doing propagate a cyborg culture affirming human-technological interfaces as the basis of further social change. This is arguably part of the process of what Fukuyama[9] calls the "Great Reconstruction" (after the "Great Disruption" caused by late capitalism and post-Fordist production from the 1960s onwards), in which "contemporary technological societies [...] replenish" social capital, in this case by propagating images of a moral and affective cyborg future. In Fukuyama's analysis, culture in its various aspects and institutions plays a crucial role in this act of remoralization; how appropriate that media technologies play a central

8 Vivian Sobchack, "Beating the meat/surviving the text, or how to get out of this century alive" in Mike Featherstone and Roger Burrows (eds), *Cyberspace/Cyberbodies/Cyberpunk: Cultures of Technological Embodiment* (London: Sage, 1995), 205–14; 211.

9 Francis Fukuyama, *The Great Disruption: Human Nature and the Reconstitution of Social Order* (New York: Free Press, 1999), 249.

role in the raising of a cyborg consciousness in American society, and of a peripheral awareness in other societies to which such texts are exported (but only fitfully, decontextualized and disassembled from their intertextual and social systems).

Asian Modernity, Traditionalism, Unequal Developments

One of the main problems raised by this cyborg romance, and indeed one of the besetting problems of technological-social change, is the unevenness of its development in and impact on different nations, regions, and people groups. This is particularly true of many of the underdeveloped countries in Asia, where even basic infrastructural amenities (health services, electricity, schooling) are unavailable in many regions, and where things like Internet access, digital media, MRI and other such forms of medical diagnosis and treatment, are unimaginable luxuries. D'Costa[10] analyzes a "self-reinforcing, cumulative" pattern of inequality in many Asian countries, arising out of "social inequality" within a country, the "mobility of technical professional talent in an IT-driven, integrating world economy," and the perpetuating effects these have on a country or class. Information Communications Technologies (ICTs), as one of the fastest-growing and most socially-transformative forms of technology, are a good yardstick with which to measure the unequal technological developments in Asia: while "some parts of Asia, notably Singapore, Hong Kong, Taiwan, and South Korea, have rates of per capita Internet access at leading international levels," and spend close to double-digit percentages of their GDP on ICT, in many other countries like Myanmar, Pakistan, Thailand, the Philippines, India and

10 Anthony P. D'Costa, "Catching up and falling behind: inequality, IT, and the Asian Diaspora" in K.C. Ho, Randolph Kluver, and Kenneth C.C. Yang (eds), *Asia.com: Asia Encounters the Internet* (London: RoutledgeCurzon, 2003), 44–66; 44–5.

China, spending on ICT is much more modest, and rates of Internet access are well behind the more developed countries in Asia.[11]

In the mid-1990s, North America and Western Europe together had more than a ninety percent share of the global Internet domains, while the whole of Asia only had a 3.5 percent share[12] – while this is changing, this statistic shows something of the huge gulf that has yet to be overcome. As with ICT spending and access rates and rates of control of Internet domains, so with other shares in global flows of communication, information dissemination and general familiarity with its technology and modes of production, particularly in the global language medium of English. It is not just the dominant language of the Internet which poses an obstacle to Asian access: as scholars have observed,[13] in many Asian nations cyberspace is to varying degrees and through varying measures a "realm of surveillance," "control" and "restriction." While cyberspace monitoring and surveillance is also carried out by other governments outside of Asia, it is certainly true that fairly tight and intrusive regulatory measures obtain in many countries in Asia (together with more "symbolic" but still cautionary and significant measures in other Asian countries) which serve to impose political

11 K.C. Ho et al., "Asia encounters the Internet" in K.C. Ho, Randolph Kluver, and Kenneth C.C. Yang (eds), *Asia.com: Asia Encounters the Internet* (London: RoutledgeCurzon, 2003), 1–20; 2–3. Tim Beal, "The state of Internet use in Asia" in K.C. Ho, Randolph Kluver, and Kenneth C.C. Yang (eds), *Asia.com: Asia Encounters the Internet* (London: RoutledgeCurzon, 2003), 23–43; 23–5.

12 Peng Hwa Ang and Chee Meng Loh, "Internet development in Asia." Paper presented at the INet96 Conference, June 25–28, 1996, http://www.isoc.org/inet96proceedings/h1/h1_1.htm (accessed: August 28, 2003).

13 Toby E. Huff, "The Internet and the public sphere: technologies of control or liberation and development" *Hybridity* 1, No. 1 (2000) 2–16; Manuel Castells, *The Internet Galaxy: Reflections on the Internet, Business, and Society* (New York: Oxford University Press, 2001); Madanmohan Rao, "Introduction: emerging markets, pockets of excellence: Asia in the global Internet economy," in M. Rao (ed.), *The Asia-Pacific Internet Handbook Episode IV: Emerging Powerhouses* (Delhi: Tata McGraw-Hill, 2002); and David Lyon, "Cyberspace, surveillance, and social control: the hidden face of the Internet in Asia" in K.C. Ho, Randolph Kluver, and Kenneth C.C. Yang (eds), *Asia.com: Asia Encounters the Internet* (London: Routledge Curzon, 2003), 67–82.

and psychological limits on netizenship and its attendant societal transformation.

In addition to the "hardware" of ICT spending and access to and familiarity with the technology, there is another sense in which many Asian countries are at a perpetual disadvantage to North America and Western Europe, and this is in terms of the (as it were) "software" of mental attitudes, received and produced images, and ideological positioning, relating to technology in society. The fact of the persistently white male cultural bias in the majority of cyberspace has been registered.[14] Chatrooms in which white men pass off as exoticized Asian women (or Asian gay boys), and in which any non-approved displays of ethnicity are greeted with hostility; games and websites which rehearse "constructed Western utopias" and a rewriting of history along the lines of the "American dream,"[15] impose on non-white participants the pervasive worldview, expectations, attitudes and assumptions of white western men. Those Asians who are well-off enough to afford Internet access, and who live in countries where the infrastructure makes this possible, thus tend to become interpellated into a white- and North American-oriented techno-ideology.

This is not only confined to the Internet and cyberspace, but is part of a larger cultural problem in which science and technology have an inescapably "Western" affiliation, and stand either as god-like and unassailably and inaccessibly other (to the majority of common people living in Asian countries), or else as a very mixed blessing which confers advantage and boon but at the cost of ideological complicity and profound identity dislocations (to the relatively small sector of Asian elites). The point about science's involvement with historical colonialism, racism and phallogocentrism has been made repeatedly, most of-

14 Lisa Nakamura, "Race in/for cyberspace: identity tourism and racial passing on the Internet," in David Bell and Barbara M. Kennedy (eds), *The Cybercultures Reader* (London: Routledge, 2000), 712–20; Ziauddin Sardar, "ALT. CIVILIZATIONS.FAQ: Cyberspace as the darker side of the West," in David Bell and Barbara M. Kennedy (eds), *The Cybercultures Reader* (London: Routledge, 2000), 732–52.

15 Sardar, "ALT.CIVILISATIONS.FAQ," 735.

ten in the context of postcolonial studies focusing on India – "a space assembled by modern institutions, infrastructures, knowledges, and practices" at the juncture of Victorian imperialism and European industrial modernization.[16] In the first place, the various discourses of science (including scientific reports, the letters and autobiographical writings of award-winning scientists, science fiction, and general discourses dependent on or applying science) are characterized by an "alliance with technology and its positivism," a "rationality and empiricism," which tend to marginalize natives (and especially native women) as lacking these qualities.[17] As such, "the alliance between science and the colonial enterprise makes journeys of exploration into voyages for conquest, with the Alien/Native/Other (people and land) becoming both the object of knowledge and the subject of the empire."[18] In the second place, for interpellated Indian elites – "subaltern" Anglophone Indians who were trained to play a role in the British colonial machinery, and after independence constituted the socio-political and economic leading class – science and technology continued to play the role of defining *homo rationalis* and thus also the civilized and modernized nation-state. As Prakash[19] puts it:

> To be a nation was to be endowed with science, which had become the touchstone of rationality. The representation of a people meant claiming that the nation possessed a body of universal thought for the rational organization of society. The idea of India as a nation, then, meant not a negation of the colonial configuration of the territory and its people but their reinscription under the authority of science [...] Thus, the Indian nation-state that came into being in 1947 was deeply connected to science's work as a metaphor, to its functioning beyond the boundaries of the laboratory as a grammar of modern power.

16 Gyan Prakash, *Another Reason: Science and the Imagination of Modern India* (Princeton: Princeton University Press, 1999).

17 Suchitra Mathur, "Caught between the goddess and the cyborg: third-world women and the politics of science in three works of Indian science fiction," *Journal of Commonwealth Literature* 39, No. 3 (2004): 119–38; 120–4.

18 Mathur, "Caught between the goddess and the cyborg," 126.

19 Prakash, *Another Reason*, 7.

This "colonization of the mind" then created a profound ambivalence in the educated class, an uneasy mix of pride in traditionalism (primarily Hinduism and the notion of a "Hindu science") and an uncritical adoption of technology.[20] The result is the present-day "hybridizations" of "Indian modernity" pulled between "the polarities of secular and religious, community and state, science and culture."[21]

A similar hybridization runs through much of the Asian modernities evinced in other nations, which were likewise subjected to European colonization in the age of industrial transfiguration (or, in some cases, by-passed colonization and stepped into the condition of "traumatic catch-up" with triumphal Western modernization), and came to independence around the mid-twentieth century with nationalizing agendas that nevertheless had the insidious programming of systematic scientism written into them. Although the specific parameters of nationalization obviously differ in each case (and there is much that is generally in common: religious and artistic traditionalism, the need to harmonize racial-cultural plurality inherited or exacerbated by colonialism, the negotiation of splits between an educated elite and the lower classes), the overarching imperative of infrastructural modernization (with the corresponding and often uncritical acceptance of "outside" technology) looms large over these nations. Familiar cultural contours then develop: the separation of a technological elite (urban, educated, cosmopolitan) from the masses who are figured as pre-technological and other; the uneasy fit of the more successful strata of that elite segment within the framework of the nation; the constant dialogical engagement between traditionalist and scientific discourses; and reactionary movements in either the traditional or the technological sides of the equation.

20 Ibid., 64, 67.
21 Ibid., 237.

The Anxiety of the Human, Asian Modernities and Hybrid Discourses

These contours have the effect of discomforting the national identity – of constantly propagating the scientific definition and desiderata of the Asian nation, while simultaneously inhibiting its development into a nation at ease with its scientific identity. Here the absence of cyborg narratives – or the presence of problematized, fissured cyberAsians – in contrast to the North American cyborg romance, is both a causal reinforcement of that discomforting identity, as well as its manifestation. The dearth of significant cyborg-type heroic figures across the expanse of Asian nations and their diasporas is altogether telling. The few cyborg heroes in Asian popular culture – among whose number we might include India's comic-book cyborg policeman Inspector Steel and TV futuristic hero Captain Vyom, China's enhanced vigilante Black Mask and quasi-cyborg Inframan, and the Philippine's vigilante-detective Biotrog[22] – are either decidedly sub-cyborg (relying mostly on martial arts-like skills with unexplained pyrotechnic powers) or else boldly copied from Western figures (Wolverine and Robocop being the most archetypal). Martial arts thus become a way of Asianizing the cyborg, implanting a distinctive feature with which to distinguish it from Western technology-driven cyborg heroes; it is also a reflection of the resurgence of traditionalism as the flag-bearer for Asian identity, and inevitably a confusion or dilution of the technological aspects of the cyborg. Inframan (like the Japanese figure of Ultraman from which it is derived) relies on a number of recognized martial arts moves such as flying kicks, and even his chief weapons the "thunderball fists" and "infra-blades," and his ability to change size,[23] are strongly reminiscent of the more arcanely powerful kung fu techniques, and not too far from their classical origins in the Monkey God of *Journey to the West.*

22 International Catalogue, "International catalogue of superheroes," http://internationalhero.co.uk (accessed: August 30, 2006).

23 Unofficial Inframan Home Page, "Inframan's weapons," http://www.stomptokyo.com/scott/infra-man/weapons.html (accessed: August 30, 2006).

Indian futuristic hero Captain Vyom, in addition to his high-tech weaponry, triumphs because of his "yogic powers of concentration" which he acquired in "a monastery in Ladakh" (International Catalogue). We might see the strong elements of martial arts and mysticism in these Asian cyborg-like figures as a nationalist impulse to resist the merely Western brand of technological empowerment, to reclaim technology under the sign of traditionalism.

The one conspicuous Asian exception is Japan, with its relatively long tradition of popular culture cyborg entities (Ultraman, Doraemon, the various characters in the *Ghost in the Shell* series, probably being the most well-known instances), although this eagerness to embrace machine identities has led to its own problems as well. In Gibson's cyberpunk imagining, Japan is synonymous with "black medicine [...] implants, nerve-splicing, and microbionics," a "magnet for the Sprawl's techno-criminal subcultures."[24] The most striking Japanese character in Gibson's novel is the machine-like enhanced ninja Hideo, and Japanese society is largely reduced to dehumanizing zaibatsus, "hives with cybernetic memories, vast single organisms, their DNA coded in silicon."[25] Gibson's account of Japanese technology – as essentially dehumanized, soulless, enigmatic – is both a dig at Japan's technological successes, as well as a caricature of this success as the supplanting of the human by the technological. In the influential *Ghost in the Shell*, a nightmarish dystopian world of AIs, cyborg fighters and robot tanks, humanity is extremely vulnerable and vestigial, the main character ("The Major") almost entirely cybernetic with the most tenuous and ephemeral human essence (the "ghost" within her machine "shell," which gives her her personality and character). The villain is a super AI known as the "Puppeteer" which can "infiltrate and influence the very minds of his victims," thus rendering the human entirely at the mercy of the cybernetic.[26] Thus Japanese popular culture's willingness to perform

24 William Gibson, *Neuromancer* (New York: Ace Books, 1984).

25 Gibson, *Neuromancer*, 203.

26 Ghost in the Shell, "Official site," http://www.manga.com/ghost/ (accessed: August 30, 2006).

the replacement of the human by the machine plays into a Western ideological thrust in which Asian technology, where successful and competitive, is somehow excessive and threatening in its threatened obliteration of the human. This image of Japanese technology is constantly reinforced by media coverage of Japanese research, as with the recent example of Professor Hiroshi Ishiguro's android created in his own image, with his own voice and movements.[27] Japanese cultural production and the image of its Research and Development thus strangely receive and corroborate Western representations of Japan as technologically advanced but inhuman and soulless, robotic rather than cyborg.

In the majority of Asian literary and cinematic productions, technology takes a back seat to various forms of nostalgic and traditionalist production: historical romances (Korea's immensely popular TV series *Jewel in the Palace*, or China's various tributes to historical epochs in movies like *Once Upon a Time in China* and *Hero*), pre-modern life (the Hindi movie *Lagaan*, subtitled "Once Upon a Time in India," Zhang Yimou's *The Road Home*), martial arts films and novels, comic or idyllic genres (the slapstick comedy of Stephen Chow, the lighthearted entertainment of Bollywood musicals). Present-day society, when it is depicted, tends to be seen through the lenses of crime docudramas, exaggerated crime thrillers, or that hugely popular Asian genre, the supernatural story. It would seem that Asian modernity still carries the heavy burden of negotiating national identities, in which various discourses and moments of "national" interest require serious or comic revisioning, while present-day society requires interrogation from dystopian and gothic angles; in all this, there is hardly the ideological and cultural space for the cyborg romance as a vision of technological identities and future social possibilities.

The Asian cyborg is thus produced at the confluence of a number of ideological "decoded flows," in Deleuze and Guattari's terms,[28] which move across societal and national boundaries in order to establish the

27 *Straits Times*, "And my android makes two," July 22, 2006, 22.

28 Giles Deleuze and Felix Guattari, *Anti-Oedipus: Capitalism and Schizophrenia* (London: Athlone, 1984), 33.

extensive system of the "capitalist machine." Together with the inevitable imitation of a Western form of technological identity comes the contrary discourse of a nationalist assertion of a traditionalism which is justified as somehow strengthening technology, even as it rewrites and reclaims it in Asian nationalist terms. At the same time, a distinctly North American form of humanistic and redemptive – almost Messianic – cyborg romance functions together with a discourse which writes other technological sites (non-white, non-American, non-masculinized) as either servile and vestigial, or (in rare cases) excessive and dehumanized. Within these ideologically-loaded cultural and narrative flows, Western capitalism's technological identity is generally confirmed as progressive and beneficial, a world-transforming force ostensibly for democracy and liberalization[29] whose potential downsides (uneven development and distribution, habits of alienation and fragmentation, loss of privacy) will more or less be automatically corrected in time, or else will be redeemed by heroic and moral (cyborg) technocrats. In contrast, a variety of "other" societies are constantly seen as less technologically advanced, less open and democratic, and altogether uncomfortable with cyborg identities, with the result of a profound malfunction of the technology, and correspondingly a loss of human moral values and goals altogether.

With the malfunction and loss of the human in "other" societies, in this imagining, comes meltdown and the large-scale threat to human life, not just in that country but around the world. While early cultural representations of technology in American culture had their share of such "meltdown" narratives – the 1979 film *The China Syndrome*, and crisis media reporting on the Three-Mile Island episode of the same year, or Stephen King's 1978 novel *The Stand*, about a killer virus which is released from a US military facility, are the classic instances – in recent years such narratives have turned to locations and episodes in non-Western countries which threaten global safety through their deficient technology and corrupt and inefficient societies. The

29 Sardar, "ALT.CIVILISATIONS.FAQ," 739–40.

1986 Chernobyl disaster obviously had much to do with such discourses, but the proliferation of texts involving life-threatening biological, nuclear, ecological or other disasters originating from threatening "other" countries – from as early as 1913 with Sax Rohmer's Fu Manchu with his various mystical and chemical plots to overthrow the West, to episodes of the 1990s TV series *The X-Files* featuring strange powers and disease infiltrating American society, to various versions of foreign technological threats (North Korean missiles, dirty bomb technology in Pakistan, biological warfare plots by any number of foreign psychopaths) – obviously reaches deeper and further than actual global events.

Clearly September 11 has also played a part in channeling Asian "meltdown" narratives, by depicting technology as a dangerous thing to be left in Asian hands, where it inevitably transforms into terrorist weaponry. International News Agencies constantly play up the horror of the fact that Asians such as Bali bomber Imam Samudra "chatted over the Internet for several months with other Islamic extremists";[30] attention is deflected from the moral judgment of terrorist violence, to the cyber-technological aspect of this Asian episode. Likewise, a *Newsweek* article assessing the impact of technology on human life mentions non-Western, non-developed countries in the explicit context of terrorist violence:

> Some of technology's most frightening political and religious uses in the developing world are well known. The 9/11 hijackers trained using flight-simulation games on home computers. Kashmiri separatists use Internet chat rooms to enlist Indian Muslims to their cause. In Lebanon, Hizbullah has even produced a videogame of its own, called SpecialForce, to romanticize its fight against Israel.[31]

While the point is ostensibly about violence and extremism, such discourses shade into a characterization of the "unstable" technological state of the "developing world," in contrast to its supposedly stable and moral functioning in the developed West: Dickey goes on to observe

30 "Jailed Bali bomber plotted attack online," *Straits Times*, August 25, 2006, 8.

31 Christopher Dickey, "Tuning in, turning on," *Newsweek* (August 25 – September 1, 2003): 48.

that "the social and political impact of the developing world's spontaneously adapted technologies is utterly unpredictable," and that "there's no good way to monitor them, and no way to stop them."[32]

The threatening "meltdown" of non-Western technology is ultimately a problem, not of technology itself (since this would bring an inevitable indictment of the nations and societies which develop and market those technologies), but must lie in some lack or deficiency in the social, political and human dimensions of non-Western peoples. Thus the image of the unstable third-world dictator with nuclear ambitions: Iran's President Mahmoud Ahmadinejad, called "defiant" by Americans who see his country's nuclear efforts as "inadequate" in its reassurances and safeguards,[33] is only the most recent in a series of nuclear dictators identified in the history of American foreign policy, including the rulers of North Korea, China and Russia. Non-Western scientists who possess nuclear technology are also defined in dehumanized terms, such as Pakistan's Abdul Qadeer Khan, who turned Pakistan into a nuclear power (and is thus regarded as a national hero) but also leaked nuclear technology to Libya, North Korea and Iran, and is now reified as a "disgraced scientist" living under house arrest and "fighting cancer."[34] If fanaticism, moral or mental instability, or political "defiance" are the threatening characteristics of non-Western nuclear nations which thus threaten a "meltdown" crisis that (it is suggested) is not a danger in the West, then "disgrace," abjection and disease (particularly the radioactively-suggestive cancer) are the perceived moral consequences of this dehumanized technological usage. Non-Western technologies, lacking the moral compass and ultimately human agendas of Western cyborgs, constitute an "unstable" mix in which the human is obliterated, somehow unable to cope by the overwhelming power of the technological.

32 Ibid.

33 Jonathan Eyal, "What next? Iran deadline expires," *Straits Times* (August 31, 2006): 14.

34 Associated Press, "Disgraced scientist fighting cancer," *Straits Times* (August 25, 2006): 21.

While this kind of Western ideological writing is not altogether surprising, although at times subtle, what is more surprising is the complicity of Asian nations in writing various discourses of national shame and guilt which would seem to confirm their sub-technological, sub-cyborg state. In India, a well-known joke concerns "jugad" technology – a Hindi word meaning makeshift, adaptable, but also entirely rudimentary and ad hoc. The embarrassment at the makeshift arrangement of wiring, machinery, generators and other equipment that is part of the everyday life throughout India, is paradoxically confirmed by the sense of national pride at the practical skill and ingenuity this technical bricolage involves, and how this distinguishes Indian society from the more sophisticated and fault-free, but also imposingly expensive and foreign imports from Europe and America. The writings of the diasporic Anglophone Indian author Amitav Ghosh – in many ways well-positioned to mediate Western political-technological culture with Indian society and life, and who foregrounds issues of science and its effect on native societies, including in his science fiction novel *The Calcutta Chromosome* – reflects this profound anxiety about scientific flows of information, methodology and capital from the West, seeing it as ideologically doubled-edged, threatening the loss of the authentic temper of Indian life and manners.[35]

A similar anxiety about flows of technology from the West is evident in China's push in Research and Development, which has the goal of reducing dependence on that technology and increasing innovations in strategic areas (one of which being computer sciences). The anxiety comes from a keen awareness of being subject to and dependent on Western technological flows, but it also manifests itself as a culture of "shaming" that reveals the ruthlessness of this enterprise. Recently China's Science and Technology Minister Xu Guanhua re-

35 Diane M. Nelson, "A social science fiction of fever, delirium and discovery: *The Calcutta Chromosome*, the colonial laboratory, and the postcolonial new human," *Science Fiction Studies* 30, No. 2 (2003): 246–66; Mathur, "Caught between the goddess and the cyborg: third-world women and the politics of science in three works of Indian science fiction," 2004.

vealed that China would "publicly shame scientists who conduct fraudulent research."[36] The catalyst was the case of Professor Chen Jin of Shanghai Jiaotong University who was found guilty of faking research on a "breakthrough" computer chip, but the episode and the state's reaction also reveal the almost inhuman pressure that Chinese society places on such strategic technological breakthroughs. A similar anxiety was revealed in the case of South Korea's Professor Hwang Woo-Suk of Seoul National University, who became a national darling after announcements of his breakthrough in cloning technology, but just as quickly became reviled and persecuted by all of Korea after it was revealed that this was based on faked results. It is clear that faked research cannot be justified by any kind of political expediency; yet the ubiquitous nature both of the faked "breakthroughs," the pride of the entire Asian nation this occasions and the subsequent national shame and cathartic vindictiveness, show the pressurizing and intensely result-oriented culture that prevails, and the willingness to excise the human face of research and its failures.

Thus, it is that Asian technology gets written as either "inadequate" or excessive, lacking proper performative thresholds or else all too successful in a dehumanizing and threateningly proliferating manner. These Western discourses of the non-Western nation's technological identity are unfortunately reinforced by the latter's varied but related cultural anxieties: that science as a Western import and ideology will also result in the loss of Asian traditional life and values; that technological competition with the West is a desperate struggle that is to be won at all cost; that the Asian nation is shamed by its inability to compete in the same scientific league with Western nations; that breakthrough, when it comes, must be at the expense and replacement of the human rather than in a happy cyborg combination; and related concerns.

36 Associated Press, "China to shame scientists publicly," *Straits Times* (July 6, 2006): 7.

"Hub" Narratives, Global Flows, Global Tribes

In the system of global techno-capital flows, a hierarchical structure thus emerges in which Asian nations – those that have in place the educational and telecommunications infrastructure, educated workforce, and technological drive and ambition – assume the role of second-tier service providers to the technological leadership of the West. Yet this subsidiary positioning is the more insidious for being implicit, concealed under ambitions and discourses of assuming a leading position. Here the ubiquitous discourse of the technology "hub" comes to the fore: the hub in mechanical terms is the central part of the wheel from which the spokes radiate. Applying this mechanical analogy to telecommunications, tourism, and information management, a hub is a place of convergence, a central holding station for various kinds of flows. Asian cities competing for pre-eminence in various industries and services – Tokyo, Singapore, Hong Kong, Shanghai for business, foreign direct investment and financial services; Bangalore, Chennai, Taipei, Sapporo and Fukuoka for ICT; Mumbai, Seoul, Manila and Hong Kong for media and entertainment; Bangkok, Singapore, Kuala Lumpur, Hong Kong, Mumbai and Chennai as travel and tourism gateways for their respective regions, to name just the main cities – all embrace the discourse of the hub in their publicity campaigns and official mission statements.

The case of Singapore may be particularly instructive here. Partly because of its small size and lack of various other resources (large population, workforce and readymade market, large hinterland with agricultural and mineral resources), Singapore has had to capitalize on its strategic location, and apply various strenuous policies, to become a "hub" for all kinds of technologies and industries: from port facilities and services, to financial services, to transportation and tourism, to biotech research, to education, to arts and culture, and several others. Its various and overlapping hub ambitions also depend upon and precipitate certain desired infrastructural and societal transformations, such as the "wired nation," an Anglophone work environment (fostered through the educational system and social regulation such as the "speak good

English" movement), the prominent spatial transformation of certain areas (especially the Marina Bay area with its present and impending landmarks of the Esplanade and the Sands Integrated Resort), and of course the military (through a hefty investment in the most up-to-date weapons technology – S$ 9.7 billion in 2006, the largest single item in the budget – and the institution of compulsory military service). The example of the military probably gives us the most vivid cyborg image, the well-trained human operator yoked to expensive and extensive weapons systems, but the Marina Bay architecture – the bionic or compound eyes of the Esplanade, and the robotic fist of the proposed casino (particularly its five-pronged ArtScience Museum), whatever else they are supposed to symbolize – in sharp contrast to the classical ideals of the neighboring civic district buildings, also offer visual indication of cyborg intentions.

Singapore's hub ambitions are thus multiple and overlapping, targeting a number of individual parts or constituents, involving extensive socio-spatial-infrastructural transformations, and expending considerable amounts of research, funding and planning. In short, they are cyborg identities, applying technologies to Singapore citizens and society in order to transform them into enhanced entities, sitting at the hub-centre of various transnational flows. This kind of cyborg future (as contrasted to other South- and East-Asian versions in which traditionalism is at some odds with modernization) is largely driven by a survivalist modernity, kick-starting select technological fields with government mandates and funding, in order to seize the advantage over potential Asian competitors. In many cases and for many fields (from bio-technology to materials engineering to computing to things like education, banking, game design and resort development and management), foreign expertise is headhunted and "parachuted" in to recruit and lead teams (which often comprise some other non-Singaporeans). The courting of expert foreigners to come and live and work in Singapore might itself be seen as a kind of technological-societal cyborg, yoking together the foreign matter of technological expertise with the local human component. So crucial is the importing of talented foreigners to Singapore's cyborg futures that the Singapore Government is setting up a Citizenship and

Population Unit in the Prime Minister's Office, as Prime Minister Lee announced in his 2006 National Day Rally message. The Unit's acronym is CPU, probably no accident in a nation rife with acronyms and one of whose targeted R&D areas is "interactive and digital media," thus reinforcing the structural parallel between importing foreign expertise into Singapore and enhancing the local body with cybernetic input.[37]

Cyborg futures bring all kinds of problems for Asian modernities, as the case of Singapore also shows. Prime Minister Lee's 2006 National Day Rally Message, announcing Singapore's need (among other things) to "bring immigrants in," was only the latest in a number of such governmental calls, and like the previous ones it provoked its share of controversy among Singaporeans, a number of whom were understandably anxious about the socio-economic impact of this influx of foreigners.[38] Apart from possible socio-economic problems (to do with inflation, employment, racial and cultural mixes and others), there is of course the danger of all kinds of stratifications and divisions of labor, including the fact that imported expertise, reluctant to share all the technological secrets which gives it its cachet, will retain longer-term controlling authority over local workers who will perpetually occupy the lower-order positions in this alliance.

Part of these problems stem from the very nature of Asian "hub" ambitions, which desire to be a central point of convergence for the region (the perimeter of the "wheel," in this analogy), but cannot envision a higher and more holistic positioning within the global capital-technological order. For the hub (both in analogical and global economic terms) is no more than a component part of the larger entity, no doubt necessary and crucial, but not the power, drive-train or steering system which control the entity's speed and direction. The structural consequences of Asian hub ambitions are already seen in certain Indian cities, which like Singapore have long harbored hub ambitions, and

37 Lee Hsien Loong, "Prime Minister Lee Hsien Loong's national day rally English speech," August 20, 2006, http://www.gov.sg (accessed: September 4, 2006).

38 Robbie B. H. Goh, *Contours of Culture: Space and Social Difference in Singapore* (Hong Kong: Hong Kong University Press, 2005), 126–30; Lee, "National day rally speech," 2006.

have a longer experience as technological hubs than Singapore. One of the most instructive, in the context of the present discussion, is "IT hub" Bangalore, which is in many ways a tremendous success story of capturing foreign direct investment, luring outside visitors of various sorts and for various durations, and building up a hub economy, image and ideology. Yet this cyborg marriage of foreign technological and capital investment with local resources has also been notorious for a number of problems of varying degrees of seriousness, including problems of various aspects of the infrastructure lagging behind the IT boom. The controlling nature of the foreign input, and the dependent or vulnerable nature of the local component, is evident in the ways that big corporations like IBM not only finance but also set the research and production agendas for the Asian hub, and tend to "exploit" local talent in the "lowest end" of production and R&D work, leading to vocal complaints by local voices.[39] As one Indian columnist astutely points out, despite its grand ambitions, there is something inherently transitory, functional and ultimately exploitative about these hubs: competition is fierce and constant, there are any number of claimants with "the potential to emerge as a hub," and one constantly has to "do more to retain […] pre-eminence."[40] Technological hubs are not in and of themselves the answer to Asia's cyborg identity and futures, although they are without doubt important initiatives to jump-start the competition for international flows of technology and capital. More fundamentally and in the longer term, hubs do not answer, and may actually exacerbate (both in their analogical position and discourses, as well as in their regional and short-term thinking) the basic problem of Asian technological identities as dehumanized, unstable, transient and expendable.

39 Harish Baliga, "Exploitation of Indian talent continues…," *India Daily*, August 21, 2006, http://www.indiadaily.com/editorial/12929.asp (accessed: September 4, 2006); Reuters, "IBM to pour $6 billion into India," *ZDNet News*, June 6, 2006, http://news.zdnet.com/2100-9595_22-6080346.html (accessed: September 4, 2006).

40 V. Jayanth, "The 'hub' concept," *The Hindu*, November 10, 2004, http://www.thehindu.com/2004/22/10/stories/2004111003991000.htm (accessed: September 4, 2006).

Conclusion: Asian Cyborgs, Intelligent Citizens, and the Return of/to the Word Warrior

Unfortunately, this is the prevailing condition of Asian cyber identities, widespread enough (not just in Asian tech hubs, but also in chatrooms, popular culture texts, porn and exotica sites, public discourses, and elsewhere) that it becomes justified to speak of the ideology of the Asian sub-cyborg. Educational traditions and pedagogical cultures are not exempt from playing a role in reinforcing this ideology: Taiwan-born and US-educated Nobel Laureate Lee Yuan-Tseh is quoted in an interview as saying that "in Asia, our biggest educational obstacle [to scientific success] is the use of the written test to select talent," and that Asian "social values" (such as peer pressure, parental determination of children's careers) also pose a problem.[41] Asian social values of control and conformity obviously also contribute to perpetuating sub-cyborg mindsets and identities: Peter Schwartz, co-founder and chairman of the Global Business Network, when invited to Singapore to discuss R&D proposal in Singapore's strategic areas, observed that Singapore "is not too good at dealing with scruffy people; you don't like people like that much around here," which poses a problem of restricting talent flows and the nurturing of local talent.[42] Efficient states and ambitious cities can create infrastructural conditions for techno-capital flows, but mindsets and cultures which obstruct Asian cyborg futures are harder to change.

The technological aptitude, and even the state will, of Asians in countries like India, China, Japan, Singapore, Taiwan and elsewhere, are undeniable. There is enough significant and rapid change in indicators like Internet penetration, R&D spending, and foreign direct investment in technology to suggest that Asia's share of the global technology pie is promising. Yet apart from a few leading Asian centers, the

41 Lee Yuen-Tseh, "A rebel with a scientific cause (interview)," *Innovations* 6, No. 3: (2006): 68–70; 70.

42 Tan Hui Leng, "Technologically tight – now loosen up, Singapore!" *Today* (July 7, 2005): 1, 3; 1.

rest of Asia is marked with huge infrastructural unevenness which constitutes a major gulf to overcome. Deeper and more extensive than this infrastructural unevenness is the culture and ideology of Asia's technological identity: caught up as it is in the internal forces of traditionalist nationalism, cultural conservatism, ultra-modernist excess, ruthless competition, and shame and guilt, as well as external forces relegating Asia's technological future to an "unstable," subsidiary and dependent position, the development of cyborg identities in Asia is more complex than the merely infrastructural level would suggest.

If "cyborg politics is the struggle [...] against the one code that translates all meaning perfectly, the central dogma of phallogocentrism," as Haraway[43] argues, then Asia (notwithstanding ambitious agendas and peaks of achievement) does not yet have cyborg power. Its bodies and texts are not under its own control, but very much produced by global technology and capital flows originating from the West, and chiefly from America. To recognize this is to argue for a less positive future for cyborg identities than some of the infrastructural developments – the "hub" discourses – might suggest, and also to argue for the need for a competitive strategy at the level of culture and discourses, instead of merely at the infrastructural level. It is to insist on the need for cultural and discursive engagements with those dominant discourses and flows, for the transformation of mindsets and cultures, for texts, media, pedagogy, ritual, and other symbolic productions. It does not seem as if Asian nations, any more than the rest of the world, can avoid their technological destiny; however, there is a big difference between being assigned the role of a robotic component, and assuming an empowered and forward-looking cyborg identity. It is the difference between an Asian modernity which is uncomfortably and perpetually dualistic, struggling to reconcile disparate parts which have been forced upon one, and one that is hybrid in an adaptive, confident and forward-looking manner. Cyborg cultures are thus yet another dimension of the socio-cultural, political and economic battle that Asian nations are faced with in the age of modernization.

43 Haraway, "Cyborg manifesto," 312.

WAI-LUK LO

Three Paradigms in Hong Kong Drama in the 1970s: Hybridity in Styles

Introduction

This paper traces the development of the three major paradigms in Hong Kong drama in the 1970s. It was a time when Hong Kong was undergoing drastic social changes and cultural transformations, and Hong Kong citizens' local cultural consciousness became apparent.

China has a long history in theater.[1] The "Drama" this essay discusses, however, is not the traditional forms, but rather those influenced by the West at the beginning of the twentieth century.

The three paradigms are: Modern Chinese drama, Western translations, and original plays with realistic concerns. The purpose of this essay is to relate their emergence to the history of Hong Kong drama, the particular cultural and political condition of Hong Kong before and during that period, the aesthetic development of world theater, and more importantly, the problematics of Chinese modernity.

In the context of this conference, it may be necessary for me to briefly point out several significant facts concerning the subjectivity of Hong Kong drama in relation to that of the Mainland.

1 It is well known that the Yuan Dynasty (1271–1368) is the first golden age of traditional Chinese Drama. The genre then is called *zaju* (mixed drama). It is sophisticated and the scripts are excellent. Nowadays, more than three hundred kinds of traditional performances that sprung from different regions are still very active among the Chinese people. Like the Yuan mixed drama, they usually combine singing, recitation, conventional gesture, dancing and martial art. In Hong Kong, the Cantonese Opera has been very popular since the mid-nineteenth century.

The Subjectivity of Hong Kong Drama

Hong Kong was ceded to the UK in 1842 and became a colony. Unlike other colonies, however, there was not that much resistance from the Chinese inhabitants. The colonial government at that time did not rule by suppression. It seemed as though Hong Kong people did not mind being ruled by foreigners as long as they could maintain their way of living. As for cultural identity, they still regarded themselves as Chinese subjects. Although Western dramas were performed in English among the English speaking expatriates and the garrison community, the Hong Kong Chinese people did not attend, let alone participated in, these performances. Instead, Cantonese opera was the most popular theatrical form for the Hong Kong Chinese.[2]

The modern form of spoken drama was born at a time of national crisis. Revolutionaries seized drama as a platform for propaganda. In Hong Kong as well as the Mainland, drama was first of all political discourse. For example, the director of the 1907 Shanghai performance of *Uncle Tom's Cabin*, Wang Zhongsheng (1884–1911), was a revolutionary. He was arrested and executed in 1911 for his participation in the Tianjin Uprising.[3] In Hong Kong, a major base of the 1911 revolution, the revolutionaries also seized the theater as a platform to arouse the people's consciousness to revolt against the Qing Dynasty.[4]

2 Law Kar and Frank Bren, *From Artform to Platform: Hong Kong Plays and Performances 1900–1941* (Hong Kong: IATC, 1999).

3 Thus, the first sentence of the Preface of the collection of essays of the History of Modern Chinese drama writes, "The Chinese Spoken Drama Movement merged with the political movement from the very beginning." *Zhongguo huaju yundong wushi nian shiliaoji di yi ji* (Beijing: Zhongguo xiju chubanshe, 1958, 1).

4 One key figure of the revolutionary theatrical performance was Chan Siu-bak (1869–1934), a close comrade of Sun Yat-Sen (1866–1925), the creator of the Republic of China. He formed an "Idealist Company" and used Cantonese Opera to promote the course. In Spring 1911, Chan established the Chan Tin Sing Pak Wa Drama Society (Striking with Heavenly Sound Spoken Drama Society). Historical records revealed that immediately after the failure of the Guangzhou Uprising (April 21, 1911), more than fifty revolutionaries gathered together and

Another period of important dramatic development in Hong Kong was in the late 1930s. After the start of the Sino-Japanese War (1937–1945), and before Japan invaded Hong Kong in December 1941, many leftist writers, journalists, filmmakers, and dramatists came to Hong Kong to promote the national defense discourse. There were many dramatic activities. Mainland professional drama troupes were well received, and local amateur groups sprang up. According to the practitioners, there were more than 150 drama groups,[5] and they named their activities *juyun* (drama movement).[6] They called for a united front in drama to urge the people to join in the fight during the national crisis.[7] The most representative performance of this time, perhaps, was the 1941 production of the anti-fascist play *Professor Mamlock* by Friedrich Wolf (1888–1953), directed by the communist director Zhang Min (1906–1975).

Drama was a form of cultural resistance to the Japanese invasion of China. During this time, Hong Kong was part of China in the minds of the Hong Kong inhabitants and the drama workers from the North.[8] Some of the performances were organized secretly, took place in classrooms or any transformed space. According to the memoirs of some of the participants, there were Japanese spies and British colonial policemen around to keep an eye on the drama movement.[9]

---

decided to form the Ching Ping Lok Bak Wa Drama Society (To turn down the Qing Dynasty and live happily, *qing ping yue bai hua ju she*). They performed themes directly related to the Chinese Revolution (Li Xi (ed.), *Li Min Wei riji.* Hong Kong: Hong Kong Film Archive, 2003).

5 Xu Yu Lian, "Yu Chan Yau Hau, Li Yuanhua tan xianggang huaju sishinian – shidai zhong de xiju," *Yue Jie* V11 (September, 1991), 92–4.

6 This term gained its popularity, and was used until the mid-1970s.

7 Xin Ying, "Jian shu xiang gang xiju tong yi zhen xian – xi wang yu xiang gang hua ju tuan lian he hui yi," *Da Zhong Ri Bao*, July 26, 1938; Hu Chun Bing, "Zhan kai xi ju zhen xian," *Da Zhong Ri Bao*, July 27, 1938.

8 Shu Lun, "xian jie duan kang zhan xi ju yun dong de xing shi yu ren wu," *Li Bao*, May 24, 1940; Shu Lun, "tan xiang gang xi ju yun dong de xin fang xiang," *Li Bao*, June 7, 1940.

9 Li Yuanhua, "xiang gang ju tan de zhui yi ji fan si," Gilbert Fong, Hardy Choi (eds), *Xiang gang hua ju lun wen ji* (Hong Kong: zhong tian zhi zuo you xian gong si, 1992), 51–68.

Immediately after the Sino-Japanese War, many leftist cultural workers came to Hong Kong again. This time, they came for political shelter to escape from the rightist Kuomintang's suppression. The dramatic activities then were leftist oriented,[10] and the Hong Kong government once again kept eyes on the Communists' activities.

Modern Chinese Drama: A Repressive Subject

In 1949 the Communists took over China, and almost all aspects of contemporary Chinese culture were reshuffled. On the one hand, many young men and women decided to return to the "motherland" to help build the "New China," on the other, many mainlanders left China for Hong Kong. It was a time of hope and confusion, fear and hatred. That was also a time of ideological conflict, and a delicate time for the Hong Kong government.

Hong Kong became a sanctuary for many mainland capitalists, liberal intellectuals, and those who connected with the Kuomintang. It was also a place for the Chinese Communist Party to communicate with the world.

William Tay argues that since 1949 Hong Kong has become a public sphere for contemporary Chinese political discourse. This space contained both the leftist and rightist views, and it also helped cultivate literary and media communications between the various political bodies. The most

10 In 1946, the Chinese Communist Party formed the Chinese Music, Dance and Drama Society *(zhong guo ge wu ju yi she)* and the Chung Yuen Dramatic Art Society *(zhong yuan ju yi she)* to promote socialism, and to recruit young people to join the course of "national liberation." The two organizations were quite active for two years. At first they performed in large theater, later they adopted the "mass line *(qun zhong lu xian)*," and developed strategies to reach the audience through informal means, e.g., roof top performance, classroom performance, and even countryside performance. They even performed works from Yan An, the headquarters of the Chinese Communist Party.

important characteristic of this sphere is that "for quite a long time, the critics of current affairs would articulate their views from the Hong Kong 'margin', to either the left (Beijing) or the right (Taipei) centres." This discursive phenomenon is different from the resistances of other colonies in the history of colonization, whose targets are the colonizers.[11]

Tay's assertion is correct in general except for the brief span of time between the mid-1960s and the early-1970s. In our context, for example, the Cantonese filmmakers that had some connection with the leftist drama movement of the 1930s continued actively to carry on the enlightenment project of the New Culture Movement of the 1920s. They adapted many modern Chinese novels and plays into films. They also introduced many Western works that had been influential in the leftist literary movement during the 1930s and 1940s, such as Cao Yu's (1910–1996) *Thunder Storm*, *Sunrise*, *The Wilderness*, and *Peking Man*, Ba Jin's (1904–2005) *Family*, *Spring* and *Autumn*, *Cold Night*, Ibsen's *Ghost*, Gogol's *Inspector General*. Gorky's *Lower Depth* was taken as a model in the creation of many realistic films.

The scene was much different in drama. Although the Hong Kong Educational Department started the Inter-school Drama Competition in 1949 upon the persuasion of scholars and drama workers, it was officially stopped after a successful ten-year run when the organizing committee adopted a liberal policy towards the competing schools. They gave all schools equal chance of entering and judged them fairly, regardless of their political affiliation. This triggered the nerves of the colonial government, and the competition had to be stopped.[12] It should be noted that in the UK drama had just been incorporated into the educational system and formally became part of the curriculum at that time.

The colonial government had a very clear idea on the difference between drama and film with respect to their modes of production. Drama was a form of participatory activity. It was intensive and forceful. To the colonial government, drama was contagious, so the stu-

11 William Tay, *"1997 qian xiang gang zai hai xia liang an de wen hua zhong jie,"* www.fl.nctu.edu.tw/acc/tswx/1997.doc

12 The competition was reinstated thirty years later, in the 1990s.

dents' minds would certainly be influenced during the rehearsal process. Therefore, while the government allowed the leftists' enlightening cinematic discourse, it kept a very close eye on the dramatic activity, especially those held within the educational sector. Li Yuanhua (1915–2006), a lecturer of the Northcote College of Education, recalled how he was reported for promoting leftist ideas when he was rehearsing Cao Yu's *The Wilderness* with his students. He staged Ibsen's (1828–1906) *Pillar of Society* instead.[13]

Drama as Enlightenment

If we juxtapose the history of Hong Kong drama to that of the Mainland's, we immediately discover a very crucial absence. While the spoken drama flourished in the 1920s and 1930s in Mainland China, it was only occasionally found in Hong Kong.[14] In the Chinese community, up to the late 1920s, even if there were performances of this form, it was limited to the small group of people that had connection to Western culture.[15]

This was a very significant difference. In Mainland China many young people participated in dramatic performances to gain the sense of liberation from the bondage of feudalism. The Chinese intellectuals commonly believed that it was only through complete Westernization that Chinese culture could be rejuvenated. They called for the "New Culture," and "Down with Confucianism!" was their slogan. Against

13 "xiang gang hua ju yun dong de zuo tian, jin tian he ming tian," (zuo tan ji lu) *Wen Xue yu Mei Shu* Vol. 2 (1976), 4–5.

14 It was not that there was no modern literature or Western art form in Hong Kong during that time. We had modern poetry and Western oil painting as early as the 1920s. (For poetry, see Yip Fai, *xin shi di tu si hui ben* (Hong Kong: Cosmo Books Ltd, 2005); for painting, www.hkartclub.com/painting/hkpaintings.html.) Certainly, there was much room for further investigation.

15 Law Kar and Frank Bren, 34.

this tide, they promoted the "Amateur Drama Movement," urging genuine drama lovers to participate in theatrical productions. They translated numerous Western plays, and wrote in the style of Western plays. In the October 1918 issue of the *New Youth* (Xinqingnian), there was an article introducing one hundred modern plays by fifty-eight playwrights from thirteen countries. Undoubtedly, the 1920s was a golden period of original scripts and translations.[16] Drama was a tool for enlightenment, and plays were published and produced. It was at that time that drama was formally called *huaju* (spoken drama).

Drama became a self-defining cultural form that enabled and accelerated the awakening of the individuality. This explained why Ibsen's *A Doll's House* was so popular since its introduction to China in the 1910s.[17] Yet, the play had not been performed in Hong Kong until quite recently.[18]

Hong Kong drama did not have that sense of enlightenment before the Sino-Japanese War, with *juyun* (Drama movement) connected primarily with the political situation of China. After the war, a group of returning intellectuals formed the Chinese Drama Group of the Sino-British Club. Its key figure was Ma Jian (1883–1959), head of the Chinese Department of the University of Hong Kong. Other members included Yao Ke (1905–1991), Liu Ts'un-Yan (b. 1917), Lui Ho-yin, Tam Kwok-chi, Hu Chunbing (1906–1960), Chan Yau Hau (b. 1915), all famous scholars and dramatists of the time. They published the *Dramatic Art Journal* and organized performances. There were also some other amateur performances, and records show that there was a drama competition among four secondary schools in 1947.[19]

16 Ma Sen, "yan yuan ju chang yu zuo jia ju chang: lun er shi nian dai de xian dai ju zuo," *Dangdai Xiju* (Taipei: shi bao wen hua chu ban she, 1991) 70–103.

17 In June 1918, *New Youth (Xinqingnian)*, the most influential journal among the Chinese young intellectuals, published a special issue on Ibsen (1828–1906), with Hu-shi's essays on Ibsenism, and translations of *A Doll's House*, *An Enemy of the People* and *Little Eyolf.*

18 Kwok-kan Tam, *Ibsen in China (1908–1997)* (Hong Kong: Chinese University Press, 2001) 216–17.

19 Ze Zhi, "zhong xue xi ju bi sai zhong, yu sai si ju qian ping – xie yu zhong xue xi ju bi sai yi hou," *Singtao Daily*, November 30, 1947, 5.

The word "Art" in the title of the *Dramatic Art Journal* was crucial. It signified that in the late 1940s Hong Kong drama had a new perspective besides consciousness shaping, for it started to develop the sense of art in drama. With the cultural logic of the time and the values embedded in Modern Chinese Drama, critical realism was regarded as the progressive style.[20] Its speed was quite fast in the beginning, and its trajectory might have followed the creative directions of modern Chinese drama if it were not for the drastic political changes in 1949.

Although the 1950s was a time of repression, looking at it from a historical perspective, however, it was also a time of cultural accumulation. What the drama workers had been doing during that particular time was like paving the way. It led to subsequent development of Hong Kong drama.

Cultural manifestations, conscious or sub-conscious, may be regarded as sign processes leading to the knowledge of the time. Dramatic themes, aesthetic forms, the organization process, or simply reenactment itself, all are cultural discourses.

The drama workers still regarded themselves as working for the course of *juyun*, except that the objective had changed from political to cultural. They delivered talks, organized courses, wrote articles, published scripts, staged plays, and encouraged the younger generation to participate in dramatic activities.[21] As such, drama became a form of enlightenment in a broader sense. The drama workers wished the younger generation took up the tool of drama to create something meaningful in their lives.[22] Due to the seriousness of the practitioners, the dramatic activities in a time of repression sowed the artistic seeds on many secondary school students, who would carry on their interest

20 Chun Bai, "fan lun wu tai zhuang zhi," *Ta Kung Pao – wen yi* Vol. 645, June 18, 1939.

21 Yao Ke jiang shu, Yu Wen bi lu, *zen yang yan chu xi ju* (Hong Kong: xiang gang ju yi she, 1957).

22 Tam Kwok-chi, "qing nian yu xi ju yun dong," *Wen Feng*, Vol. 1, p. 9, September 15, 1952.

and pursued means to produce plays when they became university students.[23]

The dramatic enlightenment brought forth an important missing tide in the next decade – Western Drama.

The Belated Western Drama Tide

In the early 1960s, we saw a new paradigm in Hong Kong drama – Contemporary Western plays. This direction was acceptable for the colonial government, who had been trying to shield the young men and women from the influence of the Socialist China since the early 1950s.

With the establishment of the City Hall Theatre, which was in the format of the nineteenth century proscenium stage, the formation of the Hong Kong Amateur Dramatic Society in 1962, which staged a series of contemporary Western plays in Cantonese, and Hong Kong University English Department's offering of *Contemporary World Drama* course in mid-1960s, Hong Kong drama arrived on the belated first tide of Western dramatic influence.

Undoubtedly, this tide was a form of artistic enlightenment, continuing what the drama workers had been doing in the repressive decade for modern Chinese drama. Thus, the drama movement took on a new meaning in the 1960s. It might not be an activity born out of the concern for what happened in the "motherland," yet it worked hard to elevate the status of drama in Hong Kong by exploring how this specific artistic form dealt with issues concerning humanity.

It should be noted that the aesthetic and thematic influences of this belated Western dramatic tide in Hong Kong were different from the

23 Perhaps that was why Chung King Fai, the first post-war Hong Kong students who went abroad to study drama in the late 1950s, called the 1960s the period of University Drama (Chung King Fai, "xiang gang hua ju de li shi he fa zhan," ibid., 23–7).

first tide of Western dramatic influence in the Mainland during the 1920s and 1930s. At that time, the end result was the triumph of realism, especially critical realism, and all other forms, i.e., symbolism, expressionism, faded out as China's political condition was getting increasingly severe with the threat of the Japanese invasion.[24]

After World War II, new dramatic paradigms such as the Theatre of the Absurd, Brecht's (1898–1956) epic theater, Artaud's (1896–1948) Theatre of Cruelty appeared in the West. They were aesthetically challenging, even opposing, to the realistic traditions of the modern drama represented by Ibsen, Chekhov (1860–1904), or Gorky (1868–1936). Moreover, there were also new developments within realism. Simply by realistically portraying the external life of men no longer satisfied the new generation of writers who strove for a deeper level of the real. Playwrights such as Wilder (1897–1975) and Williams (1911–1983) demonstrated very well how realism could be impressionistic or psychological.

In the 1960s, many contemporary Western plays were performed. The plays brought to the audience a sense of modern by the aesthetic diversities, and their refutation of the simplistic view on realism. They triggered great interests in drama among the young intellectuals. In 1966, the Federation of Post-graduate Students organized the first Inter-university Drama Competition, which marked a new page in the history of Hong Kong drama.

"Hong Kong Drama": As Subject

The delicate political situation of the 1950s repressed the production of modern Chinese drama, especially those of the leftist writers' and those from Mainland China. During that time, Hong Kong dramatists

24 Song Bao Zhen, "*zhong guo xian dai pai xi ju shuai wei ji qi yi shu qi shi*," *Er shi shi ji zhong guo hua ju hui mou* (Beijing: bei jing guang bo xue yuan chu ban she, 2000) 32–49.

wrote primarily historical plays and light comedies. Perhaps, as some scholars argued, these forms were safer, and made good shelter ports when the political sea was rough.[25] Of course, the playwrights might imbue their opinions about contemporary Chinese history, the ideological conflict between the rightists and the leftists, the KMT, the CCP, and the politics inside socialist China in the plot, the character, and the dialogue. Nevertheless, the absence of current subject matters are significant when compared with the achievement of the wide spread drama movement in the 1940s and with what was happening in Mainland China.

We may say that the dramatists deliberately chose genres to stay away from political censorship; they were well aware of the fact that they were dwelling in a colony, and were subjected to the rule of the colonial government.

It should be noted that during this time the dramatists did not stage many Western plays either. This was a significant choice. Yao Ke, for example, did not do much translated plays in the 1950s, despite his excellent command of both Chinese and English, and the fact that he had translated Bernard Shaw's (1856–1950) *The Devil's Disciple* into Chinese and Cao Yu's *Thunder Storm* into English when he was the chief editor of an English magazine in Shanghai in the 1930s. Instead he wrote historical plays. He said in the mid-1950s that he wanted to create Chinese New Drama. The plays had to be original, well known to the Chinese people, but the form was new, organically combining Eastern and Western dramatic traditional.[26]

Therefore, we could say that the drama workers might want to bring the audience's attention to "Chineseness" *(zhong guo xing)* at that particular time. Their reflection on contemporary Chinese history shaped the course of Hong Kong drama. At this time the enlightenment project of the modern drama encapsulated inside the historical subject matters. It did not need to (or even chose not to) borrow from the Western

25 Chen Li Yin, *"jian shu xiang gang de hua ju ju ben chuang zuo (1950–1974),"* ibid., 36.

26 Yao Ke, *"qian yan," Xi Shi* (Hong Kong: xiang gang ju yi she, 1957).

repertory. They did not regard the UK as the parent culture for drama, and defined themselves by sophisticated hybridization of the Western form of drama to Chinese culture. This could be understood as their subtle resistance to living in a colony.

Eventually, the creative energy responded to the social reality. Playwrights began to touch on local subject matters in the 1960s. Yao Ke, for example, was commissioned by the Anti-drug Committee to write *Mean Street* and put it on stage in 1962. With its forceful, realistic portrayal, it was regarded as the best social play of the time.[27] Its social concern, however, did not have much creative echo among the younger generation until some years later when localism came on stage.

Drama critic Cheung Ping Kuen concluded in a paper about Hong Kong drama that the 1960s and the 1970s were the beginning of "Hong Kong Drama,"[28] because during this time, Hong Kong drama workers had started to develop their concern for the place of Hong Kong and to the art of drama.[29]

1970s: The Paradigms Meet

The 1970s was the landmark of localism. In the early 1970s, after years of negotiation between local citizens and the colonial government, the Chinese language finally became the second official language in Hong Kong. Immediately, a great creative energy was released and crucial cultural discourses were articulated. They fused with the search for national identity among the young intellectuals, and formulated a new paradigm in Hong Kong Drama – original scripts that reflected society

27 Li Yuanhua, *"xiang gang ju tan de zhui yi ji fan si,"* ibid., 58.

28 Zhang bing quan, *"zhong guo guan xi yu xiang gang xi ju,"* Tian Ben Xiang (ed.), *Hua wen xi hui – di yi jie hua wen xi ju jie xue shu yan tao hui lun wen ji* (Beijing: Zhongguo xiju chubanshe, 1998) 142–53.

29 Cheung Ping Kuen, ibid. 152.

and the colonial condition. Compared with the previous two decades, the 1970s was surely a decade of original plays.[30] Since 1969, the annual Inter-University Drama Festival required the entries to compete with original works. The subjects were becoming more socially oriented. This was also the objective of the secondary school drama festival organized by The Joint School Drama Project.

In the 1970s, the Hong Kong government adopted a more liberal policy towards local cultural development. Therefore, the establishment of the major Hong Kong professional performing arts companies happened in this period. The groups listed below are still the flagship performing troupes in Hong Kong:

1973	Hong Kong Philharmonic Orchestra
1977	Hong Kong Chinese Orchestra
1977	Hong Kong Repertory Theatre
1978	Hong Kong Ballet
1979	City Contemporary Dance Company
1980	Chung Ying Theatre Company
1981	Hong Kong Dance Company

In this cultural arena, the long-suppressed paradigm of modern Chinese drama could eventually come on stage. In 1974, the Urban Council even sponsored the Cao Yu Drama Festival. This was impossible in the 1950s, when Cao Yu was then regarded as a communist writer, and simply rehearsing his plays was considered leftist. Times had changed indeed. Twenty-four amateur drama groups participated in the events, which included talks, courses, seminars, and a series of performances. This was a double act of cultural identification to Modern Chinese Drama and to the People's Republic of China.

30 According to one study, from 1949 to 1974, there were only about 200 original plays and most of them were written after 1969 when the Inter-university Drama Competition, in order to promote script writing, decided to accept only original plays. Chen Li Yin, *"jian shu xiang gang de hua ju ju ben chuang zuo (1950–1974),"* ibid., 29–49.

Thus, in the mid-1970s, three conspicuous paradigms were in operation. Like tributaries, they joined together in that particular time to motivate the development of Hong Kong Drama. They were:

1. Works from modern Chinese Drama, which signified the connection of mainland China, and Modern Chinese Cultural history;
2. Western Translations, which signified the connection to the West and the dramatic art, adopting a more diversified aesthetics;
3. Original works, which signified the connection with the present and Hong Kong. They usually employed the realistic mode.

The repressed paradigm of the modern Chinese drama, the belated but contemporary Western dramatic tide, and the newly emerged creative trend joined forces, gathered momentum, and motivated the formation of the government funded Hong Kong Repertory Theatre in 1977. In its first season, a new version of *Uncle Tom's Cabin* was staged, echoing what the pioneers had done in 1907.[31] It signified the kinship of Hong Kong Drama to Chinese Drama, and to the Chinese modernization project in general.

Conclusion

Hong Kong drama, as dramatic activities, was born in a time of National crisis; as dramatic discourses of a cultural system, however, it was born in a time when the creative energy, the concern of a place, and the

31 In 1907 a group of Chinese students formed the Spring Willow Society *(Chunliu She)* in Japan, and staged in Spring the third act of Alexander Dumas's *Camelias* in Tokyo. Well received by both the Chinese and Japanese audiences, the society adapted Harriet Beecher Stowe's *Uncle Tom's Cabin* into a five-act play and performed it in June. The play is realistic in content and the characters are true-to-life. Its central theme, the abolition of slavery, reflects the rebellious spirit of the oppressed people. 1907 is regarded as the birth year of Modern Chinese drama.

aesthetics of a form met. In whichever case, its development connected intrinsically with "modernization."

In the West, the term "modern" denotes a historical period following the Renaissance. It began as early as the sixteenth century. This period treasured the value of humanity and embraced rationalism, enlightenment, and individualism. This was also a period of social development, capitalism, industrial revolution, and scientific discovery. In China, however, "modern" was a reaction against the Western Powers. China had been continually defeated by foreign powers since the Opium War (1840). Therefore, "modernization" was first and foremost a political action.[32]

Therefore, as a form of expression, Hong Kong drama was a product of its time. It gained its historicity as a reaction to the national crisis. In its early days, Hong Kong drama was a subject of the Chinese Nation rather than the local citizens' exploration of the meaning of life or the articulation of the discontent towards the colonial ruler.

Nevertheless, Hong Kong drama had a different trajectory than that of the Mainland's. There are two crucial absences in the history of Hong Kong drama. If the absence of the modern dramatic form in Hong Kong from the 1920s to the mid 1930s is due to the lacking of the sensibility to modern drama, then the absence of Western drama in the repressive 1950s was due to the subconscious desire to uphold the subjectivity of modern Chinese drama that gained ground in the late 1930s and 1940s drama movement.

In the 1950s, as the subject of national identity, Hong Kong drama was repressive. On the one hand, the Hong Kong government was watching closely; on the other, what happened in Communist China urged the dramatists to reflect upon their cultural identity. They had no choice but to detour themselves to historical plays instead of staging works from the modern Chinese drama repertory and new works from the Mainland.

32 Huang Ji Chi, *Xian dai hua, xian dai xing, xian dai wen xue* (Hong Kong: Oxford University Press, 2003).

The subjectivity of the aesthetic form needed to be developed in order to carry through the enlightenment process. Hence the belated first tide of Western dramatic influence was very crucial to Hong Kong drama. It completed the enlightenment process of the form. It had a liberating effect. On the ground of this, when the creative energy of the new generation was directed to the present, a genuine culture of Hong Kong drama began.[33]

This paper reveals the cultural logic behind the three paradigms of Hong Kong drama in the 1970s. They are products of a particular place in world colonial history. We cannot superimpose the standard post-colonial discourse to Hong Kong drama. Repressed modern Chinese drama, contemporary Western drama, and local creations joined together at a time when Hong Kong citizens were developing a local consciousness. Their hybrid energy was so great that it changed the ecology of Hong Kong drama, and marked an important step in the de-colonization of Hong Kong culture, which is an interesting topic for further investigation.

33 For drama, besides the formation of the Hong Kong Repertory Theatre, 1977 also witnessed the opening of Hong Kong's second theater complex, Hong Kong Arts Centre. This process continued in the 1980s. We see the establishment of the Performing Arts Council (1982), the Academy for the Performing Arts (1985), and the building of various town halls, civil centers and the Hong Kong Cultural Centre. The formation of the currently influential avant-garde group Zuni Icosahedron (1982) is also significant. Zuni offers to Hong Kong drama the fourth paradigm – avant-garde theater – which stressed on contemporary performance theory, and challenged the normal expectation of theater going, it connected with the future.

Matthew M. Chew

Hybridization of Karaoke and Dance Clubbing Practices in Chinese Nightlife

Nightlife in China is slowly emerging as a legitimate topic in intellectual and media discourses in the 2000s.[1] In global media discourses, Chinese nightlife is currently portrayed in terms of extravagant and cosmopolitan dance clubs in Shanghai and Beijing, even though these elite club scenes actually make up a tiny portion of nightlife in the country.[2] A whole range of nightlife institutions, practices, and cultures – ones that complexly mix together local, Asian, and global elements – are hence hidden from view. These global media imaginaries practically reiterate a modernist, Eurocentric meta-narrative of China's opening-up to the West. Besides the modernist meta-narrative, there are additional reasons that the hybrid complexities of Chinese nightlife are being ignored in global media discourses. Hybridity in Chinese nightlife is difficult to observe because much of Chinese nightlife is carried out in semi-legal, underground ways. In addition, localized parts

1 Examples of scholarly work include James Farrer, *Opening Up: Youth Sex Culture and Market Reform in Shanghai* (Chicago and London: University of Chicago Press, 2002); Zheng Tiantian, "Performing media constructed images for first-class citizenship: political struggle of rural migrant hostesses in Dalian," *Critical Asian Studies* 39 (2007), 89; and Andrew Field "From D.D's to Y.Y. to Park 97 to Muse: dance club spaces and the construction of class in Shanghai, 1997–2007," *China: An International Journal* 6(1), 18.

2 See for example Crutch, "A minor case of culture shock," *The Bangkok Post*, (April 23, 2006), 1; David Eimer, "The great leap backward," *Mail on Sunday* (July 2, 2006), 25; Michael Sheridan, "Beijing learns the gentle art of spin," *Sunday Times* (February 15, 2004), 26; Ron Gluckman and Crystyl Mo, "China: lights, culture, action," *Asiaweek* (March 30, 2001), 1; and Nancy Collins, "The bling dynasty," *ForbesLife* (October 2006), 170.

of Chinese nightlife often do not appear to be substantially different from their global counterparts – they maintain a powerful global façade in order to satisfy locals' desire to experience global lifestyles. Moreover, Chinese nightlife in general is so commercially driven that it may not appear to qualify as the kind of hybridity celebrated by Homi Bhabha or Nestor Garcia Canclini. In this essay, I will identify and analyze a widely participated form of hybrid nightlife in China: the crossover between the nightlife cultures of karaoke and dance clubbing. The analysis will aim at deconstructing the global media imaginaries on Chinese nightlife, directing scholarly attention to the local characteristics of Chinese nightlife, and uncovering some of the positive socio-cultural implications of hybrid Chinese nightlife.

Dance Clubbing, Karaoke, and their Incommensurability

Contemporary global clubcultures – which is constituted mainly by electronic dance music, Ecstasy (the drug) culture, DJ system, and the rave party format that emerged in the United Kingdoms in the late-1980s – was first introduced into China in the mid-1990s and then attracted an increasing number of local participants in the second half of the 1990s. While a small number of cosmopolitan Chinese clubbers have been holding onto a somewhat authentically original version of global clubcultures, the rest developed and participated in localized versions of it. By 2000, imported club music, practices, and institutions have undergone significant local mutations in China. Such a process is not unique to China, as other (popular-) culturally marginal places of the world also experience local alteration of global clubcultures.[3] Despite the proliferation of studies of European and North American clubcultures, few scholars have investigated localized clubcultures in

3 See for example Kristina Sliavaite, "When global becomes local: rave culture in Lithuania," http://www.anthrobase.com/Txt/S/Sliavaite_K_01.htm

non-Western societies such as China.[4] This essay fills a part of this empirical vacuum by way of examining how global clubcultures has been transformed through hybridization with the karaoke nightlife form in China.

Karaoke establishments, dance clubs, bars, live music venues, and commercial sex establishments mutually encroach on one another in China to form a variety of crossover nightlife forms. These crossovers are prevalent in Chinese nightlife and yet they have seldom been noticed, let alone systematically investigated. This essay examines one of the most widely diffused of these crossovers: that between karaoke and dance clubbing. Karaoke, a Japanese invention and by now a predominant nightlife form in East and South East Asia, has not attracted much scholarly attention. Curiously, while current studies delve into karaoke's unique cultural characteristics, micro-social functioning, nationalist and diasporic connections, macro structural background, and global diffusion, all of them neglect to study karaoke's functioning as a major nightlife form in Asia.[5] Karaoke was introduced into China as a nightlife

4 Major works on contemporary dance club cultures include: Sarah Thornton, *Club Cultures: Music, Media, and Subcultural Capital*, (Hanover and London: University Press of New England, 1996); Ben Malbon, *Clubbing: Dancing, Ecstasy and Vitality* (London and New York: Routledge, 1999); Simon Reynolds, *Generation Ecstasy: Into the World of Techno and Rave Culture* (Boston: Little Brown, 1998); Frank Owen, *Clubland: the Fabulous Rise and Murderous Fall of Club Culture* (New York: St. Martin's Press, 2003); Dick Hobbs et al., *Bouncers: Violence and Governance in the Night-time Economy* (Oxford, UK: Oxford University Press, 2003); Paul Chatterton and Robert Hollands, *Urban Nightscapes: Youth Cultures, Pleasure Spaces and Corporate Power* (New York: Routledge, 2003). There is yet any substantial body of scholarly research on club culture in the Chinese language. See for example Lu Deping, "Disco: yizhong qingnian wenhua de fuhao xue jiedu" (Disco: semiotic reading of a youth popular culture), *Journal of China Youth College for Political Sciences 22*, No.3 (May 2003), 32–6. Robert Hollands, *Urban Nightscapes: Youth Cultures, Pleasure Spaces and Corporate Power* (New York: Routledge, 2003).

5 See William H. Kelly, *Empty Orchestras: An Anthropological Analysis of Karaoke in Japan* (Oriel College, Oxford University, 1997) for karaoke's unique cultural characteristics. See Rob Drew, *Karaoke Nights: An Ethnographic Rhapsody* (Walnut Creek, California: AltaMira Press, 2001) for karaoke's micro-social details.

form around the mid-1980s. It gained reception slowly but steadily in the 1980s and 1990s in the institutional forms of hostess bars, integrated nightlife establishments, karaoke halls, karaoke boxes (a club sectioned into numerous tiny rooms so that a large number party people can sing at the same time without affecting one another), and other local improvisations. Then it grew enormously in the late-1990s with the popularization of the karaoke box chain *(liangfan)* business model. By the time contemporary global clubcultures entered China, karaoke was already firmly established in China and it therefore acted as a nightlife institutional and cultural backdrop for the reception of global clubcultures.

I will briefly discuss how much the hybridized nightlife form composed by karaoke and clubbing – for which I would like to coin the term "klubbing" – affects Chinese nightlife in order to contextualize my subsequent analyses. A major share of dance club activities in China are carried out "in klubbing settings instead of dance clubs." Almost all Chinese clubbers I have met have experienced klubbing. There are karaoke regulars who have not experienced klubbing, but klubbing practices are

---

See Casey Man Kong Lum, *In Search of a Voice: Karaoke and the Construction of Identity in Chinese America* (Mahwah, NJ: L. Erlbaum Associates, 1996); and Deborah Anne Wong, *Speak it Louder: Asian Americans Making Music* (New York: Routledge, 2004) for its nationalist and diasporic connections. See Otake Akiko and Hosokawa Shuhei, "Karaoke in East Asia: Modernization, Japanization, or Asianization?" in Mitsui Toru and Hosokawa Shuhei (eds), *Karaoke Around the World: Global Technology, Local Singing* (London and New York: Routledge Press, 1998), 178–201; and Mitsui Toru and Hosokawa Shuhei, "Introduction" in Mitsui Toru and Hosokawa Shuhei (eds), *Karaoke Around the World: Global Technology, Local Singing* (London and New York: Routledge Press, 1998), 1–30 for karaoke's global diffusion and localization. See Chen Kuan-hsing, "The formation and consumption of KTV in Taiwan," in Chua Beng-Huat (ed.), *Consumption in Asia* (London and New York: Routledge Press, 2000), 159–82; and Hiroshi Ogawa, "Karaoke in Japan: a sociological overview," in Will Straw et al. (eds), *Popular Music – Style and Identity: International Association for the Study of Popular Music Seventh International Conference on Popular Music Studies* (Montréal, Que: The Centre for Research on Canadian Cultural Industries & Institutions, 1995) 225–8 for karaoke's macro social and structural background.

participated by a sufficiently large number of karaoke goers that klubbing is recognize as an integral part of karaoke entertainment in China. That is why equipment, music, and interior design that are suitable for dance clubbing are made available in many karaoke establishments even though they represent extra overhead costs. Apart from the elite dance clubs in a handful of Chinese metropolises (i.e. the elite club circuit), all others so called "dance clubs" in the local club circuit in China deviate substantially from the global dance club institution. Karaoke activities are routinely carried out in these dance clubs. Some clubs are devoting almost their entire interior space to segregated rooms with high quality karaoke equipment. At the very least, clubs in the local circuit encourage DJs and clubbers to sing in karaoke style on the dance floor. At the same time, many karaoke establishments in China accommodate elements of dance clubbing practices. The setting up of a "dance music" category in the karaoke selection menu – usually alongside other regular categories such as "male vocal", "female vocal", "duos" and "English language tracks" – in the majority of karaoke music systems is an example. The availability of non-stop dance mixes in an increasingly large number of karaoke box establishments is another piece of evidence. A notable minority of karaoke establishments are even designed specifically for dancing rather than karaoke singing. These are often housed within an integrated club, a hostess nightclub, or a karaoke box establishment and they function as after-hours rendezvous of veteran clubbers.

The crossover between dance clubs and karaoke is intriguing because the nightlife forms are in some important ways incommensurable. The first of these involves musical difference. While both karaoke and clubbing practices rely heavily on music, the kinds of music that they rely on are radically divergent. Karaoke establishments favor slow-tempo, melodic, sentimental, and vocal tracks in the local language. In contrast, dance clubs favor fast-tempo, rhythmic, bass-line dominated, and non-vocal tracks. These two kinds of music usually do not co-exist with each other in the same place or in the same music session. The mainstream audiences of the two kinds of music also subscribe to different socio-cultural tastes or express different psychological states; the two groups may not harmoniously mingle in a given nightlife space.

The musical conflict between karaoke and dance clubs is also more severe than that among karaoke and other nightlife forms. Bars, lounges, live-show houses, and nightclubs, for instance, can play mainstream karaoke music without needing much re-adjustment.

The second incommensurability arises from the dissimilar party practices of clubbing and karaoke. Singing and dancing are not in principle mutually excluding, but they can easily become so in the practical context of nightlife establishments. The majority of dance tracks in contemporary global clubcultures do not have any vocal lines. Even for tracks that do have vocal lines, audiences do not normally sing them. The loud music on the dance floor is a serious obstacle to any form of singing; one must sing very loudly if one wants to hear oneself or be heard. At the same time, serious karaoke singers do not want to be diverted by dancing as they need to focus on controlling their voice and reading lyrics on video screens. Karaoke settings are often not ideal for dance activities. Karaoke boxes in all but the most luxurious karaoke establishments are small rooms with limited open space for dancing. These rooms are usually packed with a sofa, table, and musical equipment. In order to put the degree of conflict between dancing and karaoke-singing in perspective, one can also contrast it with how effortlessly karaoke-singing practices can be adopted in Chinese bars or hostess nightclub establishments.

The third incommensurability derives from the different spatial arrangements favored by karaoke establishments and dance clubs. The maximum size of a karaoke hall with no soundproof spatial partitions cannot but be limited. For example, if a hall serves ten table/groups of patrons, each group only get to sing once in about forty minutes, assuming that each karaoke song lasts for about four and a half minutes. This rate is far from acceptable to karaoke enthusiasts, who would wish to sing dozens of songs in the entire karaoke night out. Under the pressure of this spatial prerequisite, the most common arrangement is to partition all space into "boxes" (a small room), with each serving an individual group of patron. Oriented to sociality, dating, and a collective atmosphere, the dance club requires a much larger, non-partitioned space than karaoke establishments. Global clubbers are predisposed to very open spatial settings because of the oceanic atmosphere of raves that accommodate thousands of participants. In order to put the degree of conflict between club spaces and karaoke spaces in perspective, one can contrast it with the different spatial requirements between karaoke and bars. There is a wide variation of sizes among bars, showing that some bar-goers enjoy the intimate atmosphere of small karaoke box-like space while others prefer a larger open space that facilitates sociability with strangers.

Two Snapshots of Klubbing: Settings, Practices, and Participants

Despite the musical, practical, and spatial incongruence between karaoke and dance clubs, Chinese nightlife participants creatively configure crossover practices that hybridize the two nightlife forms. To examine how and why Chinese nightlife participants do that, I analyze two major sites of klubbing: *baofangs* (VIP rooms or "reserved rooms") in dance clubs, and the karaoke boxes in karaoke establishments.

Baofangs in dance clubs

Baofangs in dance clubs are enclosed rooms and partitioned spaces that usually line a club's main open area. They often, though not necessarily, carry a minimum charge. Most of these rooms are karaoke-friendly, coming with a television screen, a karaoke machine, amplifiers, speakers, and microphones. Some of them also have specialized amplifiers and speakers for reproducing the deep bass sound of dance tracks. Almost all dance clubs in China – not only the provincial ones but those of the global clubbing circuit as well – have some versions of *baofangs* in them. Occupied by groups of nightlife participants who pay a hefty charge, they in effect become temporarily leased, semi-privatized spaces within a dance club. A wide variety of activities, ranging from feasting and karaoke singing to drug-taking and movie watching, can take place in *baofangs*. I cite my fieldnotes at length with the aim of recreating the details of nightlife experiences in a dance club *baofang*:

> (November 11th, 2001) A few friends and I arrived at the front door of Club Rojam at 10:00pm. Our host of the night, Cindy, told the bouncers that we reserved a *baofang*. We were immediately led inside the club by a waitress. We passed the small crowd who were lining up to pay the club's US$4 admission fee (and others who were waiting for some well-connected persons or staff to bring them inside for free). We were led upstairs through a pathway that totally bypassed the main dance hall of the club – I did not get to see any clubbers inside the club during our walk to the *baofang*. [...] Our *baofang* is about thirty square meters in size, which is one of the biggest among the several *baofangs* of the club. Cindy expected about sixteen friends to show up. The projector television was already turned on, showing three-dimensional computer animation clips. Techno is being played, at a moderate volume. No local Chinese electronic dance music was played throughout the night. The music of *baofang* was different from the live DJ sessions going on downstairs on the main dance floor, however. [...] The alcohol came promptly. We mixed the drinks by ourselves and everybody toasted to the occasion, which was Cindy's birthday. Most of us started to play drinking games such as *caiquan* [complex variants of rock-paper-scissors hand games] and liar dice. [...] For the first ninety minutes, nobody in the room danced, though some moved to the beat while seated on the sofa. Nobody suggested to go down to the main hall to dance. Two guys went downstairs to "check out the chicks" and came back up empty-handed after twenty minutes. More friends and their friends kept coming into our *baofang* until the number of people in the room reached twenty and all seats were occupied. In the meantime, a few people started to smoke marijuana and those playing drinking games were already showing initial signs of drunkenness. A few of the girls started to stand up and sway their bodies to the beat. Later on, the guys also joined in. Psychedelic, colorful, and fast-changing patterns were being played on the screen. At 12:30am, someone decided to interrupt the dance music and switched to karaoke singing. However, we soon found out the equipment did not support karaoke singing though they could play karaoke videos. There were no microphones, karaoke machines, nor a large music video collection. Nonetheless, several karaoke videos were played before we switched back to animation and dance videos. A few guys sang without using microphones. As the night wore on, people got more intoxicated. Everyone joined and played drinking game as a group. A few stood up and danced. At 2:30am, almost everyone became tired [given the group's preference of alcohol and marijuana over Ecstasy] and wanted to leave. A few went on to another party session at an after-hours club.

The music and practices described in the above passages were not totally devoid of dance clubbing elements, but their deviation from global clubcultures are nonetheless considerable. The drinking games and occasional karaoke singing diverged from global clubbing practices, even though the group was listening to global music and moving their bodies to it. The space in which the partying took place was very much like a spacious karaoke box. The atmosphere and ambience of the main dance hall downstairs were more collective, spontaneous, and typical of dance clubs. Only a few out of the twenty people in the group cared to go check out the main dance floor during the night. For others, their only interaction with the main hall was a few peeks of it on their way to the washroom. The crowd in the dance floor and our group appeared to have partied in two separate nightlife establishments. As if to ameliorate this isolation, video screens in *baofangs* often show scenes of the main dance floor (which may either be recorded earlier or televised live through CCTV) to virtually bring the main hall atmosphere inside. It is interesting that Club Rojam refrained from providing clients with karaoke equipment even though it provides *baofangs*. This inconsistency reflects Rojam's business positioning of itself as a somewhat elite yet also local-friendly club.

Those who like dance club *baofangs* tend to be affluent clubbers seeking a high status, private, and low-risk clubbing environment. Notice that our group went straight into the dance club, avoiding the queuing, and entering through a "VIP path." The *baofangs* of Club Rojam were located a storey above the main hall and far away from the dance floor. While the tables around the dance floors were densely packed, the *baofangs* were relatively spacious and buffered by a wide corridor and a small rest area to the main hall. Even after a discount, the bill was 2,900 *yuan* (or 145 *yuan,* or US$ 18 each for twenty persons), which would be approximately two times the per-capita spending in the main hall in Club Rojam. The *baofang* setting is considered low-risk because when social disapproval of drug-taking and police suppression of recreational drugs escalated after 1999, it has become risky to take drugs in the main hall of dance clubs. Even though *baofangs* are still not entirely safe if a police raid occurs, the enclosed space at least removed the threat of being spotted by acquaintances.

The previous case of *baofang* partying is socio-culturally interesting because it illustrates why even cosmopolitan, experienced, and middle-class clubbers, which are the least likely candidates to support localized club practices, tolerate and enjoy klubbing. The group in the *baofang* was familiar with the elite club circuit; they did not prefer the *baofang* setting mainly for cultural inertia or security. Most of the regulars of the local nightlife circuit are, in contrast, unfamiliar with cosmopolitan club settings and hence feel more culturally secure in hybrid, localized ones. The group in the *baofang* hybridize their otherwise global party practices with local elements (by mixing singing with dancing, altering the musical flow with karaoke tracks, and restricting sociability with a small enclosed space) for reasons such as socio-economic distinction, abundance of physical space, and risk minimization.

Karaoke boxes

The karaoke box is not the oldest institutional format of karaoke establishment but it is perhaps the most commercially viable one. Chain operators such as *Big Echo* from Japan, *Cashbox* from Taiwan, *California Red* from Hong Kong, and *Haoledi* from Beijing set up upscale karaoke box establishments across China. Numerous smaller local chains imitate them in competition and fill up lower end market segments. As a result, the karaoke box becomes one of the two major commercial institutions in China in which karaoke singing takes place. The other major institution, *baofangs* in hostess nightclubs, is as widespread in China but its business model relies much more on commercial sex/romance than karaoke singing. Neither karaoke boxes nor *baofangs* in hostess clubs avoid crossover transmutations with dance clubs, though I will only examine the karaoke box setting in this section.

The music, practices, and spatial arrangements of karaoke boxes in major Chinese cities (including Hong Kong) show certain common characteristics. Karaoke-goers are assigned a karaoke box according to their group's size when they register at the reception desk. After they are led to their karaoke box, drinks are ordered and the singing begins.

Apart from karaoke singing, a range of activities may take place in the subsequent few hours. Games such as *caiquan* and liar dice are played by almost everybody including those who do not drink. A minority might watch soccer games, play video games, or watch movies, as some karaoke management provide cable television channels and computer games. The provision of low cost or free buffet is also a trend, elevating the importance of eating inside the karaoke establishment. Club music playing and dancing are another important set of non-karaoke activities that have been transplanted to karaoke boxes in China.

> (Oct 15th, 2001) Tonight I went with a group to a karaoke box establishment operated by a Shanghainese imitation of the Taiwanese chain *Cashbox*. Kei, a Hong Kong guy who I have heard about but haven't met, hauled a small and heavy luggage into our karaoke box. From it he took out a mixer, two CD turntables, a mini stereo set for DJ-ing purposes, two hundred-CD holders full of dance CDs, a DJ headphone, a lot of wires, and a disco ball. I was astonished as well as impressed [...] He then set up the equipment and played his choice tracks during most of the time in that night. Most of the tracks he played were Cantopop and Mandopop electronic music, but he also played some of the most popular global tracks such as those of Timo Maas. People in the room danced and sang (without amplification) to the music. A few stood up while others stay seated on the sofas. [...] His DJ-ing skill was, unsurprisingly, not great. But most of the participants of that night's party, including a few veteran clubbers, appreciated his efforts and found it fun to have such an intimate DJ setup even though they have reservations of his music knowledge or DJ-ing skill level. One of the intimate characteristics was that in contrast to club DJs, Kei was extremely responsive to requests for tracks. [...] Kei did not stay idle when klubbers sang karaoke. In those moments, he added his voice over karaoke videos and acted like a radio DJ. He tried his best to entertain the crowd, free of charge.

How does the karaoke box setting constitute a nightlife environment for dance clubbing? My field notes show an extreme case in which nightlife participants forcefully reconfigured the karaoke box into a dance club-like setting – a DJ, mixed club music, dancing, and club lighting displaced singing, karaoke videos, and chatting. Usually though, Chinese nightlife participants do not go so thoroughly in transforming the karaoke box setting. An average night of klubbing in a karaoke box would include the dimming of lights, the selection of Cantopop/

Mandopop dance tracks on the karaoke machine, limiting karaoke singing to a half or two-thirds of the night's airtime, and dancing to club tracks.

The karaoke videos of Cantopop Eurobeat hits of major Hong Kong singers (e.g. Leon Lai, Kelly Chen, Sammi Cheng) as well as the Mandopop dance hits of major Taiwanese singers (e.g. Elva Hsiao, and Jolin Tsoi) are available in practically all karaoke boxes across the country. Tracks of singers that specialize in dance tracks such as B2, China Dolls, MP4, or Evonne Hsu are also accessible in many karaoke boxes. In addition to these, the management of some karaoke establishments provides electronic dance remixes (hour-long ones) created by DJs or recordings of live sessions at dance clubs. Klubbers had to informally request waiters to play them in the late-1990s. Since then, these remixes became increasingly listed in the karaoke computer system as a legitimate category, where karaoke goers can directly press a button and play them.[6] Another recent development is that some of these remixes come with live videos of dancing clubbers recorded in local dance clubs. Some karaoke establishments let klubbers play CDs that they bring or even to set up a makeshift DJ booth inside the karaoke box to mix their own sessions.

While the musical dimension of the karaoke box setting may be temporarily transformed, the social spatial aspect of it is not easily made hospitable for dance clubbing. Eager klubbers can turn off the lights in the karaoke box and re-decorate its interiors. They can smuggle into the room fluorescent gadgets, small mirror balls, and ultraviolet lights to greatly enhance the rave and psychedelic ambience of the room's physical environment. But the socio-spatially isolated nature of the karaoke box cannot be easily altered. In a typical chain-operated karaoke box establishment, there are at least a few dozen karaoke boxes and often more than a hundred ones. The total number of karaoke-goers at such an establishment on weekend nights easily rivals the capacity of the largest dance clubs in China. Yet the activities in a karaoke box

6 After 2006, karaoke box establishments became more wary of playing these dance remixes because of policy changes on the entertainment industries.

establishment are so structured around separate in-groups of friends that the collective social ambience of dance clubs is almost completely absent. The only location in a karaoke box establishment that may offer a modicum of collectivity and sociality is the waiting area at the entrance or the buffet area. However, only the largest and most popular karaoke box establishments have such waiting areas. Moreover, because there are no dance floors in the premises, even the vicarious sense of collectiveness created through CCTV broadcast of the dance floors (which is available to *baofang* klubbers in dance clubs) is unavailable.

A crucial benefit that klubbers in karaoke boxes gain from paying the price of spatial isolation is the avoiding of police suppression. Karaoke box establishments and especially the chain operated ones carry a more legitimate and healthier image than most other nightlife establishments. Since karaoke box establishments are not considered the prime spot for drugs related illegal activities, they are not often raided by the police. For example, while all dance clubs in a city must vacate their crowds at 2am during the periodic "strike hard" *(yanda)* campaigns in the period between 2000 and 2002, some karaoke box establishments were willing to let groups of clients stay until morning. A lot of clubbers indeed turn themselves into klubbers in order to take refuge in karaoke boxes during these after-hour periods. There are also other nightlife participants who prefer to party in karaoke boxes because they feel more at home in karaoke settings and yet wish to dance a bit. Yet others mix karaoke and clubbing practices in their night out as the isolation of the karaoke boxes have their own advantages over conventional dance club settings. For example, they afford more freedom than large dance clubs for groups to tailor-making their own party environment and fine-tuning the proportion of clubbing, karaoke, and other party practices.

Socio-cultural Implications of Klubbing on Chinese Nightlife

An emphasis on music reproduction in the culture of klubbing

My analysis of klubbing practices, settings, and participants supply a basis for exploring klubbing's socio-cultural impacts on Chinese nightlife. A consequential feature of klubbing practices is their emphasis on spontaneous music reproduction. While contemporary Western clubcultures take dancing as the central practice, the culture of klubbing assigns singing an equally if not more important role. The reasons for contemporary Western clubcultures to privilege dancing over all other party practices are historically contingent; this privileging does not have to be seen as an aesthetically or normatively optimal choice. Contemporary Western clubcultures tend to limit music reproductive responsibilities to DJs and do not extend much of them to the average clubber. In the party traditions of different cultures and historical periods, singing and other forms of dance music reproduction have co-existed with dancing. For example, collective playing of musical instruments and dancing come together in many festive occasions in many different cultures. With the advancement of modern technology, the role of music reproduction in party settings has been increasingly relegated to machines. But there is no normative reason for music reproduction to be entirely relegated to specialized music professionals or machines, as music reproduction is in itself an expressive activity that can be enjoyable and practicable by party participants themselves. Karaoke machines represent an exceptional case in the history of music reproductive technologies: while technology have tended to take away the opportunity of music reproduction from the average party participant, karaoke machines are invented to return that opportunity to them. Karaoke machines get rid of the vocal track of recorded dance music and re-enable partygoers to participate actively in music reproduction through singing. In this light, we may interpret klubbing as an ingenious way of reconciling and re-combining dancing with music reproductive activities.

My introduction of a macro-historical perspective at this juncture does not merely serve to justify klubbing's hybrid practices as reasonable and legitimate, but also to assess its socio-cultural contribution to nightlife. The amplification of the karaoke singers' voice and the getting rid of original vocals in dance tracks technically and functionally enable participation in music reproduction. Collective singing has been made almost technically impossible by the music reproductive preferences valorized in contemporary clubcultures. Clubbers in the West would sometimes sing to popular dance tracks that carry lyrics; they yell and instigate others to follow suit during the relatively quiet passages along tracks. However, their individual disparate voices are often overwhelmed by the greatly amplified vocals being pounded out by the sound system. Collective participation in spontaneous musical reproduction is not formally suppressed but is difficult to realize in global club settings. Klubbing settings in China provide a much more hospitable environment for group singing during dancing. There are at least two microphones in each karaoke box. Each microphone normally amplifies the voice of only one singer, but often supports three or even more voices in actual circumstances. When a dance karaoke video is played and participants stand up to dance, the ones holding the microphone are likely to be joined by one or two others. The etiquette of karaoke singing requires the microphone holder to share with others, so that the person holding the microphone would likely place the microphone in a position that allow the voices of the two newly joined to be heard. A common way to do this is to pull them in closer and put one's arm around their shoulders. Alternatively, the microphone holders may also pass the microphone around the room and let each sing a passage of the track. Through these and other social and bodily arrangements, klubbers in a karaoke box sing and dance together as a group. The climax of a klub night is often reached at moments of collective singing that signify and express powerful in-group cohesiveness. Although klubbers get few chances to socialize with strangers outside of their rooms, they develop strong ties to those who are inside.

There is a broader local cultural implication of klubbing's emphasis on spontaneous music reproduction. There might not have been a local electronic dance music in China, or at least it would not have taken its present shape and path, without the musical reproductive characteristics of klubbing. Klubbing and Chinese electronic dance music mutually nurtured each other, which is a fact that is entirely overlooked by pop music critics in China. The earliest and most broadly known sub-genre of Chinese electronic dance music, the Cantopop Eurobeat tracks produced by Mark Lui, are very karaoke-friendly. Although differing from the Cantopop mainstream in lyrical contents and musical arrangement, they are very similar to the Cantopop mainstream in musical structure, length, melodiousness, and slick presentation by idol singers. Their dance videos were played frequently in klubbing settings. At the same time, Chinese electronic dance tracks' hit status was based as significantly on their popularity in klubbing settings as their radio and television airtime. Klubbers pick and play them for their dance functionality long after their pop-chart ranking has subsided. Remaining in play in karaoke establishments for a few years, Cantopop Eurobeat dance hits' shelf-lives lasted much longer than those of regular Cantopop hits.

The mutually reinforcing effect of klubbing and the sub-genre "Cantopop rap" is even more pronounced. While Cantopop Eurobeat tracks could probably have become hits even without the presence of klubbing culture, the success of Cantopop rap depended heavily on the popularity of klubbing. Many among the general audience of Chinese popular music were not aware of the presence of Cantopop rap tracks and had never got a chance to listen to them. Among those that did, many found Cantopop rap offensive and then avoided it. Cantopop rap was mainly consumed, reproduced, and beloved in klubbing settings. The story of the sub-genre "Hi-rap" *(haidie)* in China is similar. Hi-raps usually consist of creative lyrics to be yelled over local and global electronic dance tracks. They are mostly constructed by grassroot participants of the local club circuit, and are not formally recorded and published by record companies. In the beginning, they could only be heard live in dance clubs and klubbing settings. Later on, they gained a sufficiently large cult following for pirated compact disc manufacturers to collect and record them in compact discs. The availability in compact disc format promoted Hi-rap to a broader audience, and this audience was in turn prompted by the music to participate in the local clubbing circuit.

Strong DIY (Do-It-Yourself) elements in klubbing practices

One of the most celebrated socio-cultural aspects of contemporary Western clubcultures is their DIY nature.[7] Its value lies in its circumventing of commercial interests and the empowering of grassroot party participants. China has not inherited this original DIY characteristic when they imported Western clubculture. For example, there have not been any non-commercial warehouse rave parties in China, and raves in China were either highly commercialized events or catering exclusively to affluent party crowds. Nonetheless, klubbing practices facilitate different yet equally social-culturally desirable DIY elements in Chinese nightlife. The emphasis on music reproduction discussed earlier is an example. If an average klubber is able to participate in music reproduction, she is more likely to be able to organize a party for her own group in a DIY way. But the music reproductive and DIY elements in klubbing settings do not entirely overlap; analyses of them need to be done separately.

In contemporary Western clubcultures, DJs assume the important responsibilities of picking, ordering, connecting, and embellishing the tracks to be played in a club night. DJs have become the central figureheads and the superstars in nightlife. In contrast, DJs in most types of klubbing settings play a relatively minimalist, supportive, and facilitating role. There are no professional club DJs to preside over the dance sessions in crossover karaoke lounges. Some hostess nightclubs place

7 See George McKay, "DIY culture: notes towards an intro," in George McKay (ed.), *DIY Culture: Party and Protest in Nineties Britain* (Verso, 1998), 1–53; and Hillegonda Rietveld, "Repetitive beats: free parties and the politics of contemporary DIY dance culture in Britain," in George McKay (ed.), *DIY Culture: Party and Protest in Nineties Britain* (Verso, 1998), 243–68.

"DJs" in their karaoke *baofangs*, but these "DJs" are actually young waitresses who bus the *baofang's* tables, serve drinks, and operate the karaoke system for clients. Due to their knowledge of a nightclub's karaoke video repertoire, these *baofang* DJs are sometimes entrusted to command over the picking of videos to be played. In most klubbing settings, klubbers get to select, order, and/or sing dance tracks without professional DJs' presence.

DIY klub sessions may not display the technical skills, artistry, and intellectualism associated with professional club DJ sessions, but they are no less uniquely tailor-made for the night and demanding on skills. A lot of thinking is needed for the choice of tracks for a klub night. A random playing and ordering of dance karaoke videos does not yield optimal effects. Appropriate selection of non-dance karaoke songs requires considerable knowledge of the Chinese karaoke repertoires and the matching of songs to the night's circumstances and the crowd's changing moods. For instance, non-dance songs that focus on love themes promote good atmosphere when there are many newly met or potential couples in the crowd, whereas songs that lament unconsummated love may generate better effects when the crowd consists mostly of singles. The balancing of dance and non-dance tracks in a klub night is also a challenging task. The preferred proportion of dancing to karaoke singing sessions varies among individuals within a crowd. The continuous entering and leaving of party people in the *baofang* compound the complexity. It could be as difficult for a DIY DJ to capture the flow of a *baofang* party as it is for a professional club DJ to moderate that of a rave. The constraints of local music choices represent another problem for the DIY DJ. The production rate of Cantopop and Mandopop is low, yielding no more than several hundred dance tracks in the past several years. Only a portion of this repertoire has generated karaoke videos and not every karaoke establishment features all of these videos. It is sometimes unavoidable to repeat playing the same video multiple times during a klub night. But skillful DIYers devise clever ways to avoid excessive repetitive playing. Some of them, for example, complement contemporary electronic dance tracks with danceable tracks such as Mandopop rock or classic Cantopop disco ones.

Compared with conventional karaoke, the DIY culture of klubbing lowers the prerequisite singing skill for participants. Because klubbing practices focus on dancing in addition to singing, singers are under less pressure to perform well. Klubbers who lack singing skills often yell out the lyrics of the dance tracks rather than sing to them. The tendency to collectively sing also lowers the skill prerequisite. Moreover, unlike ordinary karaoke singers, klub singers often do not mind having the original vocals un-removed (there is a button on karaoke machines that perform this function). With the original vocals remaining, the sub-par singing skills of individual participants become less conspicuous, embarrassing, or annoying to others.

Another DIY element is the playing of dance remix recordings. Many nightlife establishments in China equip their karaoke systems with dance remixes. Even hostess nightclubs – institutions that do not specifically cater to a young clubber clientele – have them. These remixes are either live recordings of DJ sessions in major clubs of the local circuit, or DJ remixes commissioned by local clubs or pirated compact disc manufacturers. Nightlife establishments either purchase these compact discs or download them in mp3 format from the numerous dance music sites in the Internet. Now, the contents of remixes in a live DJ session are not necessarily very different from those in a remix compact disk picked by an amateur DJ in a klubbing setting. But the control of the contents lies in different hands. The amateur DJ in a klubbing setting can pick, change, and pause dance remixes at will. They may pick from Cantopop, Mandopop, or global compilations, and they may also choose sessions that emphasize particular subgenres such as Hi-rap with a lot of MC-ing.

In karaoke establishments where dance remixes are not provided by the management, amateur DJs could bring their own remix discs or mp3 files and have them played in the karaoke box's system. While the largest karaoke chains may have set rules that forbid patrons to play private dance music inside their premises, these rules are in fact very loosely enforced and violated nightly. Klubbers have no problems with the nominally self-disciplining environment of karaoke chains because all it does is to make these premises less susceptible to police raids.

Klubbers would bring their own equipment and music to karaoke boxes and disregard the warnings issued by the management. Once I was with a group that broke the locked glass cabin housing of karaoke equipment in order to plug in their compact disk player to the stereo amplifier. When they had to pay the fine of a hundred *yuan* (US$ 13), they said they consider the sum "a bargain for a chance for the whole group to dance."

The most thorough case of DIY is to bring-your-own-DJ and create-your-own-DJ-booth in karaoke boxes, as exemplified by Kei (the "DIY DJ" person) described in my field notes. Although he is a non-professional, he nonetheless received a degree of respect and attention among friends that professional club DJs usually receive. Not many klubbers are as resourceful, knowledgeable, and enthusiastic as Kei, but the case is not unique because DJ-ing has become a popular youth hobby in China since the late-1990s. Quite a number of Chinese nightlife participants formally and informally learn DJ-ing. Moreover, there are low-cost DJ-ing equipment sets and club music can be obtained freely from downloading sources from the Internet. I have witnessed quite a number of instances in which klubbers brought the bare basic pieces of DJ equipment – a mini-stereo set with mixer and compact disc turntables – into a karaoke box and played club music intermittently.

Conclusion

I have shown that in contrast to global media imaginaries, Chinese nightlife is less accurately represented by the glitzy elite dance clubs in metropolitan centers than by the seemingly unremarkable klubbing institutions scattered over China. In the hybrid institutions of klubbing, we can find localized musical elements, crossover of Asian and Western nightlife practices, and resistance to global clubcultures. The majority of nightlife participants in China, including the cosmopolitan ones, participate to some extent in klubbing, as the snapshot of my night out at Club Rojam shows. Some parts of the hybrid nightlife form deviate greatly from contemporary global clubcultures. The snapshot of my night out at the karaoke box demonstrates, for example, how locals creatively use karaoke machines and music-mixing ones together to reproduce music and by-pass the global system of club DJs. While cultural mixing is not necessarily liberating, I have shown that in the case of klubbing, there are indeed positive socio-cultural potentials in its emphasis on music reproduction and DIY culture. The two socio-cultural implications also help to highlight the cultural complexities of Chinese nightlife. Klubbing's music reproductive emphasis is shaped by the characteristics of karaoke practices, music localization, and interaction with dance clubbing practices. Klubbing's DIY culture takes the general spirit of DIY from UK rave culture and embodies it in the China context with the DIY penchant of the karaoke box setting, which is in turn a Sino-cized version of the original Japanese karaoke institution. As these numerous cultural threads are loosely woven together with one other by Chinese klubbers, a hybrid nightlife culture is constructed. This culture is innovative, accommodating of club cultural differences, and generative of localized nightlife spaces.

Glossary

A note on romanization: the *pinyin* system is generally adopted except those having been transliterated by convention in Hong Kong, Taiwan and the mainland.[1]

A

Ah Q 阿 Q
Anran 安然
Au, Tak 區德

B

Ba Jin 巴金
bâi bìng 百病
baofang 包房
Beijing Renmin Publishing Co 北京人民出版社
Bencao gangmu 本草綱目
Bianluan zhong de Wenming 變亂中的文明
Bohai 渤海

C

caiquan 猜拳
Cao Yu 曹禺
Cao Yu Drama Festival 曹禺戲劇節
Ch'ang-e 嫦娥
Ch'ing *(dynasty)* 清 *(see also Qing: identical in Chinese)*
Chan, Albert Wai-yip 陳偉業
Chan, Anson 陳方安生
Chan, Yau Hau 陳有后
Chang, Chi 張繼
Chang, Ping-lin 章炳麟
Chau, Siu Ki 周少岐
Chen, Albert 陳弘毅
Chen, Di 陳第
Chen, Eugene 陳友仁
Chen, Jin 陳進
Chen, Kelly 陳慧琳
Chen, Qinzhuang 陳欽莊
Cheng, Sammi 鄭秀文
Cheng, Yi 程頤
Cheung, Chuk Ling 張祝齡
Cheung, Ping Kuen 張秉權
Chih, Lan-yin 枝蘭音
Chih-na 支那
Chi-ming ssu 雞鳴寺

1 Note: As noted by the author, "To avoid confusion, I use the Wade-Giles system of romanization, rather than the pinyin system, as Wade-Giles is the standard system in Taiwan." Thus the Wade-Giles system of romanization is used in the chapter "Civility and Self-Reflexivity: Three Texts on Women and Chinese Modernity".

Ching, Frank 秦家驄
Ching-hua yuan 鏡花緣 *(see also Jinghua yuan: identical in Chinese)*
chongtu 衝突
Chow, Stephen 周星馳
Chung Ying Theatre Company 中英劇團
Chung, Boon Chor *(alias Chung King Ue)* 鍾本初

D
Da Xue 大學
Dai, Jinghua 戴錦華
Dalong 大隆
Deng, Hanmei 鄧寒梅
Deng, Xiaoping 鄧小平
Deyi lu 得一錄
Dongbêi sanshêng 東北三省
douzheng 鬥爭
Dung, Kai-cheung 董啓章
duoji shijie 多極世界

E
Ershi Shiji Shijie Shi 二十世紀世界史

F
Fang, Junyi 方濬頤
fantan 番攤
fo-sang flowers 佛桑花
Fu, Bingchang 傅秉常
Fu Manchu 傅滿州
Fuxi yu muxi de shenhua 父系與母系的神話

G
ge-wu 格物
Grandpa Dong 阿爺董富
Gu, Yanwu 顧炎武
guangfu 光復
guanxi 關係 *(see also kuan-hsi: identical in Chinese)*
guige 閨閣
Guo, Songdao 郭嵩燾

H
Hai-Luan river system 海灤河流域
Han *(dynasty)* 漢
Han Chinese 漢族
Hangzhou Bay 杭州灣
Hanshan's temple 寒山寺
Haoledi 好樂迪
he 和
Ho, A-mei 何亞美
Ho, Andy On-tat 何安達
Ho, Fook 何福
Ho, Kai 何啓
Ho, Ko Tsun 何高俊
Ho, Miu Ling 何妙齡
Ho Miu Ling Hospital 何妙齡醫院
Hong, Ren'gan 洪仁玕
Hsiao, Elva 蕭亞軒
Hsu, Evonne 許慧欣
Hsu-hsu 栩栩
Hu, Chunbing 胡春冰
Hu, Shih 胡適
Hu, T'ai-ming 胡太明
Huai River 淮河
huaju 話劇
Huang, Phillip 黃宗智
Huangpu River 黃浦江
Hung, Jui-lin 洪瑞麟
Hung-hung 紅紅
hutong 胡同

J

Ji, Xiangxiang 計翔翔
Jiang, Yong 江永
Jiang, Zemin 江澤民
Jiangnan arsenal 江南製造局
Jianming Shijie Shi 簡明世界史
Jiaxing 嘉興
Jinghua yuan 鏡花緣 *(see also Ching-hua yuan: identical in Chinese)*
jingpin 精品
Jiuzhang suanshu 九章算術
Ju-chen 如真
jun-zi 君子
juyun 劇運

K

K'ung, Hsiang-hsi 孔祥熙
Kao, Hsin-sheng 高張信生
Ko Chan-shi 高陳氏
Kong, Ying-wah 江英華
Koo, Wellington 顧維鈞
kuan-hsi 關係 *(see also guanxi: identical in Chinese)*
Kuomintang (KMT) 國民黨
Kwan, King-leung 關景良
Kwan, Nancy 關南施 / 關家蒨
Kwok, Ka-ki 郭家麒
Kwong, Yat-sau 鄺日修

L

Lai, Fuk-chi 黎福池
Lai, Leon 黎明
Lam, Stephen Sui-lung 林瑞麟
Lan, Yin-ting 藍蔭鼎
Lan-t'ing Tea Klatch 蘭亭茶會
Lau, Chu Pak 劉鑄伯
Lau, Edwin 劉祉峰
Lau, Sai-leung 劉細良
Lee, Cheuk-yan 李卓人
Lee, Ying Yau 李應猷
Lee, Yuan-Tseh 李遠哲
Leung, Elsie 梁愛詩
li 禮
Li, Hung-wei 黎紅薇
Li, Juchen 李汝珍 *(see also Li, Ruzhen: identical in Chinese)*
Li, Ruzhen 李汝珍 *(see also Li, Juchen: identical in Chinese)*
Li, Shian 李世安
Li, Shizhen 李時珍
Li, Tze-fong 李子方
Li, Xin 李新
Li, Yuanhua 李援華
Li, Zhitan 李植枬
Liang, Qichao 梁啓超
liangfan 量販
liangji shijie 兩極世界
lien-ch'iao 連翹
 – plant: forsythia
 – noun: interconnectedness
lien-hsien 連線
Lin, Chengkun 林承坤
Liu, Hui 劉徽
Liu, Jinghua 劉景華
Liu, Ts'un-Yan 柳存仁
Liu, Xianzhou 劉仙洲
Liu, Xihong 劉錫鴻
Lo, Siu Lan 盧少蘭
Lu Hsun 魯迅 *(see also Lu xun: identical in Chinese)*
Lu xun 魯迅 *(see also Lu Hsun: identical in Chinese)*

Lui, Ho-yin 雷浩然
Lui, Mark 雷頌德

M
Ma, Jian 馬鑑
Ma, Keyao 馬克垚
Ma, Ngok 馬嶽
Ma, Ying-jeou 馬英九
mahjong 麻將
mai xiang 賣相
Manchus 滿族
maodun 矛盾
Meng, Guanglin 孟廣林
Ming *(dynasty)* 明
Mong Kok 旺角
Mu Gu Lu 木骨閭
Mu Zimei 木子美

N
Nankai University 南開大學
Nanking 南京
Nanking Journals (Nanking tsa-kan) 南京雜感
– *Wu Cho-liu's travelogue*
– *the collection of Wu Cho-liu's travel writings*
nei-sheng 內聖
Ng, Hon Tsz 伍漢墀
Ng, Mei 吳方笑薇
Ng, Ting-fang 伍廷芳
nongtang 弄堂

O
Ong, Ai-hwa 王愛華

P
Ping, Jinya 平襟亞
Ping-An li 平安里
post-Mao era 後毛澤東時期
putonghua 普通話

Q
qin min 親民
Qianlong emperor 乾隆皇帝
Qing *(dynasty)* 清 *(see also Ch'ing: identical in Chinese)*

R
Ren 仁
Renai 仁愛
Rou Ran 柔然
Ru *(surname)* 茹

S
Sai Ying Poon 西營盤
Shan-hai ching 山海經
Shanghai Jiaotong University 上海交通大學
shehui jieji 社會階級
She-Lun 社崙
Shih, Shu-mei 史書美
Shijie Lishi 世界歷史
Shijie Lishi Pingcong 世界歷史評叢
Shijie Lishi Yanjiu Dongtai 世界歷史研究動態
Shijie Tongshi 世界通史
Shijie Wenmingshi 世界文明史
– *Li, Shian & Meng, Guanglin's work*
– *Ma, Keyao's work*
shili zhuyi 實利主義
Sin, Tak Fun 冼德芬

Song *(dynasty)* 宋
Soong, Ai-ling 宋藹齡
Soong, Ch'ing-ling 宋慶齡
Soong, May-ling 宋美齡
the Soong sisters 宋家姊妹
Soong, Tse-ven 宋子文
Sun, Yat-sen 孫逸仙

T

T'ai-ming *(see Hu T'ai-ming)*
T'ang *(dynasty)* 唐
T'ang, Ao 唐敖
T'ang, Hsiao-shan 唐小山
T'ang, Kui-ch'en 唐閨臣
T'ang poetry 唐詩
T'ien-kung-k'ai-wu 天工開物
T'ien-kung-k'ai-wu hsu-hsu-ju-chen
天工開物・栩栩如真
T'ing-t'ing 亭亭
t'ung-wen-yi-tzu 同文異字
Tai Ping Shan 太平山
Tai-cheong 泰昌
Taipan 大班
Taiping insurrectionary régime
太平天國
Taipingshan Chapel 太平山福音堂
Taiwan lien-ch'iao 台灣連翹
– *plant: Taiwan forsythia*
– *Wu Cho-liu's novel*
Ta-lu Hsin-pao 大陸新報
Tam, Kwok-chi 譚國始
Tay, William 鄭樹森
tian ming 天命
Tiananmen Incident 天安門事件
To Tsai Church 道濟堂
To, Ying Fan *(alias Coxion To)* 杜應坤
tsa-kan 雜感
Tsang, Donald Yam-kuen 曾蔭權
Tsing-hua University 清華大學
Tso, Seen Wan 曹善允
Tsoi, Jolin 蔡依林
Tung, Chee-hwa 董建華
Tung Wah Hospital 東華醫院
Tz'u-hsi 慈禧

W

Waiguoshi Zhishi 外國史知識
wai-lai-hu 外來戶
wai-wang 外王
Wan, Man Kai 尹文楷
Wang, Anyi 王安憶
Wang, Bingxie 王炳燮
Wang, Qiyao 王琦瑤
Wang, Side 王斯德
Wang, Tao 王韜
Wang, Zhongsheng 王鐘聲
Wangzhu sheng 網蛛生
Wei Hui 衛慧
Wei, Yuk 韋玉
Wen, Jiabao 溫家寶
wenmingshi 文明史
Wong, Benjamin Cheonglam 黃菖林
Wong, Shing 黃勝
Wong, Siu-lun 黃紹倫
Wong, Uen Sham 王元深
Wong, Wing-Sheung 黃詠商
Wong, Yan-lung 黃仁龍
Woo, John 吳宇森
The World of Suzie Wong
蘇絲黃的世界
Wu, Cho-liu 吳濁流
Wu, Tse-t'ien 武則天

Wu-hua-kuo 無花果
– *plant: fig*
– *Wu Cho-liu's novel*
wuxu bianfa 戊戌變法

X
Xie, Zhaozhe 謝肇淛
xin min 新民
Xinqingnian 新青年
Xintan 新灘
Xiongdi 兄弟
Xu, Guanhua 徐冠華
Xue, Fucheng 薛福成

Y
Ya-hsi-ya-te-ku-erh 亞細亞的孤兒
yanda 嚴打
yangwu yundong 洋務運動
Yangzi 揚子江 / 長江
Yao, Ke 姚克
yichao duoqiang 一超多強
Yin, Johua 陰若花
Yu, Hua 余華
Yu, Ta-fu 郁達夫
Yu, Zhi 余治
yuan *(currency unit)* 元

Z
Zhan, Tianxiang 詹天翔
Zhang, Ailing 張愛玲
Zhang, Min 章泯
Zhang, Xudong 張旭東
Zhang, Yimou 張藝謀
Zhang, Zhilian 張芝聯
Zheng, Guanying 鄭觀應
Zhi 止
zhi-zhi 致知
zhong guo xing 中國性
Zhongguo Lishixue Nianjian 中國歷史學年鑑
Zhongxiao 忠孝
Zhou, Xinmin 周新民
Zhu, Guangqian 朱光潛
Zhu, Longhua 朱龍華
Zhu, Ning 朱寧
Zhu, Xi 朱熹
Zhu, Zaiyu 朱載堉
Zhu, Zhongyou 朱中有

(Compiled by C. L. Hui, graduate of the Humanities Programme, Hong Kong Baptist University)

Contributors

ALLEN CHUN is a Research Fellow in the Institute of Ethnology, Academia Sinica, Taiwan. His research interests include socio-cultural theory, national identity and (post)colonial formations. Most of his empirical work has dealt with Chinese speaking societies, contemporary and late traditional. In addition to a recent book, *Unstructuring Chinese Society: The Fictions of Colonial Practice and the Changing Realities of "Land" in the New Territories of Hong Kong* (Harwood Academic Publications 2000, reprinted by Routledge, 2002), he has edited a special double issue in *Cultural Studies* 14(3–4) entitled "(Post)colonialism and its discontents", a special issue in *Social Analysis* 46(2), entitled "Global dissonances", and co-edited a book entitled *Refashioning Pop Music in Asia: Cosmopolitan Flows, Political Tempos and Aesthetic Industries* (Routledge-Curzon). His major papers have appeared in diverse journals, including *Theory Culture & Society, boundary 2, History and Anthropology, Ethnic and Racial Studies, Current Anthropology, Journal of Historical Sociology, Anthropological Theory, Cultural Anthropology, Journal of Postcolonial Studies, Social Analysis, Communal/Plural, Inter-Asia, Late Imperial China*, and *Toung Pao*.

MATTHEW M. CHEW teaches at the Department of Sociology of Hong Kong Baptist University. He has taught courses on sociology, communications, and education in Hong Kong and Shanghai, and is currently teaching at the Department of Sociology of Baptist University of Hong Kong. His research interests include cultural sociology, globalization, cultural policy, and social theory. His works deal with a wide spectrum of empirical materials ranging from early modern universities to contemporary online computer games. His most recent publication is "Contemporary re-emergence of the *qipao*: political nationalism, cultural production, and popular consumption of a traditional Chinese dress" in *The China Quarterly*.

YIU-WAI CHU is a professor in the Department of Chinese and Head of Humanities Programme at Hong Kong Baptist University. His research focuses on postcolonialism, globalization, Hong Kong cinema, and Canto-pop lyrics. Recent publications include *The Local Myth: Discursive Production in the Age of Globalization (in Chinese)* (Taipei: Xuesheng, 2002), *Between Home and World: A Reader in Hong Kong Cinema* (co-edited with Esther Cheung) (Hong Kong: Oxford University Press, 2004), *The "China" in Contemporary Western Critical Discourse (in Chinese)* (Beijing: People's University Press, 2006), and *Interpreting Hong Kong Popular Lyrics (in Chinese)* (Hong Kong: Joint Publishing Co., 2007).

ARIF DIRLIK is Chair Professor of Chinese Studies at the Chinese University of Hong Kong, Honorary Director of the CUHK – Chiang Ching-kuo Foundation Asia Pacific Centre for Chinese Studies, Concurrent Professor, Center for Research in Marxist Social Theory, Nanjing University, and Distinguished Visiting Fellow at the Peter Wall Institute for Advanced Studies, University of British Columbia. His most recent publications are *Global Modernity: Modernity in the Age of Global Capitalism* (2007) and an edited volume, *Pedagogies of the Global: Knowledge in the Human Interest* (2006).

MARK ELVIN is Professor Emeritus of Chinese History in the Research School of Pacific and Asian Studies of the Australian National University, and an Emeritus Fellow of St Antony's College, Oxford. He is the author of *The Pattern of the Chinese Past* (1973), which restructured our understanding of China's economic history in imperial times, and of *The Retreat of the Elephants: An Environmental History of China* (2004). His more important early articles are available in *Another History: China in a European Perspective* (1996). His doctoral thesis, "The Gentry Democracy in Shanghai, 1905–14" (Cambridge University, 1969) covers a key period of China's early political modernization, and his *Changing Stories in the Chinese World* (1997) is perhaps the most relevant of his books to the topic of the chapter included in this book. His other interests include the history of science in premodern China, and the reconstruction China's population dynamics in mid-Qing times.

ROBBIE B.H. GOH is Associate Professor and Head of the Department of English Language and Literature, National University of Singapore. His recent research focuses on Christianity in Asia, cultural studies, and Anglophone writing in the Asian diaspora. Recent publications include *Asian Diasporas: Cultures, Identities, Representations* (co-edited with Shawn Wong, 2004); *Contours of Culture: Space and Social Difference in Singapore* (2005); *Christian Ministry and the Asian Nation: The Metropolitan YMCA in Singapore* (2006); and the forthcoming edited volume *Ethnic Nationalisms: Narration and Cultural Politics in Asian Societies from Independence to Globalization.*

AMY LEE has a Ph.D. in Comparative Literature from The University of Warwick, UK. Her research interest includes the Chinese Diaspora, female self-writing, contemporary fiction and culture, and narratives of marginal experiences. She has published on women's diasporic writing, life writing, gender issues in contemporary fictions and detective fiction. She has taught writing and communication courses of different kinds: professional writing and communication, creative writing and academic writing. Currently she is an assistant professor in the Humanities Programme and the Department of English Language and Literature of Hong Kong Baptist University.

PING-HUI LIAO Distinguished Professor of Literary and Critical Studies at National Tsinghua University, Taiwan is the author of nine books in Chinese and numerous essays in English. He has recently co-edited with David Der-wei Wang for Columbia University Press *Taiwan Under Japanese Colonial Rule* (2006), and with Ackbar Abbas et al. *Internationalizing Cultural Studies* (Blackwell, 2005). Among his ongoing projects is a book on Chinese diasporas and visual culture.

WAI-LUK LO is an associate professor in the Department of Cinema and Television of Hong Kong Baptist University. He is interested in film aesthetics, history and aesthetics of Chinese cinema, theater and drama, acting and body articulation, and creative writing. Selected recent publications/creative works include: *Much Ado about Nothing* (stage play; translator/director), *The Tragic Dimensions of Traditional Chinese*

Drama (theory/criticism), "Bertolt Brecht in Hong Kong" (theory/criticism), "A child without a mother, an adult without a motherland: A study of Ann Hui's films" (theory/criticism), *I Am Hongkongese II* (stage play; director), and *Being Searching* (poetry).

RICARDO K. S. MAK, who earned his Ph. D. in history from the University of Regensburg, is Professor of History at the Hong Kong Baptist University. Specializing in Sino-German relations and Western intellectual and historical thoughts, he has published more than thirty articles and reviews on related topics in academic journals in China, Taiwan, Hong Kong and the United States. He is the author of the book *The Future of the Non-Western World in the Social Sciences of 19th Century England* (1998) and co-editor of *Sino-German Relations since 1800: Multidisciplinary Explorations* (2000) and *China Reconstructs* (2003).

EVA K. W. MAN got her Ph. D. from the Chinese University of Hong Kong. She is presently a professor of the Humanities Programme and the Religion and Philosophy Department of Hong Kong Baptist University. Her academic research areas include Comparative Aesthetics, Neo-Confucian Philosophy, Feminist Aesthetics and Philosophy, Gender Studies and Cultural Studies. She has published numerous refereed journal articles, creative prose writings and academic books in philosophy and aesthetics. She is a newspaper columnist and a radio cultural programme host for local media in Hong Kong. She acted as a Fulbright Scholar at UC Berkeley, US, in 2004, and is now a life fellow of Clare Hall College, Cambridge University, UK.

MAN-KONG WONG is Associate Professor of the Department of History and Research Fellow of Modern History Research Centre, Hong Kong Baptist University. He is also a Fellow of David C. Lam Institute for East-West Studies. His recent research is on medical history of Hong Kong, history of Christian missions in China, and Sino-British relations during the 1970s. Recent publications include (co-author) *A History of Hong Kong Baptist University, 1956–2006* (Hong Kong, 2006), *Cross-cultural Perspectives on the history of Christianity in China* (Taipei, 2006), *For the Future: Sir Edward Youde and Educational Changes in Hong Kong* (Hong Kong, 2007).

WORLDS OF EAST ASIA
WELTEN OSTASIENS
MONDES DE L'EXTRÊME-ORIENT

Edited by / Herausgegeben von / Edité par

ROBERT H. GASSMANN, EDUARD KLOPFENSTEIN,
ANDREA RIEMENSCHNITTER, PIERRE-FRANÇOIS SOUYRI &
NICOLAS ZUFFEREY

The aim of the series "Worlds of East Asia" of the Swiss Asia Society is to publish high-quality, representative work issuing from academic research on all aspects of East Asia. It comprises, and receives, studies on present-day and historical East Asian cultures and societies covering the fields of art, literature and thought as well as translations and interpretations of important sources. Furthermore the series intends to present studies that offer expert knowledge on relevant themes and current questions appealing not only to the academic public, but also to an audience generally interested in East Asia.

One important goal of the series is to establish a forum for academic work in the fields of the humanities and social sciences in Switzerland. However, the series is also committed to the rich variety of studies and writing on East Asia in the international research community. The main publication languages for studies, collections (by individual or several contributors), and surveys are therefore German, French, and English.

The series is supervised and internally reviewed by an editorial board comprising leading representatives in East Asian studies.

Bd. 1 Martin Lehnert
Partitur des Lebens. Die *Liaofan si xun* von Yuan Huang (1533-1606).
2004, 299 S. ISBN 3-03910-408-X

Bd. 2 Simone Müller
Sehnsucht nach Illusion? Klassische japanische Traumlyrik aus literaturhistorischer und geschlechtsspezifischer Perspektive.
2005, 306 S. ISBN 3-03910-478-0

Bd. 3 Matthias Richter
Guan ren. Texte der altchinesischen Literatur zur Charakterkunde und Beamtenrekrutierung.
2005, 504 S. ISBN 3-03910-634-1

Bd. 4 Harald Meyer
Die „Taishō-Demokratie". Begriffsgeschichtliche Studien zur Demokratierezeption in Japan von 1900 bis 1920.
2005, 471 S. ISBN 3-03910-642-2

Bd. 5 Verena Werner
Das Verschwinden des Erzählers. Erzähltheoretische Analysen von Erzählungen Tayama Katais aus den Jahren 1902-1908.
2006, 433 S. ISBN 3-03910-667-8

Bd. 6 Ildegarda Scheidegger
Bokutotsusô. Studies on the Calligraphy of the Zen Master Musô Soseki (1275–1351).
2005, 207 S. ISBN 3-03910-692-9 / US-ISBN 0-8204-7563-7

Bd. 7 Samuel Guex
Entre nonchalance et désespoir. Les intellectuels japonais sinologues face à la guerre (1930-1950).
2006, 300 S. ISBN 3-03910-829-8

Bd. 8 Satomi Ishikawa
Seeking the Self. Individualism and Popular Culture in Japan.
2007, 253 S. ISBN 978-3-03910-874-9

Bd. 9 Helmut Brinker
Laozi flankt, Konfuzius dribbelt. China scheinbar abseits: Vom Fussball und seiner heimlichen Wiege.
2006, 180 S. ISBN 3-03910-890-5

Bd. 10 Wojciech Jan Simson
Die Geschichte der Aussprüche des Konfuzius *(Lunyu)*.
2006, 339 S. ISBN 3-03910-967-7

Bd. 11 Robert H. Gassmann
Verwandtschaft und Gesellschaft im alten China. Begriffe, Strukturen und Prozesse.
2006, 593 S. ISBN 3-03911-170-1

Bd. 12 Judith Fröhlich
Rulers, Peasants and the Use of the Written Word in Medieval Japan.
Ategawa no shō 1004–1304.
2007, 223 S. ISBN 978-3-03911-194-7

Bd. 13 Wang Hui: Translating Chinese Classics in a Colonial Context:
James Legge and His Two Versions of the *Zhongyong*.
2008, 224 S. ISBN 978-3-03911-631-7

Bd. 14 Martina Wernsdörfer: Experiment Tibet. Felder und Akteure auf dem Schachbrett der Bildung 1951-2003.
2008, 547 S. ISBN 978-3-03911-671-3

Bd. 15 Roland Altenburger: The Sword or the Needle. The Female Knight-errant (*xia*) in Traditional Chinese Narrative.
2009, 425 S. ISBN 978-3-0343-0036-0

Bd. 16 Yiu-wai Chu & Eva Kit-wah Man (eds):
Contemporary Asian Modernities. Transnationality, Interculturality, and Hybridity.
2010, 318 S. ISBN 978-3-0343-0093-3